TWENTIETH-CENTURY SPAIN

POLITICS AND SOCIETY IN SPAIN, 1898–1998

Francisco J. Romero Salvadó

Lecturer in Modern European History
London Guildhall University

St. Martin's Press
New York

St. Martin's Press, Scholarly and Reference Division,
175 Fifth Avenue, New York, N.Y. 10010

First published in the United States of America in 1999

This book is printed on paper suitable for recycling and made from fully managed and sustained forest sources.

Printed in Hong Kong

ISBN 0–312–21626–2 clothbound
ISBN 0–312–21629–7 paperback

Library of Congress Cataloging-in-Publication Data
Romero Salvadó, Francisco J., 1960–
Twentieth-century Spain : politics and society in Spain, 1898–1998
/ Francisco J. Romero Salvadó.
p.   cm. — (European history in perspective)
Includes bibliographical references and index.
ISBN 0–312–21626–2 (cloth). — ISBN 0–312–21629–7 (pbk.)
1. Spain—Politics and government—20th century.   I. Title.
II. Series.
DP233.R59   1998
946.08—dc21   98–17662
                                                                    CIP

Uxori Carissime Alison

CONTENTS

PREFACE

After teaching a course on contemporary Spain for a number of years, I have become well aware of the lack of a general textbook to introduce undergraduate students to the subject. Recent research has advanced greatly the field of Spanish history and has pushed the subject into the mainstream of modern European Studies. As the demand grows for courses in Modern Spain, both in departments of Hispanic Studies and History and Politics, I hope this book will reflect recent scholarship and provide a comprehensive and up-to-date companion. It is also intended to be accessible to the general reader with an interest in this field.

The book aims to examine Spain's long and difficult struggle to modernity. Without ignoring its crucial and rich internal peculiarities, the Spanish case will be analysed very much as an integral part of the Western world. The structure that has been adopted is chronological so as to facilitate a sense of Spain's evolution. Chapter 1 provides an introduction to the regional diversity of Spain and the historical background to the twentieth century. Chapter 2 deals with the aftermath of the colonial disaster of 1898 and the struggle of the Liberal Monarchy to survive the resulting social and political challenges. The First World War would be the final watershed which brought about its crisis of authority and its collapse in 1923. Chapter 3 examines the dictatorship of Primo de Rivera as a failed authoritarian response to the crisis of the old Liberal order. Chapter 4 explores the brief exercise in democratic politics that the Second Republic represented. The battle for power between Left and Right and the process by which Spaniards came to accept that their differences could only be resolved by war are investigated. Chapter 5 analyses the Civil War in both its domestic and international dimensions. The conflict is explained as the clash between two diametrically opposed visions of Spain's past and her future potential. Foreign involvement transformed the Spanish Civil War into the last battle between democracy and Socialism against the rising power of

Fascism before the outbreak of the Second World War. Chapter 6 looks at the nature of the regime of the victor and the impact on the economy, society and culture. Finally, Chapter 7 focuses on the process of political transition and consolidation of democracy after Franco's death in 1975.

FRANCISCO J. ROMERO SALVADÓ

ACKNOWLEDGEMENTS

I would like to thank all those whose contributions have helped make this book possible. I am deeply grateful to the financial assistance provided by the British–Spanish Joint Research Programme (Acciones Integradas) which allowed me to make several visits to Spain. I am indebted to the help received in different archives and libraries while engaged in my research there. In this context, I have to mention particularly the staff at both the Fundación Pablo Iglesias in Madrid and the Centre d'Estudis d'Historia Contemporánia (Biblioteca Figueras) in Barcelona.

I owe a debt of gratitude to several friends and colleagues. Above all, I want to thank Paul Preston for many years of support and encouragement. I am grateful to Angela Cenarro, Helen Graham, Enrique Moradiellos and Regina Tolosa who helped me locate sources or gave expert comments on specific issues. I want to thank Jonathan Smele for providing the maps for this text. I would also like to express my gratitude to Iwan Morgan, Head of the Politics and Modern History Department at London Guildhall University, who granted me a sabbatical which greatly aided the progress of this book. Finally, I would like to mention my wife Alison Pinington. Without her endurance, sense of humour and continuous tolerance of my voluble moods this project would have never been completed.

LIST OF ABBREVIATIONS

ACNP   Asociación Católica Nacional de Propagandistas (National and Catholic Association of Propagandists): influential Catholic lay association created in 1909. It was behind the creation of the CEDA and then played an important part, particularly between 1946 and 1957, in Francoist governments.

AP   Alianza Popular (Popular Alliance): centre–right party created by ex-Francoist ministers in 1976 and led by Manuel Fraga Iribarne.

CC.OO   Comisiones Obreras (Workers' Commissions): Communist-controlled trade union which first emerged in the late 1950s.

CDS   Centro Democrático y Social (Democratic and Social Centre): a centre–left party headed by Adolfo Suárez who broke away from UCD in the summer of 1982.

CEDA   Confederación Española de Derechas Autónomas (Spanish Confederation of Autonomous Rightist Parties): right-wing and Catholic coalition founded in 1933 and led by José María Gil Robles.

CEOE   Confederación Española de Organizaciones Empresariales (Spanish Confederation of Employers' Organizations): main industrialist body founded in 1977.

CiU   Convergéncia i Unió Democrática de Catalunya (Convergence and Democratic Union of Cataluña): coalition of centre Nationalist parties which under Jordi Pujol has been the dominant political force in Catalan politics since the democracy.

CNCA   Confederación Nacional Católica Agraria (National Catholic Confederation of Agrarians): founded in 1917 and closely connected to the ACNP. It provided the mass base of the CEDA.

CNT	Confederación Nacional del Trabajo (National Labour Confederation): anarcho-syndicalist trade union created in 1910.
CRT	Confederación Regional del Trabajo (Regional Confederation of Labour): Catalan branch of the CNT.
CTV	Corpo di Truppe Volontarie (Volunteer Troop Corps): Italian forces sent to Spain to fight for the Nationalists during the Civil War.
EE	Euzkadiko Ezkuerra (Basque Left): party formed in 1977 closely linked to the political–military branch of ETA. It merged with a section of the Basque Communists in 1981 and was absorbed by the PSOE in 1993.
EEC	European Economic Community
ETA	Euzkadi Ta Askatasuna (Basque Nation and Liberty): Basque radical movement founded in 1959. It began the armed struggle in 1968.
FAI	Federación Anarquista Ibérica (Iberian Anarchist Federation): group of Anarchists created in 1927 and who came to control the CNT in the 1930s.
FET	Falange Española Tradicionalista (Spanish Traditionalist Falange): Francoist single party also known as the 'National Movement' created by the merging of different right-wing groups in April 1937.
FNTT	Federación Nacional de Trabajadores de la Tierra (National Federation of Land Workers): agrarian section of the UGT.
FRAP	Frente Revolucionario Anti-Fascista y Patriótico (Anti-Fascist and Patriotic Revolutionary Front): ultra-left terrorist group which appeared in the late 1960s.
GAL	Grupos Antiterroristas de Liberación (Anti-terrorist Liberation Groups): state-sponsored illegal anti-terrorist group active in the 1980s.
GRAPO	Grupos de Resistencia Antifascista Primero de Octubre (Groups of Anti-Fascist Resistance First of October): ultra-left terrorist group which began its activities in the mid-1970s and was thought to be infiltrated by the police.
HB	Herri Batasuna (Popular Unity): coalition of radical nationalist groups formed in 1978 to serve as a political front for ETA.
HOAC	Hermandades Obreras de Acción Católica (Workers' Brotherhood of Catholic Action): Catholic workers' associations which began to function in the 1940s.

INI	Instituto Nacional de Industria (National Industrial Institute): a national corporation created under Franco to supervise and regulate industrial production.
IU	Izquierda Unida (United Left): coalition of left-wing groups created after the Nato Referendum in 1986. Its main component is the PCE.
JAP	Juventudes de Acción Popular (Popular Action Youth): youth section of the CEDA.
JOC	Juventud Obrera Católica (Catholic Workers' Youth Movement): Catholic workers' association which began its activities in the 1940s.
NATO	North Atlantic Treaty Organization: Western defensive alliance created in 1949.
PCE	Partido Comunista de España (Spanish Communist Party): founded in 1921.
PNV	Partido Nacionalista Vasco (Basque Nationalist Party): leading Nationalist group in the Basque Country founded by Sabino Arana in 1895.
POUM	Partido Obrero Unificado Marxista (Workers' Party of Marxist Unification): small revolutionary Marxist group fiercely opposed to the PCE and created in 1935 by the merger of the Left Communist Party led by the former Trotskyist Andreu Nin and Joaquín Maurín's Bloc of Workers and Peasants.
PP	Partido Popular (Popular Party): successor of AP in 1989 and led by a new generation of young Conservatives.
PSOE	Partido Socialista Obrero Español (Spanish Socialist Workers Party): founded in 1879.
PSP	Partido Socialista Popular (Popular Socialist Party): independent Socialist party founded by Professor Tierno Galván in 1968. It joined the PSOE in 1978.
PSUC	Partido Socialista Unificado de Cataluña (United Socialist Party of Cataluña): formed in July 1936 by the fusion of the Catalan section of the PCE and that of the PSOE.
UCD	Unión de Centro Democrático (Union of the Democratic Centre): centrist coalition formed by Adolfo Suárez in 1977.
UGT	Unión General de Trabajadores (General Union of Labourers): socialist-controlled trade union created in 1889.

UMD   Unión Militar Democrática (Democratic Military Union): clandestine organization of democratic military officers which came to the surface in the summer of 1975.

UP   Unión Patriótica (Patriotic Union): political movement created in the 1920s to support the dictatorship of General Primo de Rivera.

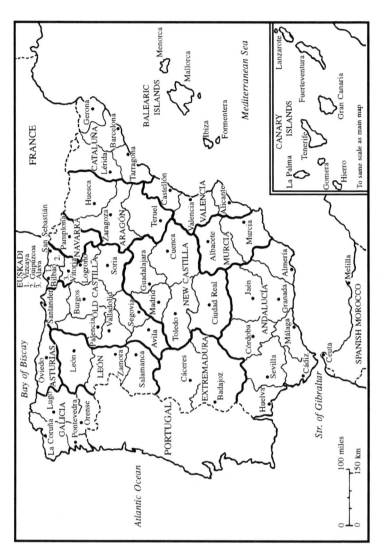

MAP 1 Regions and Provinces of Spain

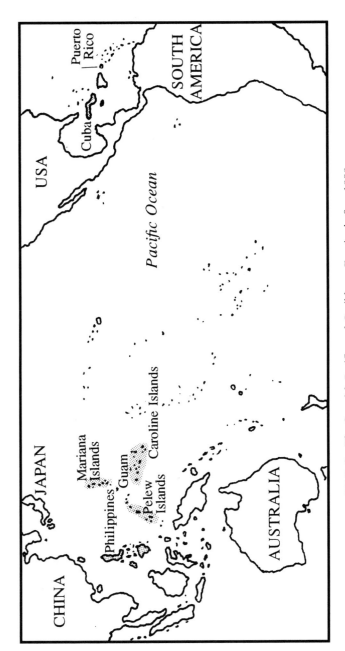

MAP 2 The Spanish Pacific and Caribbean Empire before 1898

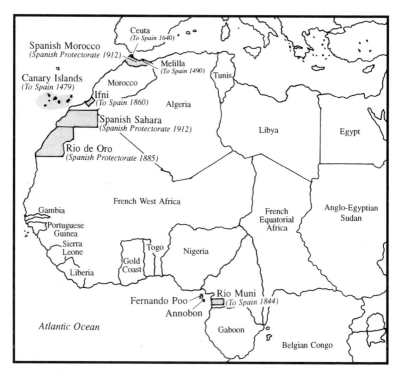

MAP 3 The Spanish African and Atlantic Empire in 1912

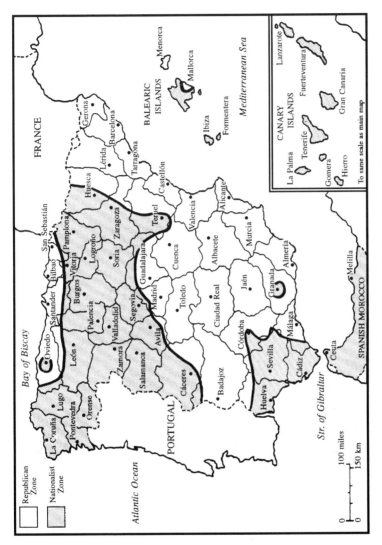

MAP 4 The Division of Spain, end of July 1936

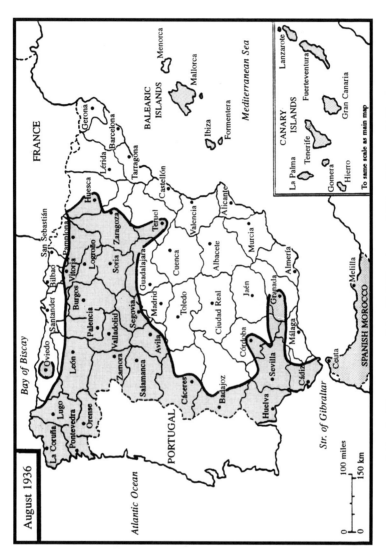

MAP 5 The Progress of the Civil War, August 1936 to February 1939

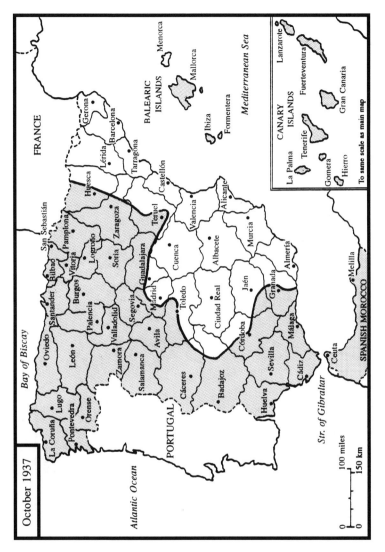

October 1937

Bay of Biscay

Atlantic Ocean

FRANCE

PORTUGAL

Mediterranean Sea

BALEARIC ISLANDS

Menorca

Mallorca

Ibiza

Formentera

CANARY ISLANDS

Lanzarote

Fuerteventura

Gran Canaria

La Palma

Tenerife

Gomera

Hierro

To same scale as main map

SPANISH MOROCCO

Str. of Gibraltar

Melilla

Ceuta

La Coruña

Lugo

Pontevedra

Orense

Oviedo

León

Santander

Bilbao

San Sebastián

Pamplona

Huesca

Vitoria

Logroño

Burgos

Palencia

Valladolid

Zamora

Salamanca

Cáceres

Badajoz

Huelva

Sevilla

Cádiz

Córdoba

Málaga

Granada

Almería

Jaén

Ciudad Real

Toledo

Madrid

Segovia

Ávila

Soria

Zaragoza

Guadalajara

Teruel

Cuenca

Albacete

Murcia

Valencia

Alicante

Castellón

Tarragona

Lérida

Barcelona

Gerona

100 miles

150 km

0

0

MAP 5 *cont.*

xxi

July 1938

Bay of Biscay

FRANCE

Atlantic Ocean

Mediterranean Sea

BALEARIC ISLANDS

Menorca
Mallorca
Ibiza
Formentera

CANARY ISLANDS

Lanzarote
Fuerteventura
Gran Canaria
La Palma
Tenerife
Gomera
Hierro

To same scale as main map

San Sebastián
Pamplona
Gerona
Barcelona
Lérida
Tarragona
Castellón
Huesca
Vitoria
Logroño
Zaragoza
Teruel
Bilbao
Soria
Valencia
Alicante
Santander
Burgos
Guadalajara
Cuenca
Murcia
Oviedo
Palencia
Segovia
Madrid
Albacete
Valladolid
Ávila
Toledo
Ciudad Real
Jaén
Almería
León
Zamora
Granada
Lugo
Salamanca
Cáceres
Córdoba
Málaga
La Coruña
Pontevedra
Orense
Badajoz
Sevilla
Huelva
Cádiz
Ceuta
Melilla

PORTUGAL

Str. of Gibraltar

SPANISH MOROCCO

0   100 miles
0   150 km

MAP 5 *cont.*

xxii

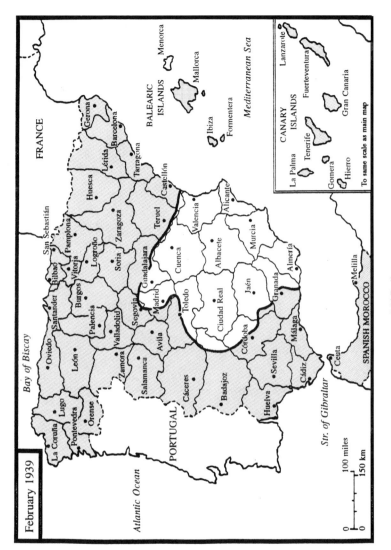

February 1939

Bay of Biscay

Atlantic Ocean

FRANCE

PORTUGAL

SPANISH MOROCCO

Str. of Gibraltar

Mediterranean Sea

BALEARIC ISLANDS

Menorca
Mallorca
Ibiza
Formentera

CANARY ISLANDS

Lanzarote
Fuerteventura
Gran Canaria
Tenerife
La Palma
Gomera
Hierro

To same scale as main map

La Coruña
Lugo
Pontevedra
Orense
Oviedo
Santander
San Sebastián
Bilbao
Vitoria
Pamplona
Logroño
Gerona
Barcelona
Lérida
Huesca
Zaragoza
Soria
Burgos
León
Palencia
Valladolid
Zamora
Salamanca
Segovia
Ávila
Cáceres
Badajoz
Huelva
Sevilla
Cádiz
Ceuta
Melilla
Córdoba
Málaga
Granada
Almería
Jaén
Ciudad Real
Toledo
Madrid
Guadalajara
Cuenca
Albacete
Murcia
Valencia
Alicante
Teruel
Tarragona
Castellón

100 miles
150 km
0

MAP 5 *cont.*

xxiii

1

INTRODUCTION

Any traveller to Spain can easily notice its dramatic regional disparities. The contrasts are such that this traveller might well believe himself to have visited different countries. Indeed, Spain is a state formed by different nations with diverse cultures, climates, traditions and even languages. They emerged during the long eight-hundred-year struggle to expel the Moors from the peninsula, the legendary medieval feat known as *la reconquista* ('the reconquest'). In 1474, the Catholic rulers, Isabel and Fernando joined by marriage the two most important of these kingdoms, Castilla and Aragón. Yet it never went beyond a marriage of convenience and their heirs were never kings of Spain as such, but sovereigns of a commonwealth of nations whose parliaments and ancient laws they swore to uphold in return for their allegiance. In fact, the vast empire of the sixteenth and seventeenth centuries in America and Asia was only part of the Crown of Castilla. The nation of Spain was only to emerge in 1715 with the victory of the Bourbon candidate to the throne during the War of Succession. In this conflict, the Castilians succeeded in crushing the regions of the periphery which had backed the Habsburg claimant. Yet the imperial outposts on the continent were lost as well as the island of Menorca and the strategic rock of Gibraltar. However, although Spain was now centralized under Bourbon hegemony, the harsh peninsular topography with its many long rivers and mountain chains made the creation of an integrated national market difficult and perpetuated the reality of distinct nations evolving with different languages, traditions and economies.

In simple terms and avoiding sub-regional differences, the Spanish state consists of the following areas: Galicia, located in the northwestern corner of the peninsula. Here a language close to Portuguese is spoken. Its Atlantic climate brings abundant rain which favours the raising of livestock. Yet the traditional division of the land into small plots or *minifundios* made it impossible to sustain population growth, forcing Galicians to supplement their income by becoming fishermen. Historically, Galicia has been the main area of emigration abroad.

Moving eastwards, Asturias and Cantabria are still green and fertile, but the former with the development of mining and the emergence of a coal industry, became an heroic stronghold of the working class. Next to them and bordering with France are Euskadi (Basque Country) and Navarra. Basque, not a Latin language, is spoken. Surrounded by mountains which preserved the Basque heritage from being 'contaminated' by the numerous invasions and migrations which characterized Europe in ancient and medieval times led to the claim that the Basques constitute the 'purest' European race. A wealthy and productive land, the Basque provinces resembled the mythical arcadia inhabited by devoutly Catholic and well-off peasants, proud of their ancient laws and stubbornly opposed to the changes brought about by economic and ideological modernization. Navarrese and Basque peasants became the cannon folder of the Absolutist or Carlist armies. In the last part of the nineteenth century, while Navarre remained agrarian and loyal to Carlism, Euskadi went through a rapid phase of industrialization based on metal, steel and ship-building. Many there turned to Basque Nationalism.

Aragón is a poorer and more sparsely populated land. With an extreme continental climate, this was an area of more disparate economic differences: a backward countryside in which large land properties subsisted with a more prosperous capital, Zaragoza, of artisans and small-scale manufacturers.

In the eastern part of the country and also part of the former kingdom of Aragón, we find Cataluña, Valencia and the Balearic islands. The vernacular language is Catalan. Here the Mediterranean climate, hot summers and mild winters, favoured the development of a fertile and competitive agriculture of citrus fruits, rice and vine resulting in a relatively wealthy countryside. The existence of important maritime centres and a long border with France, meant that this was one of the most dynamic areas of trade and commerce open to foreign influences and exchanges. Based on textile production, this area was the first to go through industrial modernization. Barcelona and to a lesser extent Valencia emerged as two important industrial centres attracting cheap labour from their hinterland and then from other poorer areas of the country. Proud of their national peculiarities and resentful of the political control exercised from Madrid, Catalans expressed their discontent by supporting anti-centralist tendencies such as Federalism, Anarcho-Syndicalism and Catalan Nationalism.

In Central Spain, there is the vast area which used to be the former kingdom of León and Castilla. As its name implies, this is the land of castles. During the many centuries of *la reconquista*, the Castilians developed a culture of stoicism, mysticism and resilience. This was the frontier where the brunt of the struggle against the Moors took place. Side by side with the nobility, the common peasant played a crucial role in this fight. Half monk, half warrior, they were given small plots of land as the frontier moved southwards. Being in military terms superior to its neighbours, Castilla emerged as the dominant area in Spain, imposing its language, its rulers and its Catholic intransigence. A vast colonial empire was conquered and for almost two centuries Castilian armies were hegemonic in Europe. Nevertheless, Castilla remained a poor, underpopulated and arid land with inhospitable continental weather, whose main crop was wheat. Its peasants always lived dangerously close to the poverty line, often dependent on money-lenders to survive and strongly affected by the actions of wheat-hoarders and wealthier landowners. Yet proud of their past and keen defenders of their status as property owners, Castilla became the heartland of Catholic Spain and the stronghold of the Conservative Right.

As we advance southwards into New Castilla, Extremadura, Murcia and, above all, Andalucía, we enter into the land of the stereotype. This is the area of sun, flamenco and bull-fighting well known by tourists. It is also the poorest and most divided region due to brutal social and economic contrasts and thus where the class struggle has been the most fierce. The origins can be found in *la reconquista*. Its last phase, the conquest of the south, was altogether a much faster and different affair. Rather than the Crown or the peasants, this task was left to both nobility and ecclesiastical orders. In return, they were given permanent control of large amounts of land as well as judicial and political power over the local inhabitants. The new feudal owners had absolute authority in their *latifundios* or large estates, whose main products were wine and olive oil. Controlling the means of production and being the main source of work and authority, the descendants of the Castilian Knights became a very wealthy social class with paramount influence in national politics. In contrast, the landless peasants enjoyed the lowest living standards in Spain, working in high temperatures from sunrise to sunset for starvation wages. Andalucía was thus a recipe for social violence, the stronghold of rural anarchism and banditry, in which bloody rural *jacqueries* (popular peasant uprisings) and the cruel repressive responses of the authorities succeeded each other with alarming frequency.

At the start of the nineteenth century, the possession of still the largest colonial empire on earth and the existence of a subsoil rich with mineral resources (coal, lead, mercury and copper) seemed to indicate that Spain was a good candidate to lead the march towards economic modernization. Yet one hundred years later the country had been relegated to the periphery of Europe. It was a former great power in decline. A combination of political and economic errors ensured that Spain remained poor, backward and underdeveloped.

It was not until the year 1808 that the different Spanish nations found a common objective. The inefficient Bourbon King Carlos IV was deposed by Napoleon who replaced him by his own brother Joseph. The population of Madrid rose against the French, initiating the badly termed 'War of Independence'. One region after another revolted against the foreign invader. Two new concepts were coined then in Spain: Guerrillas and Liberals. The former were the local fighters who replaced the regular army, once it had been defeated, and kept harassing the supply lines and the rear of the French troops; Liberals were the delegates of the local and provincial juntas which sprang up to organize the resistance against the invaders. They finally gathered in Cádiz in 1812 where a *Cortes* or parliament had been summoned in order to draw up a modern constitution. The delegates declared their allegiance to the Bourbon heir, Fernando, but they also voted for the abolition of the old feudal order, thus putting an end to the economic and political privileges of the clergy and aristocracy and to the absolute power of the Crown.

Fernando VII, known during the war against the French as 'the desired', proved to be one of the most infamous monarchs in Spanish history. His Bourbon ancestors had been dubbed 'enlightened despots'. Fernando was certainly a despot but not an enlightened one. Cruel and mean, as soon as he returned to the country Fernando repudiated the constitution, restored absolutism and imprisoned and executed the very same people who had been fighting on his behalf for almost six years. His rule was a period of obscurantism and tyranny marked by mismanagement, risings against his government and brutal repression. Fernando's troops, with the exception of a brief liberal stage between

1820 and 1823, succeeded in suppressing insurrections in Spain but in the meantime lost all the colonies in mainland America.

Fernando's death in 1833 was followed by a dynastic dispute which led to a civil war. The Liberals embraced the cause of the King's daughter, the one-year-old Isabel, while the Absolutists supported his brother Don Carlos. The Carlist war was a long and cruel conflict that assured the economic backwardness and the political instability of the country.

In the 1830s a bourgeois revolution did take place in Spain, but it was a revolution *manqué*. The basic legislation to dismantle the feudal apparatus was introduced, but it left the structure of landholding unchanged and was not followed by sweeping political reforms. The elimination of the old seigneurial regime did not produce a real political revolution and a modern capitalist society. Land, the most important source of wealth, became a commodity which could be freely sold or bought in the market. The disentailment of the land and the expropriation of ecclesiastical property held in mortmain or of municipal land failed to produce the creation of a new rural middle class of small landowners which could have laid the foundations for the successful economic modernization and industrialization of the country. Instead, the land was sold in large chunks at public auction to the highest bidder. The new enlarged ruling class was a landed oligarchy which consisted of the very same old feudal class together with urban speculators, financiers and wealthy peasants who could afford the high prices to buy the land. Most of them were absentee landowners who regarded their property as a source of authority and prestige and neglected agricultural improvements and investment.

This outcome was not exceptional but followed the trend adopted in almost all the rest of Europe, where a weak bourgeoisie formed a ready alliance with the old ruling feudal class adopting in the process some of the cultural, political and economic values of the previous regime.[1] It was worse in Spain than in other states as the laws of disentailment were introduced amidst a savage civil war and therefore had as their main objective the dual aim of rescuing the State Treasury and of ensuring the throne of Isabel II. The system of sale brought profit to only a few and hence accentuated the concentration of land in the hands of a class of absentee landlords.[2] Production growth was a consequence of the increase of land under cultivation, but there was no relative improvement in productivity as it was easier and cheaper to resort to the vast surplus of impoverished peasants, many little better than serfs, than to provide investment in new farming technology. Seasonal employment and starvation wages caused in large measure the lack of growth in the demand for industrial products, making it almost impossible for the take-off of a national industrial sector.[3] The recurrence of food crises throughout the nineteenth century and the subsequent popular riots were ample proof of the failure of the liberal revolution to produce the economic modernization of the country.

It was no surprise that the traditional ruling classes, the Castilian and Andalusian nobility, backed the Liberal cause. Their sudden conversion was far from a miracle. The triumph of Liberalism sealed the alliance between the upper urban bourgeoisie and the rural aristocracy. The latter was more than prepared to accept the loss of their ancestral and seigneurial privileges, and in return, the nobility saw their hereditary rights transformed into titles of property, they were reimbursed for a number of feudal dues by the state and managed, in most cases, not only to retain their lands intact but even to expand their holdings.[4] The old ruling class, with a few exceptional casualties, saw its economic, social and political position strengthened by the new Liberal order. The urban elite was incorporated into the new power bloc and took on its mentality which was anything but democratic.[5] The great losers of the Liberal revolution were the clergy and the peasants. The Church's land was expropriated and the clergy had to relinquish a great deal of its former economic and political power. Liberalism also brought about sweeping changes harmful to the peasantry, now fully exposed to the forces of the market. They were now taxed, hired or sacked. Their common lands were sold, and the long-term leases and inherited rights enshrined in the old feudal order were gone forever.[6]

The civil war lasted almost seven years. Carlism found enthusiastic support both among those devout Catholics who resented the attacks upon the authority and the property of the Church and those who were unhappy with the abolition of the medieval legislation which protected regional and local peculiarities. Thus the Absolutist cause was firmly backed in the rural areas of Navarra, the Basque Country, Cataluña and Valencia. These were regions which were not only distrustful of the Centre, but whose well-off peasants were deeply suspicious of the modern and centralizing ideas which Liberalism represented. The Carlists never had the manpower or the resources to control any major city or threaten the central state, but proved extremely successful in holding out in their strongholds of the north and the north-east. Unlike the poorly motivated Liberal armies, the Carlist troops fought stubbornly for what they almost regarded as a holy cause. By 1839, both sides were exhausted and affected by war weariness. Aware of the impossibility of winning the war, on 29 August the Carlist generals in the north agreed to abandon the cause of the Absolutist pretender. In return, they obtained guarantees of no future reprisals and were absorbed with full pay into the Liberal army. A year later the Carlists had been defeated in their last redoubts in the east.

The end of the civil war failed to produce normalization of the country. Economic mismanagement, widespread discontent and political turmoil continued unabated. In a system in which only a small minority were entitled to vote, political parties were small groups with scarce popular followings.[7] Once one of these factions achieved power it sought to exclude the others and perpetuate its rule. In contrast, the army emerged from the war as the best organized and disciplined institution. As Liberalism failed to arouse the enthusiasm of the majority of the population, the military became the final guarantor of the Liberal order. They had ensured victory in the dynastic dispute, and then put down the frequent popular revolts which kept occurring in the southern half of the country. Indeed, banditry and rebellions became such an endemic problem that in 1844 the Civil Guard, a new armed police force commanded by military officers, was created with the task of patrolling the countryside. It was popularly hated particularly by the exploited Andalusian peasants who regarded them as little more than the private army of the landowners.

Political parties unable to gain power by legal means had to resort to force. With generals emerging as leaders of the different factions, the army became the final arbiter of politics. For nearly three decades, *pronunciamientos* or military coups were the only valid means of political change. A succession of short-lived administrations and continuous praetorian intervention was not the best combination for economic progress. Governments, dependent on the goodwill of the officers, had to devote more than 50 per cent of the budget to maintaining an inflated and overmanned standing army. A growing budget deficit and constant indebtedness forced the hand of politicians always eager to find short-term solutions. A resort to credit became normal and all the other needs of the country were ignored for its sake. Thus spurred by its monetary difficulties, the state became the main recipient of the capital market which otherwise could have been diverted into more productive forces.[8] Furthermore, the pressure of a needy Treasury, added to bureaucratic and administrative short-sightedness, meant that authorities openly bartered mineral concessions for short-term pecuniary relief. Initial indiscriminate sale gave way in 1868 to the passing of a mining law which amounted simply to a speculators' charter. The result was to transfer Spain's best resources and their potential profits to the hands of foreign capitalists. By 1913, 29 per cent of Spanish mining companies and about half of Spanish mining capital lay in overseas control.[9] From its former imperial greatness, Spain had become a financial colony herself.

To make matters worse, unlike in other European states, railway construction failed to generate an industrial boom. The general Railway Law of 3 June 1855 payed little attention to national needs, nor did it aid the economic integration of the country. On the contrary, it granted all kinds of concessions to foreign companies by offering a rebate of all duties on the import into Spain of all capital goods, rolling stock and fuel. Railways proved inadequate for Spanish needs. Instead of a network, built on the economic realities of the country, the system radiated from Madrid, with terminal points at the sea-ports. It responded both to the centralizing designs of the political elites and to the interests of foreign capital. Export, to which the Spanish railway system was subjugated, was mainly concerned with the products of mining mostly owned by foreign companies. Hence the railway was turned into an instrument of colonization and exploitation, much more than an instrument of true development.[10]

In September 1868, a new *pronunciamiento* developed into a revolution when the officers' revolt was followed by popular insurrections in all the major cities. The so-called 'Glorious Revolution' of 1868 represented the Spanish version of the European revolutions of 1848. Its demands went beyond a mere change of government and brought about the end of the reign of Isabel II. By then, surrounded by favourites and sycophants, and her reputation tarnished by sexual and financial scandals, the Queen had spent all her political credit. The period 1868–74 marked the first serious attempt to overthrow the rule of the traditional oligarchy and establish a genuine democratic regime. Yet as in the rest of Europe, all efforts to establish a new stable political system collapsed.

Once the objective of overthrowing Isabel was accomplished, the revolutionary coalition began to fall apart. The victorious generals imposed upon their more radical partners a monarchist regime. After a long search for a suitable candidate, Amadeo of Savoy, second son of the Italian king, accepted the offer to become Spanish monarch. By the time he arrived in Madrid, a brutal revolt had erupted in the most important remaining colony, Cuba, and his most influential backer, General Juan Prim, had been assassinated.[11] The hapless Amadeo behaved as the first sincere constitutional king in Spanish history. Yet his short rule was marred by constant shows of disloyalty, continuous political infighting and from 1872 by a new Carlist rising in their rural strongholds. On 11 February 1873 a tired Amadeo abdicated and quietly left the country. Almost by default a republic was then proclaimed.

The new regime proved to be even less stable than the monarchy. In a hitherto centralized state, the move towards a federal republic opened the gates for regional anarchy. The new Republican leaders soon lost control of the situation. All over eastern Spain, cities declared themselves municipalities or cantons practically independent from Madrid. Simultaneously, peasants revolted in the south seizing the much coveted land. With the country threatened by Carlism in the north and anarchy in the south, the army once more took matters into its own hands. On 2 January 1874 General Manuel Pavía stormed parliament and disbanded the deputies. On 29 December of that year, another general, Arsenio Martínez Campos, staged a *pronunciamiento* restoring the Bourbon dynasty in favour of the son of Isabel II, Alfonso XII. Spain's most valiant attempt in the nineteenth century to set up a democratic system free from the control of oligarchic groups had ended in failure.[12]

The so-called Restoration or Liberal Monarchy represented the most successful and lasting era of social peace and political stability in modern Spanish history. To a great extent, the success of the new regime was the work of its architect Antonio Cánovas del Castillo. A shrewd politician from Málaga, active during the reign of Isabel II and then the leading element plotting the Bourbonic Restoration, Cánovas sought to avoid the mistakes of the past. His main objective was to devise a political solution which could put an end to the years of civil strife, military *pronunciamientos* and general instability which had characterized the earlier part of the century.

Cánovas broke with a tradition marked by political intolerance and exclusiveness. He created and led the Conservative party. However, instead of perpetuating the political domination of his party, he helped a former political opponent, Práxedes Mateo Sagasta, to organize and head a rival group, the Liberals. In fact, Cánovas worked out a political system which seemed to be modern and democratic. The Constitution of 1876 conceded freedom of expression and association; Catholicism was declared the state religion but private practice of other faiths was allowed; political parties and trade unions were permitted to exist, and, in 1890, universal male suffrage and trial by jury were introduced. In 1885 following the sudden death of the young King Alfonso, Cánovas and Sagasta sealed a formal agreement, known as the Pact of the Pardo, by which their two monarchist or dynastic parties agreed to alternate peacefully and systematically in office in what was described as the *turno pacífico* ('peaceful rotation').

In reality, the Canovite system was anything but democratic. The Spanish political order represented the local variety of oligarchic liberalism then hegemonic in Europe. All the constitutional paraphernalia actually had as its main purpose the concealment of the monopoly of politics enjoyed by a governing elite. That political class was formed by the representatives of the ruling landowning oligarchies of Castilian wheat growers and Andalusian wine and olive oil producers. As the years went by, the group also included large financial interests such as banks, state companies or big concerns like railways.[13] Thus Liberalism in Spain, as in most European countries at the time, was actually a sham and a way to disguise a blatant reality in which the privileged groups in society maintained their supremacy. It perpetuated a social infrastructure that permitted the co-existence of modern political institutions with a semi-feudal socio-economic order.

Cánovas' great achievement was to conceive a political formula through which the ruling elites could enjoy power without the need to resort to praetorian intervention as an instrument of change. For the next four decades, political power was monopolized by the two dynastic parties, Conservatives and Liberals, who agreed upon a system of regulated rotation through which they shared the spoils of office, patronage and administrative graft. Neither dynastic formation was a modern political group seeking to win the vote with clear-cut programmes. On the contrary, apart from the slightly anti-clerical rhetoric of the Liberals, there was hardly any difference between them. They were artificial groups created from above. Dynastic politicians did not even bother to campaign before polling day as the system was based on electoral falsification. During the Restoration period elections did not produce governments in Spain, it was the government which made the elections. The *Ministro de la Gobernación* ('Minister of the Interior') manipulated the results so that the government always obtained an overall majority. The ruling system avoided confrontation and instead sought compromise and stability. The party in power at election time respected the strongholds of the dynastic opposition and even the most important seats of such enemies as the Republicans on the Left and the Carlists on the Right. At the top of the Canovite edifice, the Crown played a crucial role. The monarch was not only Commander in Chief of the army but also had the power to veto laws and appoint and dismiss governments. He was the one who ensured the smooth functioning of the *turno*. When the monarch felt that the party in power was 'exhausted' he called the opposition to office. Any prime minister, to whom the king gave the decree of dissolution of parliament, knew that the new elections would inevitably give him an overall majority to rule comfortably. At the bottom, the *caciques* were the kingpins of the entire political structure. They were the local notables, the bigwigs and influential bosses of each locality. They could be landowners or their agents, officials, money-lenders, lawyers or even priests. It was they who delivered the expected majorities to the governments in Madrid. The *caciques* made universal adult male suffrage inoperative. They ran their areas as personal fiefs having unlimited powers to settle local affairs, choose judges, appoint officials, undertake public works and even levy taxes in accordance with their will. No government dared to move against them as its position in office depended on them. They filled the gap left by the lack of real political mobilization and took advantage of their key role as the link between the central administration and the country. Hence the *caciques* could systematically violate the law with impunity and build a clientelist network, the so-called *amigos políticos* ('political friends'), based on patronage and self-interest. Their friends were rewarded and promoted and their enemies coerced, arrested and in some cases even murdered.[14]

The first two decades after 1876 constituted the golden era of the Restoration Monarchy. Widespread political passiveness and the lack of any organized opposition allowed the smooth working of the *turno*. Elections were systematically rigged and results known in advance in the capital. In practice, the real electoral contest took place during the bargaining and negotiations which went on before the actual polling day. If necessary all kinds of sophisticated methods of fraud and coercion, popularly known as *pucherazos*, were undertaken to obtain the election of the official candidate. Yet during this period *pucherazos* were the exception. It was a misconception that *caciques* prevented people from expressing their will in the ballot box by the use of sheer force. It would be impossible to understand how a regime which allowed freedom of association and expression could simply resort systematically to constant repression against the voters and get away with it. In most cases, *caciques* could deliver the right results without any organized resistance just by the exercise of their power of patronage as the local representatives of the central administration. The continuity of the Canovite system depended on mass apathy and political demobilization, and, only when necessary, on physical repression. The hegemony of the Liberal order was facilitated by the nature of Spanish society in the last quarter of the nineteenth century. It benefited from the economic and cultural backwardness and the lack of national integration which favoured the development of the patron–client network in which *caciques* were perceived by their fellow citizens as the only valid link between their communities and the distant central state.[15]

During the last quarter of the century, a 'dual economy' emerged and consequently the gap between the wealthier and poorer regions of the state widened. A modern capitalist economy developed around the cotton-textile industry of Cataluña and the iron and steel factories of the Basque Country. The relative prosperity and modernization of these areas contrasted with the backward and traditional economic subservience of central and southern Spain. The possibility of industrial expansion and growth was seriously impeded by the reality of small industrial enclaves amidst an overall poor and rural nation. Thus industry found itself caught in a vicious circle: Catalan or Basque goods could not compete with British or German products for foreign outlets while they were left at the mercy of the low purchasing power of the domestic market. Hence the growth of industry ended up stifled by the inelasticity of demand.[16]

Up to the early 1880s there was a certain overall rural economic development which basically reflected the breaking of new ground following the disentailment. However, starved of technical improvements and capital investment, agrarian returns always remained too low. Spanish exports of wine benefited for a while when *Phylloxera* invaded the French vineyards and a large gap was left in the international market. However, the boom was short-lived as *Phylloxera* spread southwards destroying Spanish wine production. Furthermore, as in the rest of Europe, economic problems increased dramatically with the onset of the so-called Great Depression. The transport revolution and the dramatic reduction of freight charges produced by steam navigation meant the arrival of cheap grain from Russia and the American continent which devastated the agrarian sector in Europe. It cost less to bring wheat from the United States to Spanish ports than from the centre of Spain to the coastal regions.[17] Home prices and farmers' incomes fell by half, bringing financial bankruptcy and desperation to the countryside. As Catalan or Basque industry was unable to absorb the sudden surplus of labour, over one and a half million Spaniards emigrated between 1880 and 1913 to different American countries.

The economic crisis produced the alliance of Basque and Catalan industrialists with Castilian wheat-growers in a common demand for state protection. Their efforts were rewarded with the introduction of high tariff barriers in 1891, which were increased again in 1907, transforming the Spanish economy into the most heavily protected on the continent. Thus the leading economic elites settled for the easy benefits of protection which sheltered all national production behind tariff barriers. By opting for protection, Spanish policy-makers consciously made a choice for social stability and the preservation of the *status quo* against rapid economic and social change. Free trade and social dislocation could have promoted fast economic growth by allowing a better reallocation of resources; but this involved a high-risk operation: rapid migration which could have provoked a political explosion.[18]

However, if protection in the short-term avoided the collapse of agriculture, it also served to hide its deficiencies and encouraged the survival of an inefficient and backward agrarian sector which retarded the overall growth of the economy, and which still in 1914 engaged 66 per cent of the active population. High transport costs and food taxes combined to deny cheap food to the industry of the periphery; but industry did not care, since it had been equally successful in the cry for protection for its products.[19]

It was obvious that as the country advanced economically, socially and culturally, the ruling system, largely based on preventing such evolution, would begin to run into increasing difficulties. The *turno pacífico* meant that national politics were dominated by large agrarian interests unresponsive to the wishes of the population. Systematic political change at the top was an artificial mechanism which did not produce any meaningful change in the lives of the citizens. Parliament remained a talking-shop in which dynastic politicians spent their time bartering for concessions and graft while making verbose and empty speeches. The result was an explosive social reality with a deeply rooted agrarian problem barely concealed, but not solved, by a political system not responsible to the demands of the majority. There always existed a strong possibility of violence and conflict, as the only choice left for the masses was apathy or violence. Hence in order to meet the challenge from below, the Canovite system sought and obtained the support of key institutions: Church and army.

Cánovas saw religion as an important bulwark of the ruling order. The constitution of 1876 represented a successful attempt to accommodate liberal opinion and win over the support of the Catholic Church for the new regime: Catholicism was retained as the state religion and bishops were given seats in the Upper House, but other faiths were allowed to be practised in private. Furthermore, the Restoration Monarchy encouraged the expansion of religious congregations and granted the clergy almost total control of primary and secondary education. Most of the wealth which had been lost by the confiscation and loss of ecclesiastical land was recovered and re-invested in speculation and trade. It was believed that by 1912 the Church controlled almost one-third of the wealth of the country.[20] Pope Leo XIII soon urged Spanish Catholics to rally to the Liberal Monarchy. The result was, with the exception of opposition of some of the ultra-orthodox, the Catholic hierarchy finally abandoned the Carlist cause and aligned with the regime.[21] Indeed, the identification of the Catholic clergy with the ruling oligarchy meant that outbursts of popular violence often resulted in anti-clerical riots and the burning of churches. Additionally, the Catholic domination of culture and education pushed the intellectuals towards the anti-monarchist opposition.

At the same time, the collaboration of the military was crucial to safeguard the existing political settlement. Hence, right from the start, the army was absorbed into the ruling power bloc. Officers were rewarded with promotions, seats in the Senate, aristocratic titles and representation in both dynastic parties. Politics remained in the hands of civilians but in exchange they were not to interfere in military matters. The post of War Minister was occupied by a general between 1875 and 1917. Furthermore, the Law of the Constitution of the Army of 29 November 1878 underlined the importance of the military in the Liberal Monarchy. Its second clause stated that the armed forces, beside the normal tasks performed in a constitutional state, had as their primary function the defence of the nation from its internal enemies. The maintenance of public order was left entirely in their hands. The Civil Guard was placed under the control of the Ministry of War. During the history of the Restoration era both parties quickly responded to any social or political unrest with the suspension of constitutional guarantees and the declaration of martial law which granted the army a totally free hand. This militarization of public life revealed the fragility of the constitutional system and facilitated the intervention of the army in politics.[22]

The success of the Canovite system in winning over the support of the military was proved by the fact that only one anti-monarchist *pronunciamiento* took place between the years 1875 and 1923: the pro-Republican revolt of 1883 in Badajoz led by General Villacampa which was easily put down. The officers became the ultimate guarantors of the existing order and the praetorian guard of the ruling oligarchy, repressing with utter brutality any popular rebellion.

Thirst for social justice and redistribution of the land, in addition to the devastating effects of the economic crisis, meant the continuous explosion of social violence. Ironically, the two most affected regions were the poorest, Andalucía, and the wealthiest, Cataluña.

There were successive uprisings in Andalucía by a semi-enslaved landless peasantry living at the mercy of feudal landowners who imposed upon them miserable wages and who could always resort to the services of the hated Civil Guard. In 1882 the police claimed to have discovered an anarchist secret society, *La Mano Negra* ('The Black Hand'), whose objective was to murder the main landowners. Thousands of arrests were made, hundreds imprisoned and eighteen executed. The last important rural insurrection in the nineteenth century took place in 1891 at Jerez when four thousand peasants marched into the city with anarchist slogans and demanded an improvement to their lot. There were hundreds of prison sentences and four more executions.

Class struggle was equally fierce in Cataluña. Industrialists, many of them heading small and medium-sized family concerns and therefore conscious of their narrow profit margin, saw in the economic demands of the workers not only a threat to their authority but also to their business survival. Employers' intransigence combined with the miserable conditions in which the proletariat, many of them emigrants, were living ensured the persistence of social confrontation. Unlike Andalucía, workers in Cataluña had a tradition of federalism and trade unionism. However, there was a minority who believed in the so-called 'propaganda by the deed': shaking the working classes by some violent feat. During the late 1880s and the 1890s an epidemic of bombing and terrorist actions began. Nevertheless, the nature of some of these actions pointed to the possible activity of *agent provocateurs* on the authorities' payroll. Some of the bombs had clear bourgeois or military targets, but others were indiscriminate attacks in which the labouring classes were on the receiving end and whose perpetrators were never identified. In fact, the perpetuation of a climate of terror provided the authorities with an excuse to crush the labour movement while reminding a frightened Catalan bourgeoisie how much they were dependent on central governments for the restoration of social peace. The ruthlessness and cruelty of state repression and the widespread use of torture in the dungeons of Montjuich shocked Europe. Left-wing militants were arrested by their thousands, tried by military courts and many executed. A young Italian Anarchist, Michelle Angiolillo, determined to avenge the brutalities inflicted upon thousands of workers, travelled to Spain and did not stop until he found and shot dead Cánovas, the Spanish Prime Minister on 8 August 1897.[23]

Yet it was foreign rather than domestic causes which contributed crucially to end the golden era of the *turno pacífico*. Since 1875 the strategy adopted by the dynastic politicians in the field of foreign affairs had been one of *recogimiento internacional* ('international retrenchment'), that is isolation and neutrality avoiding any entanglements with either of the camps then emerging on the continent. The obvious danger in that approach was that if Spain was to find herself in any major confrontation, she would have neither allies nor friends.

Since the loss of its vast possessions on the American continent, the Spanish empire had been reduced to the islands of Cuba and Puerto Rico in the Caribbean, some archipelagos in the Pacific (the most important of them being the Philippine islands), and a few small enclaves in Africa. Throughout the nineteenth century, Spain failed to modernize its antiquated and semi-feudal colonial system. Any political or economic demands for autonomy and free trade were systematically rejected. Furthermore, the colonies were economically exploited, remaining captive markets for Spanish products.[24]

It was not surprising that there were frequent complaints against an obsolete and corrupt colonial administration. Widespread discontent often erupted into violence. The first ominous warning appeared in 1868 with the outbreak of the first full-scale revolt against Spanish authority in Cuba, the most precious of Spanish possessions. It took ten years to reach a compromise: the so-called Pact of Zanjón which offered a general amnesty and vague promises of autonomy. They were never fulfilled. Power was not shared with the Creole elites, but remained concentrated in the hands of the so-called *peninsulares* – those who had been born in the Iberian peninsula. They retained a privileged status and dominated the local administration, the Church, the military and commerce.[25]

To make matters worse, there was a growing interest in the United States in the future of Cuba. Many believed that it was America's manifest destiny to wrest control of such a wealthy caribbean island, just a few miles from the coast of Florida, from a backward and ailing Spain. There had been several attempts to purchase Cuba in the past and much support for the independentist Cuban movement. Despite the introduction of high tariff barriers, it was an established fact that the Cuban economy was moving into the orbit of the northern industrial colossus and that Spain could do little to reverse that trend. In 1894, 43.1 per cent of Cuba's imports came from Spain while, despite the heavy protection, 37.4 per cent came from the United States. That same year Cuba exported 88.1 per cent of its produce (mostly sugar, tobacco and coffee) to the United States, while only 8.9 per cent went to Spain.[26] In the 1890s the imperialist lobby in the United States included important economic groups, press barons such as William Randolph Hearst, and outstanding political figures such as the Vice-President Theodore Roosevelt.[27] They just needed an excuse to intervene.

A new independentist insurrection broke out in Cuba in February 1895 and, the following year, a similar movement erupted in the Philippines. The Spanish governing classes responded by closing ranks and declaring in bold speeches that if necessary Spain would fight to the last man and the last peseta to retain control of their colonies.[28] But tough words were not matched by victories in the battlefield.

In fact, different military tactics were implemented: an initial strategy of new vague economic and political concessions to divide the insurgents was then followed by brutal repression and the 'reconcentration' of the population in fortified camps close to cities with large Spanish garrisons. Neither of them succeeded and the insurrection continued unabated. Eventually the rebels put into practice a modern guerrilla kind of warfare, avoiding frontal clashes and instead using hit-and-run tactics which gave them almost total control of the countryside in which the material superiority of the Spanish army could not be put into use.[29] Furthermore, the military stalemate was generating serious social and economic tensions back in the metropolis, as well as fuelling the determination of the imperialist lobby in the United States to intervene.

Between 1895 and 1898 more than two hundred thousand troops were sent overseas to quell the revolts. Due to the unjust system of military recruitment, in which those from wealthy origins could buy exemption from the armed services, recruits were drawn mainly from poor backgrounds. They were badly paid, ill-fed and ill-clothed, fighting a fierce and often invisible enemy in an unfamiliar country. Moreover, the deficient state of medical services meant that they ran the risk of contracting one of many tropical diseases. In fact, for every single Spanish soldier killed in combat, it was estimated that ten died from disease.[30] Combined with the social tragedy of war and death that affected thousands of Spanish families, there was a grave financial haemorrhage to sustain the war effort.

Like his predecessor, Grover Cleveland, the US President William McKinley had, since March 1897, shown no desire to meddle in Cuban affairs nor any particular sympathy for the insurgents. Yet the growing media and political campaign, feeding American public opinion with a steady diet of atrocities committed by the authorities in the island as well as the failure of the Spanish administration to crush the revolt, persuaded him in January 1898 to dispatch the battleship *Maine* in order to protect the lives and properties of US citizens on the island. On 15 February 1898, an explosion destroyed the *Maine* in Havana harbour. The imperialist lobby had, at last, found the perfect excuse to intervene. Although, the sinking of the American vessel was probably due to an accident, McKinley found himself unable or unwilling to oppose the growing calls for military retaliation. By April the United States was at war with Spain.[31]

Without solid European allies and with outdated defensive capabilities, it was clearly an act of temerity, if not an utterly foolish enterprise, to wage war against the United States. Yet the Sagasta administration faced a dilemma. On the one hand, the government was aware that Spain was economically and militarily too weak to defeat the rebels, let alone the United States, and clearly unable to sustain a long-drawn-out campaign. On the other, because of the growing jingoistic mood of public opinion and within the armed forces, shared largely by the Carlist and Republican oppositions, they knew that they could not give way without putting the stability and very survival of the Restoration regime in jeopardy.[32]

In the end, the Spanish governing elites found it easier to lend themselves to a tragi-comedy of pompous rhetoric and hollow patriotism. The decision to wage war against the United States was made not

on emotional grounds, but on the basis of cool calculations: war with
'cheap soldiers and obsolete warships' would be a disaster, only out-
weighed by the military reaction that would be sparked off by surren-
dering without a fight. Hence the Sagasta administration embarked
upon a suicidal war against the Americans in order to put an end to the
dispute in an honourable fashion, and most importantly in a manner
unlikely to endanger the continuity of the regime. Such a quixotic act
would enjoy national support and the government would only have to
surrender in the face of overwhelmingly superior forces.[33]

Thus the dynastic politicians adopted a machiavellian military strategy: the longer the war would last, the greater the political risk. Hence
the plan was to go along with the general patriotic mood, put up a
token armed resistance to please the army's honour and dignity, and
seek a direct naval confrontation which would lead to the destruction of
the Spanish fleet and the impossibility of continuing the war.[34]

Indeed, the Spanish naval forces, concentrated in the bay of Cavite
in the Philippines and the port of Santiago in Cuba, were sacrificed in all but name. On 1 May and 3 July respectively, two American
fleets, which were overwhelmingly superior in numbers and firepower,
destroyed the obsolete Spanish warships almost without opposition in
a matter of hours.[35] In these circumstances almost no one objected
when Sagasta sued for peace in early August. The loss of both fleets
made it impossible to continue the war in a part of the world so far
from the metropolis and so near the enemy's homeland.[36]

Spain had not lost her last peseta or her last drop of blood in the
conflict, but the price was extremely high. By the Treaty of Paris of
10 December 1898 Cuba, Puerto Rico, Guam and the Philippines
were transferred to American control.[37] Six months afterwards, Spain
liquidated its former overseas empire by selling the Caroline Islands
and other small enclaves in the Pacific to Germany. After spending
2000 million pesetas in a frustrated colonial adventure, the national
debt had almost doubled. Additionally, some sixty thousand soldiers
had died, only ten thousand of them in combat. This was the logical
and sad conclusion of an antiquated colonial policy and an inefficient
administration.

2

THE LIBERAL MONARCHY: THE POLITICS OF NOTABLES, 1898–1923

The Aftermath of the Colonial Disaster

It could be argued that the twentieth century began in Spain two years earlier than in the rest of Europe. Indeed, the year 1898 proved a watershed. Almost overnight, the nation lost its vast overseas empire. The magnitude of this disaster has to be understood in the context of an era in which the possession of colonies was seen as the hallmark of a vigorous nation. Hence, in an age marked by imperialist expansion and 'Social Darwinism', the loss of the empire reduced Spain from the status of Great Power to that of a second-rate nation. The defeat had an immediate effect on the peninsula. Rather than a military setback, the colonial disaster was felt as a deep psychological trauma. Spaniards were awoken brutally from the self-delusion that the country was still at the centre of world affairs. News of the shocking military setbacks were swiftly followed by the sad spectacle of the return of thousands of emaciated and sick soldiers crammed on the decks of ships. They were in such an appalling physical condition that many were hardly able to make their way home.[1] It was this widespread feeling of impotence and decline that gave birth to the movement of criticism against the ruling system known as '*Regeneracionismo*' (regeneration). In 1898 the ideological hegemony of the regime sank together with the Spanish fleet. Yet despite suffering a crushing blow, the lack of organization and the dispersion of the opposition forces enabled the survival of the ruling notables for another twenty-five years.[2]

Resenting the close links between Church and state and now shocked by the overwhelming defeat, the leading cultural elites in the country (writers, poets, philosophers) led the assault upon the ruling regime. Intellectuals denounced the ruling system as the epitome of all that was wrong in the country: *caciquismo*, backwardness, clericalism and decline. By focusing their attention on the short-comings of the Restoration Monarchy, they crucially contributed to the production of the crisis of legitimacy of the regime. These intellectuals were known as the Generation of '98. They represented a golden era for Spanish culture with outstanding names such as Miguel de Unamuno, Antonio Machado, José Ortega y Gasset, Angel Ganivet and Pío Baroja. Their work put the whole system into question. They led the criticism against a political order which perpetuated the political and economic backwardness of the country and gave their support to different groups in the opposition.

Outstanding in this task of national regeneration was the Aragonese publicist and lawyer Joaquín Costa. He tried to mobilize the widespread discontent of the middle classes that followed the colonial disaster and the rising taxes and deflationary policies introduced by the governments to deal with the resulting national debt. As early as 1899, Costa used the Chambers of Commerce and Agriculture to found a party of 'producers', the National Union, with which to challenge the political hegemony of the dynastic parties. They drew up a programme based on economic modernization through the development of irrigation canals and reservoirs, public works and reforms of state education. Yet farmers and tradesmen were impotent to break by legal means the deeply rooted power of the local *caciques*.[3] A frustrated Costa then joined the Republican movement. In 1901 he published his famous, *Oligarquía y caciquismo como la forma actual de gobierno en España*, the first proper critical analysis of the ruling oligarchy. Although a democrat, Costa's conclusion that a national *caudillo* or an 'iron surgeon' might be needed to implement surgical methods to extirpate the corruption of politics, would become a rallying cry for those seeking regeneration by authoritarian means.

Simultaneously, the colonial disaster gave impetus to centrifugal tendencies within Spain which rejected the Liberal model of the nation-state. The cultural and economic gap between the historical regions, the Basque Country and Cataluña, and the rest of the country had widened during the second half of the nineteenth century. After 1898, the rule of what was perceived as an incompetent and corrupt centralist oligarchy was challenged by the emergence of nationalist parties in these areas. In the Basque case, nationalism inherited many elements from Carlism: ultra-Catholicism and reaction against the transformations brought about by modernization. Yet unlike Carlism, it adopted a virulent racialist and separatist position. The Basque Nationalist Party (PNV), founded by Sabino de Arana in 1894, warned that the 'purity' and superiority of the Basque race was threatened by the growing number of immigrants attracted by the success of Basque industry. The PNV did not make its electoral breakthrough until 1918.

A more important and modernizing force in Restoration politics was Catalan Nationalism. Having lost its lucrative colonial markets, the Catalan industrial bourgeoisie moved away from a regime which could not even defend its economic interests. It threw its support behind the *Lliga Regionalista*. Founded in 1901, the year in which it had already obtained an astounding electoral victory in Barcelona, and led by one of the most intelligent politicians of the era, Francesc Cambó, the *Lliga* was a socially conservative group with a pragmatic political line. Its final objective was to achieve a decentralized political system and the economic modernization of the country under the hegemony of Catalan industry. In order to achieve that purpose, the *Lliga* was aware that it had to destroy the monopoly of power held by the agrarian-based and centralist oligarchy. In the short-term, the Catalanist strategy was to use the autonomist, sometimes quasi-separatist, lever to exert pressure on the central governments and obtain economic and political concessions for the Catalan industrialists. The accidentalist character of the *Lliga* meant the emergence of rival left-wing Catalanist groups. Paradoxically, the conservative *Lliga* was often regarded by the landowning elites in Madrid as a dangerous revolutionary and separatist group.

The Colonial Disaster also injected new life into Republicanism. The collapse of the First Republic had been followed by bitter infighting, mutual recriminations and factionalism. In 1903 the most important Republican groups established an electoral alliance, led by a former President of the First Republic, Nicolás Salmerón. The introduction of universal suffrage began to pay off as Republicans increased notably their parliamentary representation, gaining ground in all the main cities where results were more difficult to manipulate.[4] New leaders emerged: the Asturian Melquiades Alvarez backed an accidentalist position prepared to accept the monarchy as long as the regime was genuinely committed to a real process of democratization. In 1912 he created the Reformist party which obtained the support of many intellectuals.

More decisive in Spanish politics was the rise of the controversial Alejandro Lerroux. A maverick and corrupt politician and yet extremely able and competent, he arrived in Barcelona in 1901 to organize the ailing Republican movement. He proved remarkably efficient as an orator and organizer, building up a formidable electoral machinery. His party, the Republican Radical, was to dispute the hegemony of Catalan politics with the Nationalist groups, especially the *Lliga*, for the next twenty years. A professional politician above all, very much like the dynastic notables he professed to combat, Lerroux was constantly involved in local financial scandals during his domination of the municipal government. Moreover, his shady reputation was enhanced by the fact that he was funded by the Liberal administrations in Madrid. The latter were more than happy to stir up trouble in Cataluña against the rising Nationalist movement and to back a demagogue who could divert the proletariat from Anarcho-Syndicalism. His skills in attracting and mobilizing the lower classes, at least until 1914, cannot be disputed. It earned Lerroux the nickname of the 'Emperor of the Paralelo', the proletarian quarter of the city. A master of propaganda, he spoke in defence of workers' rights, organized impressive rallies and created in 1906, one year before the Socialists, *Casas del Pueblo* in each neighbourhood where workers could gather and obtain recreational and cultural services. Simultaneously, loyal to a tradition of revolutionary Republicanism which rejected neither violent conspiracy nor the support of a military coup, he sought to establish good relations with both local Anarchists and army officers. Thus Lerroux's rhetoric stood out by its fiery and populist demagoguery, in which vague promises for a forthcoming social revolution were efficiently replaced by brutal anticlericalism, a patriotic defence of Spanish unity denouncing Catalan separatism, and the continuous display of street violence which characterized the Radical Youth, the so-called 'Young Barbarians'.[5]

Unlike other states, the Spanish ruling classes, after the catastrophic toll of the colonial wars, could not channel the aspirations of the lower classes into imperialist adventures. By the turn of the century, the labour movement, thoroughly ignored by the Canovite Settlement, began to make important strides. The most striking feature of the Spanish working class was not just its ideological and geographical division between two antagonistic camps – a Socialist tendency concentrated in Castilla, Asturias and the Basque Country and an Anarcho-Syndicalist current in Cataluña, Valencia, Aragón and Andalucía – but the relatively slow and painful, although consistent, growth of Socialism in comparison to the progress of the Anarcho-Syndicalist movement characterized by periods of great activity, followed by others of repression and retreat.

Anarchist success could initially by explained by the fact that Giuseppe Fannelli, the man sent to Spain to spread the new ideas of the First International, was a Bakunian. Hence Anarchist ideology was dominant in the first two Federations of Spanish Workers which existed between the 1860s and 1880s.[6] It would be a mistake, however, to conclude that the earlier arrival of Anarchism explains solely the slow development of Marxism in Spain. In fact, theoretical and functional deficiencies hindered the prospects of a successful Socialist expansion.

In 1879, the Spanish Socialist Party (PSOE) was created, followed by the establishment of a trade union, *La Unión General de Trabajadores* (UGT) in 1888. From its inception, the PSOE interpreted Marxism through the analyses of French Socialists which bore little relation to the Spanish situation and led them into reductionist and deterministic concepts. Believing blindly in the inevitability of the final triumph of the proletariat, the Socialists adopted a rhetoric full of revolutionary, fervour but in practice, however, they followed scrupulously a legalist and moderate strategy. They concentrated on the daily struggle to improve living standards and succeed in wages disputes, avoiding a head-on confrontation with the state. Hence the ultimate goal of revolution was displaced by an instinct for bureaucratic survival and the preservation of the organization became an end in itself.[7] The result was the emergence of a kind of 'decaffeinated' Marxism that, whilst proclaiming the necessity and inevitability of Socialist revolution, was engaged in precisely the legalist reformism which their own arguments dismissed as useless. This contradiction led Socialists to their overriding and obsessive preoccupation with organizational matters and the poverty of their analysis made them overlook such vital issues as the agrarian problem and regional diversity in Spain.[8]

Furthermore, Spanish Socialists, under the tight grip of their leader Pablo Iglesias and the Madrid-based national executive, fixed upon the idea of state power, threw themselves with admirable courage into the political contest despite a reality where electoral falsification was rife. To make matters worse, in seeking to preserve the purity of the movement, the PSOE rejected tactical coalitions with other forces which might 'contaminate' it with bourgeois ideas.[9] This reformist strategy meant very slow, if also steady, progress. In the political arena, the first successes did not take place until the local elections of 1905 when Iglesias and other Socialists obtained seats in the municipal administration of several cities. Ironically, Iglesias had to resort to the same fraudulent methods as his opponents to secure election.[10] Socialist expansion was limited to the labour aristocracy of the capital, Madrid, the national federation of railway workers, and then, as a result of the prestige won after a series of successful strikes, to the Asturian miners and workers of the shipping concerns and iron foundries of the Basque Country, where local leaders often followed more militant tactics than those prescribed by the National Executive in Madrid.[11]

Yet, participating in the politics of the era could hardly appeal to a majority of workers. The millenarian and uncompromising character of Anarchism not only appealed to the downtrodden peasants of Andalucía, unsurprisingly suspicious of politics which preserved the economic and social power of the great state proprietors, but also gained widespread support among Catalan workers with a tradition of federalism and militancy. In fact, Anarchist ideas resembled a sort of new messianic religion which provided an ideological coherence to a tradition in which the popular classes, distrusting the state, relied on direct action to redress grievances.[12]

By the turn of the century, Anarchism was in retreat in Cataluña and Andalucía since two decades of endless violence carried out by a minority of acolytes of 'propaganda by the deed' had brought only repression and distress to the workers.[13] Yet the UGT–PSOE found it almost impossible to make inroads in these areas. The absence of an agrarian strategy and concentration on the electoral struggle barred its expansion in the south. On the other hand, in Cataluña, the vacuum left by the decline of Anarchism was temporarily filled by the Republican Radical Party.[14] On 3 August 1907 Catalan workers launched *Solidaridad Obrera*. It was largely a reaction against the false revolutionary potential and the demagoguery of Lerroux. *Solidaridad Obrera* was a trade union heavily influenced by the Syndicalist principles of the French *Confédération Générale du Travail* (CGT). It urged the unity of Catalan workers from all political persuasions and the adoption of methods of direct action in the economic struggle.[15]

The ascension to the throne of Alfonso XIII in 1902 also contributed to undermine the foundations of the political system. Not being indifferent to power, he wished to govern as well as to reign. With the demise of the two historical leaders of the *turno pacífico*, Cánovas and Sagasta, the young monarch found it relatively easy to implement the maxim 'divide and conquer'. Alfonso used and abused his constitutional prerogatives to appoint and dismiss cabinets. It enhanced his role as the ultimate arbiter of politics, as well as furthering the natural factionalism of the dynastic parties.[16] Moreover, in the disputes between officers and politicians, the king always sided with the former. The year 1898 also marked the return of the army into politics. The unreformed and over-staffed officer corps was embittered by the colonial defeats which they blamed upon the corrupt and incompetent Liberal politicians.[17] Extremely sensitive to any civilian criticism, the military became increasingly alienated from the rest of society, developing an ideology in which they identified themselves as being above politics and the guardians of the sacred values of the fatherland. As guarantors of national unity and social order, army officers were likely to clash with the emergence of the organized labour movement and regionalist parties. In the process, the army began to consider the existing constitutional practices as inadequate to crush the 'pernicious effects' of nationalism and class conflict.

The first serious confrontation took place in November 1905. Some three hundred officers, incensed by the publication of an anti-militarist cartoon in the satirical Catalanist magazine *Cut-Cut*, decided to take the law into their own hands. They ransacked the offices of that magazine and of the main Catalanist newspaper, *La Veu de Catalunya*. The Liberal government found itself caught between the solidarity of the army corps and the widespread Catalan outcries for punishment of the perpetrators of such violent action. There were rumours that the military were prepared to storm parliament. Alfonso took an active role, dismissing the existing Prime Minister, Eugenio Montero Ríos, and replacing him by another Liberal notable, Segismundo Moret, more ready to placate the army. The latter passed in March 1906 the Law of Jurisdictions whereby any offense against the army, the monarchy or the fatherland was to come under military jurisdiction. This concession to army brutality was a devastating blow to civilian supremacy in Spain.[18] The indignation was such in Cataluña that all political parties from Carlists and Nationalists to Republicans decided to form a political alliance, *Solidaridad Catalana*. The only exception was Lerroux's Radicals. In the elections of April 1907, *Solidaridad* obtained forty-one of the forty-four seats contested in the region. If a similar process had taken place in other regions, the monarchy would have been in danger of falling.[19]

Whereas most dynastic politicians were happy simply to carry on with business as usual, a minority became conscious that the flood of criticism unleashed by the Disaster of 1898 meant that the survival of the system depended on its successful reform. The leading advocate of this regeneration from within was Antonio Maura, leader of the Conservative party since 1903, and the most important statesman of the period. His calls for 'revolution from above' represented the most important attempt undertaken by a dynastic politician to seek the mobilization of part of the electorate (the Catholic middle classes) in order to replace the artificial foundations of *caciquismo*.[20]

Maura's experiment failed. In his second and longest premiership (1907–9), he managed to alienate almost every political force. His uncompromising and autocratic style and clerical leanings upset the Left, while his plans to clean up the system infuriated the Liberal party and even many Conservatives, who were well aware that they risked losing their privileged position in a clean ballot. His two most ambitious projects never materialized. The Bill of Local Administration, an attempt to introduce corporate suffrage in municipal elections in order to quash local *caciquismo*, was blocked in parliament. Yet it achieved certain support from the *Lliga*, hence splitting *Solidaridad Catalana*.[21] In the long term, it led to the establishment by another Conservative cabinet in 1913 of the Catalan *Mancomunidad*, a local institution which fell far short of granting autonomy but returned some limited administrative powers. His Bill of Repression of Terrorism produced the creation of a Leftist Bloc in which Republicans and Liberals shared the platform in public rallies, condemning the harshness of Maura's measures.

Ironically, Maura's fall was produced by a colonial issue. Under the terms of the Treaty of Cartagena of 1907, the Great Powers had allotted to Spain, which already possessed there the enclaves of Ceuta and Melilla, the task of policing Northern Morocco. By 1909 the government found itself facing a full-scale rebellion of the local tribes. With memories of the tragic losses of 1898 still fresh, the call-up of working-class reservists in July was met by violent protests. Furthermore, unlike the historical links with Cuba, the Moroccan adventure was regarded as the personal enterprise of the king and some aristocratic and clerical groups who owned the iron mines there.

A planned nation-wide general strike failed everywhere but in Cataluña. Being the main port of embarkation, the anti-militarist revolt spiralled out of control in Barcelona and neighbouring towns on 26 July. Misunderstandings between the authorities helped to worsen the incidents: the tolerant Civil Governor, Angel Ossorio, opposed to taking any hasty actions which could inflame the situation, was overruled by Juan de la Cierva, the authoritarian Minister of the Interior, who regarded the strike as a separatist and revolutionary insurrection. Once martial law was declared Ossorio simply withdrew to his villa outside the city while the Captain General, Luis Santiago, acted with unexpected timidity and slowness. The result was that the leaderless masses became the virtual owners of the city. Syndicalists and Socialist leaders were confused, having no plans beyond a twenty-four hour anti-war protest. The Radicals showed the hollowness of their rhetoric when they refused to give it political leadership. The result was the so-called 'Tragic Week': days of anarchy and chaos in which the Young Barbarians finally put into practice a decade of fierce anti-clerical rhetoric, directing the anger of the crowds into the burning of churches and convents. The revolt was finally crushed with great violence resulting in hundreds of casualties, thousands of arrests and the execution of five people, including the famous Anarchist schoolteacher, Francisco Ferrer Guardia.[22]

The immediate consequences of the Tragic Week proved crucial. A national and international campaign ensued to protest against Ferrer's execution. The monarch forced the resignation of Maura and replaced him with a Liberal cabinet led by Moret. A frustrated Maura refused then to alternate with the Liberal party in power, the basis of the *turno pacífico*. Alfonso intervened even further to divide the Liberal party, traditionally a much more fragmented group led by different local notables than the Conservatives, by refusing the decree of dissolution to Moret and instead backing José Canalejas, another Liberal baron.[23] Canalejas himself failed to appease the Left with some mild anti-clerical and social legislation.[24] In 1911 and 1912, Spain was rocked by continuous strikes and Canalejas incensed the labour movement by increasing intervention in Morocco where Spain established a formal Protectorate and by solving a railway strike by conscripting workers. The Liberal Prime Minister was then assassinated by an Anarchist in November 1912. Alfonso again intervened to ensure the leadership of the party passed to the maverick and cunning Count Romanones.[25] The Liberal party was irretrievably divided and Romanones was forced out of office in October 1913. Maura once more refused to succeed in power, but was shocked when his party, eager to enjoy the spoils of power and patronage, abandoned him in order to form a government under the leadership of a former minister and wealthy company lawyer, Eduardo Dato.[26]

Something unique in the Restoration period then took place when a group of young and energetic monarchists decided to follow Maura's lead. Maura became the only dynastic politician to mobilize the support of a legion of devout followers. The *Mauristas* constituted the first modern right-wing group in Spanish politics. Yet they never formed a coherent party, but a broad church united by their devotion to Maura and their bitter criticism of the corruption of the *turno*. There was a modernizing, reformist and Christian Democratic faction led by Angel Ossorio, and an authoritarian, nationalist and anti-liberal tendency headed by the intolerant Antonio Goicoechea.[27]

The aftermath of the 'Tragic Week', by debunking its 'radicalism', initiated the slow but steady eclipse of the Radical Party. *Solidaridad Obrera* decided to expand its organization to the rest of the country. With this goal in mind, the Anarcho-Syndicalist trade union *La Confederación Nacional del Trabajo* (CNT) was created in October 1910. Under the leadership of revolutionary Syndicalists, the CNT rejected parliamentary politics and instead put all their efforts into the economic struggle by means of direct action. The growth of the CNT was rapid. In a few months 139 workers' societies affiliated, which gave it a total of 25 915 members. However, the CNT was soon behind a series of ill-timed strikes. Then, following the assassination of the Prime Minister Canalejas, a crackdown on the organization forced the CNT into clandestinity.[28]

The Socialists abandoned in November 1909 their traditional sectarianism and established a *conjunción* or alliance with the Republicans, from which only the Radicals, tarnished by their shady reputation, were excluded.[29] The PSOE's new strategy was produced by the awareness that even if the transition to Socialism remained inevitable, Spain still had to pass through the vital preliminary stage of bourgeois revolution. Hence Socialists had to ally with Republican parties and work for democratic reforms. After 1909 the UGT made more systematic use of the strike weapon, taking part in a series of nation-wide strikes in 1911 and 1912. Yet their main concerns remained their political activities: the active campaign against the war in Morocco and their electoral involvement in the *conjunción*. A first success was obtained in May 1910 when Pablo Iglesias was finally elected the first Socialist deputy.[30]

The First World War: Neutrality and Revolution

As war broke out on the continent, Prime Minister Dato rapidly declared Spain's official neutrality. A distant conflict in the Balkans was no reason to break with the traditional policy of international isolation.

Furthermore, the government was well aware of the country's economic and military inability to wage a modern war. There existed the belief that the conflict would be over before Christmas. There was nothing to be won on the battlefield, while in case of a military stalemate, by maintaining an impartial position, Spain could play a leading role in the peace negotiations.[31]

Maintaining neutrality, virtually at any price, was supported by most dynastic politicians who agreed that only harmful consequences could result from the continental conflict. They succeeded in this but it was beyond their power to prevent the conflict from entering Spain. Neutrality did not save the political system. Spain did not enter the war, but the war entered Spain and its political and socio-economic impact undermined the foundations of a regime which until then had been based on the apathy and political demobilization of the population.[32]

In the summer of 1914 nearly all the political forces readily accepted the decision to remain neutral. However, as the war went on, the initial consensus broke down. For the leading cultural and political elites it became a question of obsessive concern. The war was perceived as an ideological clash in which each of the warring factions came to symbolize certain transcendent ideas and values. The quarrel between the partisans of the Allies and the Central Powers generated such a violent debate that it almost acquired the moral quality of a civil war: 'a civil war of words'. It represented a verbal clash between the two Spains, which was a portent of the real civil war that still lay a generation in the future.[33]

Unlike most dynastic politicians, trying to ignore the conflict setting the continent ablaze, public opinion began to split between *Francophiles* and *Germanophiles*. In very broad terms, the Right wanted a victory for the Central Powers and the Left for the Allies. *Germanophiles* were predominant among the privileged social groups (the clergy, the aristocracy, the court, the upper bourgeoisie, the army, the landowning oligarchy) and right-wing parties such as the Carlists and the *Mauristas*. For them, a German victory constituted the best guarantee for the consolidation of values such as monarchism, religion and conservatism. In contrast, *Francophiles* were those social and political groups hostile to the *status quo*: the intellectuals, the professional middle classes, Republicans, Socialists and Regionalists. They expected the triumph of the Entente to produce democracy and political freedom throughout Europe.[34]

By 1916 the term 'neutrality' changed its initial meaning and the ideological polarization increased. With the entry of Italy and Portugal into the war, even the most rabid *Germanophiles* realized that, with the country surrounded by the Allies, to join forces with Germany would be military suicide. Hence they became champions of strict neutrality since this was seen as the best way to support the German cause. In contrast, the *Francophiles* declared strict neutrality a sham and switched to positions ranging from benevolent neutrality towards the Allies to diplomatic rupture with the Central Empires and even open intervention.[35]

The war dramatically altered Spain's economy and society. The country benefited from her neutral status by supplying both camps, and new outlets, which had to be abandoned by the belligerent nations, were taken over. The radical drop in imports together with the rise in the volume and prices of exports meant that a poor nation almost overnight saw a sudden flow of gold across her frontiers and the balance of trade went from a situation of chronic deficit to one registering fabulous profits. However, this sudden prosperity only emphasized the weaknesses of the Spanish economy and widened the gap between rich and poor areas. The difficulty in importing staple commodities, the unregulated export of large quantities of Spain's domestic production and the increasing amount of money in circulation brought about galloping inflation and rocketing prices. The precarious transport system almost collapsed under the new pressures. The industrial regions of northern and eastern Spain entered a phase of feverish activity, while other areas of the peninsula were devastated by shortages and unemployment, forcing thousands of workers to emigrate mainly to Barcelona and Bilbao. The consequence was that whereas industrialists and financiers experienced a previously unknown period of opulence and wealth, for many, especially among the working classes, these were years of worsening living standards and shortages of staple products.[36] This was a golden age for profiteers and speculators who managed to amass huge fortunes. In particular, rural *caciques* reaped enormous profits by hoarding grain and then selling their production when prices peaked. Governments proved unable or unwilling to introduce forceful measures against the very same *caciques* to whom the governing elites owed the votes which sustained them in power. After 1915 the signs of popular discontent increased, turning soon into food riots and attacks on shops.

The working classes had to bear the brunt of the shortages and the rising costs of living. Rocketing inflation pushed the proletariat to fight in order to protect their living standards. Militancy was also boosted by employers' willingness to satisfy workers' demands for fear of losing markets at this extraordinary moment of profits. Notwithstanding the constant struggle, salaries could not keep up with rising prices, while the lack of staple commodities produced widespread misery and distress.[37] Under pressure from the rank-and-file, the UGT and the CNT, concluded for the first time a historical Labour Pact in July 1916 in order to force the government to implement measures to solve the problem of inflation and shortages. The reformist UGT leadership loathed the idea of collaborating with the CNT but it could not ignore the constant demands for workers' unity and drastic action from the membership. Reservations were finally overcome when the smaller CNT, led then by pragmatic Syndicalist leaders and not Anarchist zealots, accepted Socialist leadership in the alliance.[38]

For the next six months, the always cautious Socialists followed a strategy of popular rallies combined with constant visits to ministers to let them know the distress of the proletariat. Failing to achieve any redress, the labour movement shifted to more radical tactics. On 18 December 1916 a successful twenty-four hour nationwide stoppage took place. Three months later, Julián Besteiro, a leading Socialist and Professor of Logic at the University of Madrid, drew up a manifesto on behalf of the united working class. It was the most radical document ever subscribed to by Spanish Socialism. The regime was accused of being the cause of the widespread distress of the population and warned that, at a convenient moment, the proletariat would overthrow it by means of a general strike. In fact, Besteiro was far from thinking in terms of a social revolution. Socialists distinguished between a reactionary plutocracy, identified with the dynastic politicians in power, and a progressive bourgeoisie, represented by Catalan Regionalists and Republicans. The manifesto was an open invitation to the commercial and industrial bourgeoisie to take power and establish a genuine democratic system with the support of the labour movement.[39]

The Catalan industrial bourgeoisie, represented politically by the *Lliga Regionalista*, as the main beneficiary of the economic profits reaped from their control of war production, sought to translate the new reality into political terms. Under Cambó's astute leadership, they believed that the moment to destroy the monopoly of power enjoyed by the centralist landowning oligarchy and its representatives, the *turno* parties, had arrived. The ambitious plans of the Minister of Economy, Santiago Alba, the rising star of the Liberal party, gained the Catalan bourgeoisie allies across the country.

In 1916, Alba expected to consolidate his personal prestige and become the leading figure of his party by introducing a vast far-reaching economic programme. His so-called Plan of National Reconstruction consisted of a ten-year project for public works, naval, military and cultural reforms representing a total expenditure of 2134 million pesetas, which was partly to be paid for by levying a tax on excess war profits made by industry and trade but not, significantly, by agriculture.[40] Naturally, industry and trade were not prepared to bear the brunt of the costs of Alba's programme while the landed oligarchy was to be unaffected. Cambó and his associates cleverly singled out Alba as the man to bring down. Hence the *Lliga* pursued a strategy of obstructionism in parliament while organizing throughout the country a formidable coalition of industrial groups against the government. The Regionalists were assisted in their plan by the fact that rivalries and intrigues among the Liberals left Alba isolated. Many Liberal notables, including Prime Minister Romanones, were delighted to see Alba's meteoric rise brought to an end by the obstructionism pursued by the Regionalists in the chamber.[41] By early 1917 it was clear that not only had Alba been defeated and his career impeded, but also that the Liberal party was bitterly demoralized and divided, having failed even to pass the annual budget. Cambó could then boast that the dynastic parties could no longer rule without the goodwill of the *Lliga*.

Inflation and shortages also drastically affected the living standards of army officers. Furthermore, as the proximity of the continental struggle revealed the incapacity of the Spanish military to engage in a modern war, dynastic governments sought, for the very first time, to break the tradition of non-intervention in army matters and introduce a comprehensive programme of reform and modernization. In 1916 a Bill of Military Reform was passed to deal with the sensitive question of reducing the vastly overmanned officer corps by introducing tests of physical and intellectual ability. Any reform which struck at the security of bureaucratic middle-ranking officers who now also suffered from worsening living standards was bound to infuriate them.[42] To add insult to injury, they had been observing for months how the organized proletariat could obtain pay rises through strike action. Thus deeply disturbed by their increasing economic hardship and incensed by the government reforms, they began gradually to absorb some syndicalist principles. From the second half of 1916, *Juntas Militares de Defensa* – officers' trade unions – were created. They quickly denounced the corruption of the ruling politicians and attacked the favouritism enjoyed by the privileged members of the Palace clique and the elite troops serving in Africa.[43]

It was, however, the international question which finally initiated the chain of events which led to the beginning of the end of the politics of notables in Spain. In fact, the arrival to power of Count Romanones in December 1915 intensified the debate on neutrality. Unlike the other dynastic leaders, Romanones took an active role in foreign policy, favouring rapproachment with the Allies. As early as August 1914, he had openly stated his pro-Allied views in a famous editorial called 'Fatal Neutralities'. According to the Count, the war offered Spain a golden opportunity to expand her Empire in North Africa and strengthen her economy through closer collaboration with the Allies. Although he did not advocate diplomatic rupture with the Central Powers, Romanones made clear that Spain should abandon isolation and move towards the Entente.[44] Romanones' sympathy for the Allied cause was certainly reinforced by his economic links with France. He was one of the largest shareholders of mining concerns in Andalucía and northern Morocco, partly exploited with French capital, and the production of his companies in Asturias went mainly to France to support her war effort.

Romanones' premiership was characterized by a gigantic struggle between him and the *Germanophile* forces in Spain. At the same time, regardless of Spain's neutral status, the number of German atrocities piled up: a sophisticated spy network was established, merchant vessels were sunk in international waters, Anarchists were funded to disrupt Catalan industrial output for the French war effort, and Moorish gangs were armed and trained to revolt in Morocco. Additionally, taking advantage of the rising cost of paper, the Central Powers bought a large number of newspapers. Through control of part of the national press, Germany not only defended her illegal activities but could launch a campaign in which neutrality was equated with patriotism and the final goal of which was to bring about Romanones' downfall.

Events reached a climax in 1917. The war entered a more violent phase with Germany's announcement in February of an all-out submarine offensive. One month later, a spontaneous insurrection in Petrograd overthrew the Tsarist autocracy and in April the United States abandoned its traditional isolationism and intervened in the conflict. In Spain, *Francophiles* regarded these developments as confirmation that the war in Europe had become an ideological struggle between democracies and autocracies; *Germanophiles* insisted that the country should be kept out of the European conflict.

The intensification of the German submarine offensive against neutral shipping and the subsequent interventionist attitude adopted by

the United States and several Latin American Republics, persuaded
Romanones that the time had come to break off diplomatic relations
with Germany. The sinking of the *San Fulgencio*, a vessel carrying a much-
needed cargo of British coal, torpedoed despite having a German safe
conduct and being already in Spanish waters, seemed to Romanones the
right psychological moment to exploit popular opinion and take the final
step against the Central Powers.[45]

The Count miscalculated the situation. Revolutionary events in Russia
had sent waves of panic among Spanish ruling elites. More than ever
they were determined to stay out of the European nightmare. They
concluded that with a militant working class, a restless Catalan bourgeoisie and an unreliable officer corps, it was madness even to consider
entry into a war for which, after all, Spain was neither militarily nor
economically prepared. Hence Romanones, only counting on the support
of the regime's enemies, Republicans and Socialists, was opposed by
the neutralist section of his party led by the rather colourless Marquis
of Alhucemas and by the king himself. On 19 April 1917 Romanones
was dismissed and replaced by a new Liberal cabinet presided over by
the Marquis of Alhucemas.

After the fall of the Tsar, a frightened Alfonso XIII threw his support
behind the German cause. It was his personal intervention that led to
the Count's fall.[46] On 27 May, at a pro-Allied gathering at the bullring
in Madrid attended by over 20 000 people, the king was accused of
being the major obstacle to the democratization of the country and
warned that he might soon be following the fate of the monarchs of
Russia and Greece. The meeting went on to affirm that only by joining
forces with the Allies could Spain become a democracy and take an
active part in the construction of a new world order.[47]

As he became the main target of the *Francophiles*, Alfonso was increasingly worried by the existence of officers' trade unions whose leaders
openly talked about ending royal favouritism and cleansing the army.
They reminded him of the Russian Soviets and hence he ordered their
dissolution. On 1 June, the governing classes were shocked when after
arresting the leading *Junteros* for refusing to disband their unions,
almost the entire officer corps revolted. The army sent an ultimatum
demanding the release of their arrested leaders and even made preparations for a military coup.[48] The Alhucemas cabinet resigned after less
than two months in power.

The *Juntas'* victory was all but in name a *pronunciamiento* and a devastating blow to civilian sovereignty. Their movement was above all an

outburst in defence of the corporate interests of the army. Yet the reformist language used in their mouthpiece, *La Correspondencia Militar*, marked by constant attacks on the ruling oligarchy, galvanized all the anti-*turno* political forces. They welcomed the officers' rebellion believing that the army was no longer the praetorian guard of the regime and instead was leading the way to national regeneration.[49]

Furthermore, amidst a deafening clamour in the country for new men and new political methods, Alfonso, as if nothing had changed, followed scrupulously the traditional *turno* fiction and entrusted Dato with the formation of a new government. The latter promptly acted with the usual practices: closing parliament, suspending the constitution and introducing tight censorship. Real public opinion was infuriated. All the groups excluded from power by the *turno pacífico* seemed to agree that political reform was imperative. Revolution in Spain was not only desirable but had in some form or other become inescapable. Army officers, the *Mauristas*, the Catalan bourgeoisie, Republicans and Socialists coincided for the first time in their opposition to the *status quo*. It was evident that if they managed to co-ordinate their activities the ruling system was doomed.

It was the *Lliga Regionalista* which took the lead in the offensive against the ruling order. In fact, the *Lliga* was not necessarily anti-monarchist and certainly not revolutionary, but it was aware that the existing political unrest and widespread turmoil facilitated the undertaking of their ultimate objective: a realignment of politics by wresting power from the landed oligarchy. Moreover, being a reformist but a conservative force, the *Lliga* sought to carry out a political revolution precisely in order to prevent a deeper social revolt which would have undermined the industrial bourgeoisie's own power and status. Its leader, Cambó, regarded the rigid maintenance of a discredited political formula as the gravest danger to social order. He even declared that to be a revolutionary in such circumstances was the most conservative thing to be. The *Lliga* wanted a Constituent Assembly to transform the political structure of the country, not the 'storming of the Bastille'.[50]

The Catalan offensive gathered momentum when, in open defiance of the authority of the government, the *Lliga* summoned an alternative parliament in Barcelona in which deputies were to discuss the political renovation of the country. The so-called 'Assembly of Parliamentarians' took place on 19 July and constituted the most important attempt in the Restoration era to carry out a thorough political reform by peaceful means. Sixty-eight parliamentarians gathered that day in Barcelona to reject the continuity of the *turno* fiction and demand the summoning of a Constituent *Cortes* organized by a national government whose members should represent the real popular forces of the nation. A clean vote would be ensured by the appointment of a non-political representative at the Home Office. Finally, they set up three commissions to study, among other crucial matters, the concession of home rule to Cataluña and constitutional reform.[51] Republicans and Socialists, being averse to organizing a violent insurrection, were delighted to participate in an initiative led by the Catalan bourgeoisie. Yet Cambó and his partners failed to obtain the collaboration of Antonio Maura.

To a large extent, Maura's stand in the summer of 1917 could have changed the course of the Liberal monarchy. The *Juntas*, lacking political contacts, turned to him for leadership. Simultaneously, the parliamentarians sought to persuade Maura to join their cause. At this crucial moment, most *Mauristas*, eager to destroy the *turno* sham, were prepared to join a popular initiative to regenerate Spain. Hence Maura could have become the link between officers and parliamentarians. Besides, his support for the Assembly could have guaranteed that the movement was seen neither as a separatist plot nor a threat to the social order. Without Maura, it was unthinkable that the army could participate in a movement led by Catalans, Republicans and Socialists. Yet despite the urging of some leading *Mauristas*, including Ossorio and his own son Miguel, Maura declined all the approaches of both *Juntas* and Assembly. Notwithstanding all his fierce attacks on the *turno*, Maura was above all a devout monarchist and old-fashioned Liberal. Thus, even though he saw the need for political reform, he was unwilling to sanction any illegal manoeuvre which might endanger the throne or the supremacy of civil power.[52]

Maura's passivity not only paralysed and disarmed the *Maurista* movement, but also gave a temporary respite to the government. Eventually, the Dato administration, aware of its immense unpopularity, was to resort to any means, including hypocrisy, deception and trickery, in order to cling to power. Firstly, officers were mollified by the recognition of their *Juntas* and all kinds of promises, which in some cases reached scandalous proportions. On 10 July, behind the back of his own War Minister, Dato sent a letter via the Civil Governor of Barcelona to the *Juntas* promising to meet all their demands, by Royal Decrees if necessary. Dato was prepared to send to the reserve those generals blacklisted by the *Juntas* and to replace his War Minister with another more to the liking of the officers. Then, by cynical use and control of media censorship, the government conducted a campaign of deceit, harassment and misinformation, erecting a *cordon sanitaire* around Cataluña and portraying the Assembly as a pact between Catalan separatists and Red revolutionaries. A peak in this strategy of deception was reached by José Sánchez Guerra, Minister of the Interior, when he declared in the Conservative mouthpiece, *La Epoca*, that the Assembly had never taken place.

Despite governmental chicanery, the truth of the Assembly and its resolutions began to emerge. The Dato administration, desperately fighting for survival, feared that the parliamentarians, winning more popular support by the day, would be able to hold a second meeting in Oviedo on 16 August. But the government still had a last card to play: provoking the labour movement into an ill-timed general strike in order to scare the bourgeoisie, implicating the officers in the repression and then being able to claim to be the saviour of social order.[53]

Indeed, the sudden outbreak of a transport strike in Valencia coinciding with the celebration of the Assembly in Barcelona, gave the government the opportunity to regain the initiative. It is unclear whether the labour conflict in Valencia was the work of *agents provocateurs*.[54] There are hardly any doubts, however, that the government, outmanoeuvering the moderate UGT leaders, pushed the workers into a general strike. In the dispute between the railwaymen and the *Compañía del Norte*, the Socialists went to painful extremes to avoid the expansion of the transport conflict, but they constantly ran into the intransigence of the company; an intransigence which was supported, if not inspired, by the Conservative administration.[55] The Socialists were prepared to postpone the strike in order to have more time to reach a compromise, but they were rebuffed. They even expressed their willingness to accept the dismissal of their militants, the main cause of the conflict, if the company gave a written explanation. Not only was this denied, but the government also insisted that the UGT either accepted an unconditional surrender or went ahead with the strike at the announced date. The former could not be accepted as the UGT was well aware that it would mean the practical destruction of the railway union. Hence, having exhausted all means of negotiation and under pressure from the CNT, the Socialists decided to link the transport dispute with the General Strike announced in March. Overconfidence and optimism certainly influenced the decision to launch a General Strike on 13 August. After the previous events of the summer, they believed that they could count on the support of the bourgeoisie and at least the neutrality of the officers.[56]

On 13 August 1917, for the first time, Socialists led a revolutionary strike to overthrow the regime. Careful instructions were given encouraging workers to avoid violence and instead fraternize with the troops. Moreover, they refrained from any far-reaching social and economic demands, limiting their objectives to the implementation of the resolutions taken by the Assembly in July.[57] The Socialist 'baptism of fire' went wrong from the start. There was not to be a Spanish Petrograd. Badly organized, the movement failed to spread beyond the main urban centres and, with the exception of Asturias, was easily crushed in less than a week. The bourgeoisie maintained an ambivalent position, waiting for the situation to develop without making any specific commitments. The officers forgot all their anti-oligarchical language of the previous two months and followed the orders of their generals. The military response was, if anything, shocking in its unexpected brutality.[58] Rumours spread by the government that foreign gold was behind the disturbances removed their last hesitations. Most of them concluded that it was better to shoot workers in Spain than to dig trenches in France.

The collapse of the General Strike represented the failure to impose democratization from below. Yet the government's victory was short-lived. Once the revolutionary spasm of August was over, both the Catalan bourgeoisie and the *Juntas* continued their offensive against the ruling system. Cambó began a tour of propaganda throughout Spain in order to keep alive the spirit of the Assembly. In an atmosphere of growing optimism, the parliamentarians gathered for a second and last time in Madrid in mid-October, where they confirmed their commitment to carry out the conclusions adopted in July. The attitude adopted by the army was even more alarming. The officers soon discovered that the popularity they had enjoyed in June had evaporated after the brutal repression of the strike. Moreover, they also realized that they had been used by the government to put down a rebellion which it had itself provoked. Their resolution to act was confirmed when a cable from the Minister of the Interior advising the Civil Governors to bide their time until the moment to crush the *Juntas* arrived, was intercepted. The final and anticipated deadly blow to the government arrived on the night of October 26, when a document signed by all the corps of the army was delivered to the king. The message was an ultimatum in which Alfonso was very respectfully advised to appoint within the next seventy-two hours a new cabinet more in tune with the wishes of the nation, otherwise the officers would take the initiative themselves.[59] For the second time in a few months, the military had overthrown a government. The Liberal monarchy lay in tatters.

The Structural Crisis of the Liberal Monarchy

Before 1914, cultural progress, demographic changes and economic modernization, meant that existing forms of elitist politics were beginning to break down in Europe. The growing consciousness and organization of those classes excluded by the ruling systems was reflected in increasing calls for social reform and political change. The Great War accelerated and made irreversible that trend. Such a devastating conflict produced massive economic dislocation and social distress, which in turn intensified ideological militancy and class struggle. It heralded the arrival of a new era of mass politics in which traditional rulers, confronted with the unwelcome prospect of genuine democracy and with the threat of radical political change, found it impossible to turn back the clock of history.

In Spain, the ultimatum of the army not only represented the death warrant for the Dato cabinet but also the end of an era. In November 1917, the political hegemony of the dynastic parties ended. The *turno pacífico*, the monolithic foundation of the Liberal order since 1875, was destroyed. Yet the potential for democratization died with the crushing of the August strike and the collapse of the Assembly movement.

The great losers of the 1917 events were the dynastic parties. Although still dominant in all the administrations until 1923, they were mere caricatures of their former selves. Increasingly divided into rival factions, they never managed to reconstruct the *turno*. Furthermore, they failed to meet the growing demands generated by the social mobilization and political consciousness brought about by the war.[60] The real winners were the Catalan industrial bourgeoisie, the Crown and the army.

After a record political vacuum of eight days without government, the solution was a monarchist coalition cabinet presided over by Alhucemas. In that cabinet, the Catalan Nationalists were represented for the first time. The *Lliga*'s sudden about-face in November 1917 was decisive in saving the regime and dashing all hopes for political renovation. It switched sides once its main objectives were achieved: the political monopoly enjoyed by the *turno* broken and now Catalan Regionalists holding two portfolios which included control of the economy. The *Lliga* both created the Assembly and, with its participation in the new government, contributed to its final demise. In fact, the U-turn of the Catalan Regionalists, although shocking for their allies on the Left, only followed the bourgeoisie's historical trend. The proletariat was used as a travelling companion to put more pressure on the governing elites. Once the power of the latter had been seriously impaired, it was easier for the party of Catalan industry to seek an accommodation with the landowning classes than to continue its uneasy alliance with the labour movement.[61]

The crisis of 1917 also sealed the anti-Liberal alliance of Crown and army. Constitutional practices were preserved, but the king and the officers saw their authority strengthened at the expense of the discredited governing elites. By eliminating the reformist peril enshrined by the Assembly, Alfonso conserved his privileged position as the ultimate arbiter of politics. At the same time, the *Juntas* were represented in the cabinet by Juan de la Cierva, a former Conservative minister and now leader of his own faction on the extreme Right of dynastic politics. Cierva, lacking Maura's liberal scruples, agreed to be the officers' representative and ensured that their economic and corporatist demands were met.[62] Henceforth, the officers and the king increasingly acted as an anti-constitutional party with power of veto to make and topple cabinets. The result was social conflict, political instability and, in the end, the destruction of the political system.[63]

The Alhucemas coalition never went beyond a temporary patchwork put together to tide over the existing crisis. In the general elections of February 1918, Republicans and Socialists confirmed their advance in the main cities, but rural *caciques* remained omnipotent, delivering their votes to Conservatives and Liberals. Yet the former were now divided into three rival factions and the latter into five. Hence, far from renovation, the destruction of the *turno* led to political deadlock and instability. Soon after, the War Minister, Cierva, taking advantage of the existing political fragmentation and of his special status, began to behave as a dictator unaccountable for his decisions. In early March and behind the back of the other ministers, Cierva introduced by Royal Decree a Military Reform Bill. It did not reform anything but pleased the officers by meeting their economic demands.[64] At the same time, the War Minister pushed aside his fellow cabinet members and decided to solve an ongoing postal and telegraph strike by ordering the militarization of these services. A unique situation then occurred when the government resigned, but with one minister, Cierva, refusing to do so.

Amidst the ensuing panic and chaos, the eyes of the entire political class turned for salvation to Maura, the only leader with enough charisma and reputation to form a new coalition which could avert the emergence of a dictatorship by Cierva backed by the officers.[65] The result was the creation on 22 March 1918 of the most impressive government of the Restoration era. Presided over by Maura, it contained three former Prime Ministers and other outstanding politicians such as Santiago Alba and Francesc Cambó. The so-called *Ministerio de Primates* ('Cabinet of Titans') was received with popular enthusiasm. However, the flamboyant new government never matched expectations. In fact, its achievements were extremely poor and it lasted in power little more than six months. Its failure and disintegration revealed the full extent of the crisis of the liberal system.

In foreign policy, the impotence and fragility of such a 'formidable' coalition was fully displayed. Despite glaring evidence of Germany's illegal activities in Spain, the government could not take any stern measures. Thus Germany behaved almost with impunity: her submarines causing havoc among the Spanish merchant fleet and her intelligence services hiring gangsters, Anarchists and even policemen to inform on and disrupt industrial activity which could help the Allied war effort.[66] Nevertheless, not even at the eleventh hour when the conflict was reaching its conclusion in the continent was Spain's strict neutrality abandoned. In reality, king and army vetoed any hasty decision which might endanger 'the good relations' with the Central Powers.[67] The spectre of the Russian Revolution and the awareness of military incapacity determined Alfonso's resolution to stick to a neutrality which was proving not only fatal but humiliating and ridiculous.

In domestic matters, apart from the concession of an amnesty in May for those implicated in the revolutionary events of the earlier year, little more was accomplished. Once the panic which had sealed monarchist unity faded, traditional internal squabbles and petty rivalries resurfaced, making it impossible to undertake any enterprise with success. During the summer the coalition began to fall apart. When parliament reopened in October, a frustrated Maura attended the sad spectacle of ministers attacking one another and all claiming the succession of the still existing coalition.[68] The 'Cabinet of Titans' collapsed in shame.

The fall of the Maura administration coincided with conclusion of the Great War. However, the armistice of November 1918 did not put an end to the struggle in Europe, it only changed its appearance. It was henceforth no longer a frontal confrontation between two warring camps, but an era of class struggle, revolutionary zeal and ideological militancy. Bolshevism found a ready audience among the war-weary populations and began to spread westwards, initiating the richest period of revolutionary activity since 1848. Falling living standards and shortages of food and fuel prompted soldiers, workers and peasants throughout Europe to engage in riots, mutinies and uprisings on a scale previously unknown. By 1921 the revolutionary *élan* began to peter out. A period of economic and political reaction followed. In many countries, the post-war social struggle had produced waves of panic among the ruling classes. Hence their rejection of parliamentary and constitutional methods as a valid system of defending their interests, and their support for authoritarian formulas.

The Spanish case was the regional version of the general crisis which engulfed the rest of Europe. Spain was caught in the spiral of social violence and ideological militancy which swept across the continent. After 1918 the social and economic situation worsened dramatically. The kind of artificial protection which had existed during the war years disappeared and the country's traditional deficit in trade reappeared. Prices continued to increase, reaching a peak in 1920, while salaries lagged far behind.[69] News of the Bolshevik triumph in Russia and the post-war economic recession intensified the class struggle. Shortages and inflation forced the distressed population to acts of violence. From 1918, food riots and assaults on shops and bakeries often involving women and children became a common feature.

It was evident by Autumn 1918 that Spain was sliding into a revolutionary situation which, unlike in 1917, possessed both an urban and a rural dimension.[70] However, it was not the UGT–PSOE but the more militant Anarcho-Syndicalist CNT that capitalized on the growing discontent. The brutal suppression of the revolutionary strike of August 1917 halted the militant impetus of the Socialist leaders. After 1917, they were absolutely opposed to any further revolutionary adventure. By contrast, the experiences of 1917 only reinforced the CNT's anti-parliamentarian leanings and its determination to continue the struggle against the regime.[71] Hence, in this moment of mass mobilization and social conflict, Anarcho-Syndicalism became the leading force within the organized working class, even making inroads into traditional Socialist strongholds. In December 1919, the membership of the UGT (with 211 342 members) lagged far behind that of the CNT (which boasted a membership of 790 948). Ironically, the spread of Bolshevism failed to generate a strong Communist movement in Spain.

A Communist Party was eventually created in April 1921 after a split in the PSOE.[72] It remained a tiny group attracting only a minority of the Asturian and Basque sections of the Socialist movement. Fist fights and even shootings between Socialists and Communists in these areas became commonplace. The Communist cause equally failed to win over the CNT. Initially, the Anarcho-Syndicalists mistook Bolshevism as a confirmation of their vision of revolutionary spontaneity. Thus the CNT adhered provisionally to the Communist International in December 1919. In June 1922, after hearing the report submitted by Angel Pestaña during his stay in Moscow in the summer of 1920, the CNT abandoned the Communist organization.[73] Communism thus failed dramatically to establish a solid foothold in Spain in the 1920s. There was simply no ideological room for it squeezed between the legalism and moderation of the UGT–PSOE and the radicalism and militancy of the CNT.

Class struggle and social violence was at its fiercest in the rural south. Hundreds of enthusiastic Anarchists travelled from village to village spreading the news of the revolution and the subsequent repartition of land among the peasants in Russia. It provided the always restless Andalusian peasantry with the necessary myth and hope to spark a rebellion. Between 1918 and 1920, the starving peasants rose throughout southern Spain demanding 'land and bread'. Both local authorities and bourgeoisie were thunderstruck by the determination and organization of the peasants. Many fled in panic to the safety of the cities. Real power lay in the workers' trade unions which had sprung up amidst the revolutionary euphoria. Temporarily a dictatorship of the toiling masses existed in all but name.[74]

At the same time, the CNT's growth was astonishing in the industrial centres, particularly in Cataluña. In the summer of 1918, the *Confederación Regional del Trabajo* (CRT), the Catalan branch of the CNT, under the leadership of pragmatists such as Angel Pestaña and Salvador Seguí, was reconstructed. The old craft trade unions were replaced by modern industrial unions (*Sindicato Unico*) whose objective was to include all the workers in a given area working in different jobs but in the same industry. The entire labour force was divided into thirteen industrial activities or *ramos*. Thus in times of social struggle, the duration of the conflict could be longer and the strength of the movement greater.[75] CRT membership trebled in little more than a year to 345 000. The formidable strength of the new *Sindicato Unico* was fully revealed when a strike broke out in February 1919 at the Anglo-Canadian hydroelectric concern in Barcelona known as 'La Canadiense'. The mobilization of the Catalan proletariat was stunning. The strike lasted forty-four days, leaving the city totally paralysed and gaining the workers a remarkable victory.[76]

The Spanish ruling classes, like their European counterparts, were in a state of panic and frenzy. For them, revolution seemed imminent. To make matters worse, there was an imminent economic recession on the horizon which they planned to counter by massive lay-offs of workers and cuts in production. However, in order to do so, the Anarcho-Syndicalist movement had first to be crushed. Thus the Spanish bourgeoisie in general, and the Catalans in particular, frightened by the growing power of the CNT, dropped any reformist intentions that they might have harboured in the past and sought to defend their economic interests. Industrialists and landowners resorted to sheer violence. They hired gangs of thugs and sponsored paramilitary groups, and, ultimately, turned to the army for protection. Employers would settle for nothing less than the CNT's total destruction. A miniature civil war was in the offing.[77]

Between 1919 and 1923, short-lived governments in Madrid were unable to control the increasing violence and terror which reigned in the country. The alliance between employers and army officers not only operated behind the backs of these governments, but even began to behave as an anti-state lobby forcing the fall of those cabinets opposed to their plans. In 1919 alone, two governments, one Liberal led by Romanones and the other Conservative led by Joaquín Sánchez de Toca, attempted to seek a conciliatory solution to the social crisis and were forced to resign. A detachment of 20 000 troops was sent to Andalucía where towns were occupied after pitched battles, workers' unions were closed and hundreds of militants imprisoned. At the same time, the streets of Barcelona became a battlefield. In November 1919, the Catalan employers launched a massive lock-out which lasted two months and left 200 000 workers jobless. One month later, the so-called *Sindicatos Libres* were established in Barcelona. A new trade union controlled by Catholic and Carlist workers, the *Libres* presented the employers with a great opportunity to split the labour movement. Under the protection of General Severiano Martínez Anido, who became Civil Governor of Barcelona in October 1920, gunmen of the *Libres* were trained and armed in military barracks and the notorious '*Ley de Fugas*' (the shooting in custody of captured Syndicalists 'while trying to escape') was introduced. For two years, this bloodthirsty and vicious officer ran Barcelona as his private fiefdom. Thousands of Syndicalists and left-wing sympathizers were imprisoned or deported to distant provinces (making the journey on foot and in chains). Hundreds of the best militants of the CNT, including three General Secretaries, were killed. Ironically, the brutal and indiscriminate repression boosted the position of the radical Anarchists in the CNT. The better-known and more moderate and pragmatist Syndicalist leaders became the targets of employers' gunmen. By contrast, it benefited the extremists in the CNT who were best equipped to operate clandestinely and most disposed to meet violence with violence. From 1919, Anarchist groups of action responded in kind and industrialists, overseers and strikebreakers were gunned down. Among these, the most outstanding victims were the Conservative Prime Minister Eduardo Dato and the Archbishop of Saragossa, shot dead in March 1921 and June 1923 respectively. The spiral of violence spread from Cataluña to other regions. Spain resembled a country in civil war: seldom did a day pass without the newspapers reporting fresh assassinations or new acts of vandalism.[78]

A further devastating blow to the ailing regime came from Morocco. Since 1909 Spanish troops had been engaged in an unpopular and massively underfunded campaign against the local tribes. In the summer of 1921, the country was shocked when news arrived of a major rout at Annual, where over 12 000 Spanish troops had been massacred. The impact of the defeat led to a national uproar demanding that those responsible be brought to account for such a disaster. It was the last nail in the coffin of a system accused of leading Spain to international humiliation. Alfonso was, for many, the real target of the popular demands for investigation into responsibility for the disaster. He, and he alone, had encouraged General Silvestre to initiate the reckless adventure which had turned into such slaughter.[79]

After Annual, calls for a military take-over became deafening. The dynastic politicians saw their role reduced to that of verbally abusing one another in the *Cortes* which, now more than ever, functioned as a mere talking shop. Parallels with the Italian case, where Mussolini seized power in October 1922, were drawn continually in the right-wing press. In December 1922 a coalition of Liberal factions under the leadership of the hapless Alhucemas came to office. The new government presented a vast programme of social, economic and constitutional reforms which were intended to produce modernization of the regime. There were also hopes that after four years of violence a peaceful solution could be reached in the labour conflict. Nothing of the kind happened. During the following months every progressive scheme was abandoned or put aside. In fact, the government was only successful in using the traditional methods of patronage and falsification to win the general elections of April 1923. The failure to deliver any of their promises only confirmed the unwillingness or incapacity to reform the regime from within. By the summer, the government was discredited, broken and divided.[80]

It was in this climate of political disarray, social warfare and economic dislocation that the same groups which had benefited from the crisis of October 1917 – the Crown, the Catalan industrial bourgeoisie and the army – decided to end the constitutional façade and support an authoritarian solution in September 1923. General Miguel Primo de Rivera did not overthrow the last constitutional government, he merely filled the vacuum which had existed since 1917.

3

FROM DICTATORSHIP TO REPUBLIC, 1923–31

Regeneration from Above: The Arrival of an 'Iron Surgeon'

The establishment of a dictatorship in Spain in September 1923 should be viewed in the wider context of the general European situation. The social and economic distress produced by the Great War, the spread of Bolshevik ideas and the power vacuum created by the collapse of the Central Powers, initiated a period of massive class struggle and political turmoil which heralded the arrival of mass politics and the death-knell for the oligarchic Liberal orders on the continent. It was not so much the threat of revolution, which had clearly subsided by the early 1920s, as the fear caused by the growing strength of the organized labour movement and the challenge presented by the advent of genuine democracy which persuaded the ruling economic and social classes to support authoritarian formulas. Ironically, one of the more bizarre consequences of the Bolshevik Revolution was that the interwar years were an era of virtually uninterrupted working class defeats.[1] The destruction of the Soviet regime in Hungary in the summer of 1919 and its replacement by Admiral Horthy's dictatorship inaugurated an era of political and economic reaction which swept Europe during the 1920s and 1930s.

Primo de Rivera's coup formed part of that general pattern. It was the response of the frightened dominant classes in a society in transition between oligarchic and democratic politics.[2] The surprise was not that a military *pronunciamiento* took place in Spain, but that it arrived so late.[3] Calls for a dictatorship in right-wing circles had been growing since 1919. They became deafening after the disaster at Annual and the increasing spiral of social violence.

When Primo made his bid for power nobody was prepared to defend an ailing and corrupt constitutional system deeply affected by a crisis of authority. On the contrary, it was welcomed by a broad spectrum of public opinion. The passivity or benevolence with which the coup was received revealed the insurmountable gap between society and dynastic politics, as well as the popular will to welcome political change.[4] To the gauntlet thrown down by Primo, the Liberal cabinet responded with defeatism, impotence and a reluctance to force a showdown with the military plotters. Nobody expressed that feeling better than the Prime Minister, who seemed to be relieved to pass the burden of government onto somebody else. Indeed, the Marquis of Alhucemas summed up the frustration of the governing elites when he greeted the rebellion with a mixture of cynicism and relief, remarking that he had a new saint to commend himself: Saint Miguel Primo de Rivera, because he had released him from the nightmare of governing.[5]

The working classes had no reason to mobilize in defence of an elitist order. Apart from an aborted attempt by the Communists to organize a one-day general strike in Bilbao, in general the organized labour movement received the coup with apathy. After years of social warfare and brutal repression, the CNT was exhausted and unwilling to take on the army, while the more cautious Socialists adopted a strategy of 'wait and see' and forbade their militants to join any revolutionary initiative.[6] On the other hand, the Catholic Church, the Chambers of Commerce, and financial and employers' organizations responded with enthusiasm and jubilation.[7] In Cataluña, where Primo de Rivera had been Captain General since March 1922, the *pronunciamiento* counted on the active complicity and participation of the wealthy classes. Since the removal of Martínez Anido in October 1922, they had turned to Primo for help and guidance in their violent struggle against the CNT. Outstanding elements of the Catalan bourgeoisie accompanied the general from the moment when he 'pronounced' against the government until his triumphal departure from the train station bound to Madrid to form a new administration.[8]

Crucial to the outcome of events was the attitude of both the army and king. After 1917 with the growth of social warfare and the existing political deadlock, the role of the military in decision-making and their encroachment upon civilian sovereignty had been unstoppable. However, when the rebellion took place, Primo could only be sure of the support of a minority of the armed forces. Yet his move was more than mere bluff. The Captain General of Barcelona knew he could rely on the passivity of the majority of the army in what could be termed a 'negative *pronunciamiento*': in fear of dividing itself, the army refrained from taking sides, thus sending a message to the government that officers were not expected to fight fellow officers.[9] With this attitude, the army was leaving the final decision in the hands of the king as head of state and main source of power in the Canovite system. Hence the monarch was the master of the situation and responsible for its outcome.[10]

Alfonso XIII, if technically innocent of being behind the military rebellion, was at least well aware of its preparations and did nothing to oppose it. On the contrary, he quickly showed his readiness to welcome a dictatorship.[11] Since his crowning in 1902, Alfonso had shown his willingness to govern by the use and abuse of his royal prerogatives and his preference for the army to the detriment of politicians.[12] The solution to the crisis of 1917 sealed the alliance between king and officers. In the following years, scared by the advance of Bolshevism, Alfonso did not conceal his contempt for parliamentary politics, lambasting in public and private the constitutional system. The colonial disaster in Morocco and the possibility of being incriminated in the issue of responsibilities confirmed his opinion that the sterile dynastic parties offered him no protection against the enemies of the throne. In the summer of 1923, Alfonso even toyed with the idea of taking on himself the role of national saviour and setting up a personal dictatorship. He was dissuaded by Antonio Maura and instead let 'those who do not let others govern assume the responsibility of government themselves'.[13]

The coup, just a few days before the opening of parliament which after the summer recess was to discuss the recommendations of the parliamentary commission working on the Colonial Disaster, definitely counted upon the king's sympathy. He was eager to see that debate buried.[14] During the night of 13 September, Alfonso deliberately took a long time to arrive in Madrid, refusing to back any exceptional measure which could be adopted by his government and making clear that his primary allegiance was to 'his army'. Once in the capital he rapidly dismissed the Liberal administration and invited Primo de Rivera to form a military government.

In his first trip abroad to Italy in November 1923, a jubilant Alfonso introduced Primo de Rivera as 'my Mussolini'. Indeed, like Fascism in Italy, the Spanish dictatorship constituted the local solution to the crisis of oligarchic liberalism. Primo admired Mussolini, banned any attacks on the Fascist regime in the Spanish press, established excellent relations with Italy and during his years in power tried to copy some of the principles of the Italian model. However, his regime never attempted to create the kind of totalitarian new order envisaged by the Fascist ideology and was closer to other military dictatorships then established in Europe. Primo's *pronunciamiento* certainly represented a break with the tradition of nineteenth-century praetorian intervention. The officers no longer seized power as the representatives of a political faction, but claimed to be above partisan politics and defenders of the sacred values of the nation endangered by the corruption and mismanagement of the existing ruling system. The army thus became both the symbol and the pillar of national unity and regeneration from above. In line with the anti-parliamentarian tendencies of this era, its objective was the establishment of a strong, authoritarian and centralized state, which by destroying both the inefficient liberal system and the threat of the organized labour movement and separatism offered the road to economic modernization from above, but stopped short of the revolutionary mobilization of Fascism.

Primo seemed to be the ideal candidate to lead a new regime. As an Andalusian landowner, a devout Catholic, a good monarchist and then Captain General of Barcelona, and thus the spokesman for the Catalan industrial bourgeoisie, he seemed to possess the right qualifications to remould the power bloc and build a new equilibrium of forces by accommodating interests of the landowning classes with those of the industrial bourgeoisie and bring to an end the political deadlock of the previous six years.[15]

From the start, it was obvious that Primo lacked a clear political philosophy. He created a military administration with representatives of the different branches of the armed forces, suspended the constitution, ended jury trials, dissolved the *Cortes* and declared martial law over all the country. In his first manifesto to the nation, the dictator expressed the main features which were to define his rule: paternalism, populism, machismo and political amateurism. Moreover, by insisting on saving Spain from the hands of the professional politicians who, since the Disaster of 1898, had been ruling the country for their own benefit, Primo claimed the mantle of Joaquín Costa's 'Iron Surgeon' – the interpreter of the general aspirations of a country weary with the reigning political corruption. The dictatorship portrayed itself as an attempt to undertake national regeneration from above by performing radical surgery. Primo even implied that his rule would be a short parenthesis in the life of the nation during which, supported by all citizens of goodwill, quick solutions would be found to deal with Spain's maladies (social disorder, economic recession, the colonial war in Morocco, etc).[16]

The first years of the dictatorship were quite successful. In this period, Primo de Rivera confined his role to that of 'Iron Surgeon' heading a Military Directory as a temporary surgical operation to release Spain from the grip of old politics.[17] His populism and bon-homie was welcomed by most Spaniards tired of the elitism of the previous system. The dictator, unlike the dynastic politicians, possessed charm and sympathy, spoke the language of the street, and did not attempt to conceal the vulgarity of his manners or his fondness for celebrations, alcohol and women. He even declared that he had learnt the art of government at the casino of his natal town, Jerez.[18]

His campaign against *caciquismo* and old politics was more a success in terms of propaganda than in reality. In order to consolidate his status of 'Iron Surgeon', the previous governing classes were continually denigrated and criticized in the official press as unscrupulous politicians misgoverning the country by fraudulent methods of clientelism and nepotism. Their power-bases of patronage were demolished when former politicians and public servants were forbidden to act as company directors. Town councils all over the country were dissolved. Between September 1923 and April 1924 generals took over as civil governors. Some of them then began to be replaced by civilians, particularly after December 1925, but the percentage of civil governorships in the hands of the military always remained very high. At the same time the decree of militarization of the administration of October 1923 meant that army officers were sent as *Delegados Gubernativos* to every province to supervise and conduct the election of new councillors, civil servants and administrative staff. As the shock-troops of the anti-*caciquista* crusade, they became 'pocket iron surgeons' whose objective was to bring about the moralization of public life by seeking and supporting outstanding and good-willed citizens.[19] Notwithstanding all the regenerationist aura, in most cases, these *Delegados Gubernativos* soon abused their authority, thus creating a new type of *caciquismo*. Furthermore, they rarely confronted the influence of the traditional *caciques*. In reality, the delegates seldom challenged the position of the local landowners or notables. On the contrary, they established a working relationship with the entrenched vested interests who were eager to join the rising bandwagon and so continued their dominance of rural life.[20]

After years of class struggle and warfare, the dictatorship restored law and order and initiated a golden era of social peace. General Martínez Anido was in charge of the Home Office as a guarantee to root out the opposition. Martial law and emergency measures lasted until May 1925. The Communist Party and the CNT were banned and hundreds of their militants imprisoned. Yet state repression, quite low in terms of bloodshed compared with the previous years, did not explain solely the dramatic improvement in labour disputes and industrial relations. In fact, one of the regime's greatest innovations was its experiment with social policies and its attempt to find support among the organized labour movement. There was a real concern to create a fairer society and reach a social deal to improve the living standards of the working classes. In order to do so, the Socialist movement was singled out as a responsible and reformist organization which could be drawn into a *modus vivendi* with the state. After initial hesitations, the reluctance to collaborate with the regime of the political wing of the party led by the ex-deputy for Bilbao, Indalecio Prieto, was defeated. The moderate leadership of Julián Besteiro and the trade unionist wing led by Francisco Largo Caballero welcomed the opportunity to establish their hegemony within the working classes while gaining concessions for them. Their view was that Socialists could best defend the interests of workers and peasants if they attained positions of influence within the state. Thus Socialists found their way into the social and economic institutions of the regime. The form of the state mattered less than the continued existence of the Socialist organisation within it.[21]

The dictatorship borrowed from Fascism the idea of corporatism or the establishment of arbitration committees of workers and industrialists concerned with improving class relations, solving social disputes and discussing legislation. It was the ideal conclusion of a centralized and interventionist state pursuing a social policy of conciliation. However, when the so-called *comités paritarios* or joint committees were finally consolidated by law in November 1926, they never adopted the all-embracing style of the Italian regime but were characterized by a benevolent paternalism. Unlike Italy, syndicalist freedom was respected and workers were not represented by a single Fascist union. In fact, the Socialist UGT acquired the lion's share of labour representation above the *Libres* or the Catholic trade unions. Moreover, while employers bore the burden of financing the committees and had to abide by decisions largely favourable to the workers, the proletariat still had the right to resort to strike action.[22] Even the CNT's old guard led by Angel Pestaña contemplated the idea of participating in the regime's corporatism and accepting its arbitration machinery. Yet this was furiously opposed by the Anarchist hard-liners. The latter founded, in a secret meeting in Valencia in July 1927, the *Federación Anarquista Ibérica* (FAI) with the objective of capturing the leadership of the organization once it could resume its activities legally.[23]

Social peace lasted practically until the end of the regime. Urban workers had years of gradual improvement in living standards and safe employment. Prices of basic commodities dropped, there were significant increases in public spending on education, social benefits and health, ambitious public works projects were undertaken and workers' rights were defended in the *comités paritarios*. Nevertheless, the countryside remained untouched by these paternalist experiments. The dictatorship avoided infuriating the landed interests by ignoring key issues such as *latifundismo*, social injustices or agrarian reform.[24]

In economic terms, this was an era of industrial expansion. Old ideas of *laissez faire* were abandoned and replaced by protectionism and state intervention. The dictatorship represented the triumph of autarky: economic nationalism based on state control, commitment to very high tariffs, support for national industry and enlargement of the public sector.[25] It was largely the programme traditionally defended by the Catalan bourgeoisie and was also in line with Costa's schemes of economic modernization through the development of national resources and the reactivation of the economy by governmental investment in public works such as road construction and the overhauling of the railway system.

In 1924 the National Council of the Economy was created to defend national agrarian and industrial interests. Spain became one of Europe's most heavily protected economies with the third largest public sector after the Soviet Union and Italy. Full employment and vast ambitious programmes benefited ordinary workers, but large companies were the big winners as the state assisted and encouraged combines, industrial take-overs and monopolies. The regime's corporativism, control of production and regulation of markets ended in abundant examples of favouritism and excessive bureaucratism. The orgy in public spending was mostly paid for by the so-called 'extra-ordinary budget' which expected to raise capital from the surpluses in the ordinary budget and by public loans and credit. Consequently, the durability of the regime and its economic programmes depended on the confidence of the wealthy classes.

The last immediate problem for the dictatorship was the colonial war in Morocco. On this issue, Primo de Rivera was considered to be an *abandonista*, siding with the peninsular and bureaucratic officers who had formed the *Juntas de Defensa* and was prepared to contemplate the idea of pulling out, partially or totally, of Morocco. Primo had made speeches in the past making clear his position against the continuity of the conflict in Morocco, a constant financial and human haemorrhage that the country could not afford. The exposition of his *abandonista* ideas, which included plans for exchanging Gibraltar for Ceuta, cost him his post as Military Governor of Cádiz in 1917 and the Captain-Generalcy of Madrid in 1921.[26] Despite this record, many of the so-called *africanistas* or colonial officers, fearful of possible incrimination for the colonial defeat at Annual and the erratic policies and permanent underfunding pursued by the civilian governments, supported the coup. They soon felt outraged when the dictator filled his administration with *Junteros* and ordered a general retreat to new defensive lines and the repatriation of large numbers of conscripts. Their objections were vociferous and immediate. Francisco Franco and other leading colonial officers took advantage of Primo's tour of the Protectorate in July 1924 to openly express their discontent. In almost every garrison that the dictator visited the reception was marred by some snub and constant lack of respect.[27]

Fortune seemed to smile on the dictator. The Spanish retreat was contemplated by Abd-el-Krim, the rebel chieftain, as proof of weakness. Hence he not only continued harassing the Spanish troops but, emboldened by his successes, began the invasion of French Morocco. The outcome was a Franco-Spanish Conference which met in Madrid between 17 June and 25 July 1925 and led to a joint military operation. On 8 September Franco headed the landing on Alhucemas Bay, while the French army advanced from the south pushing the rebels into the Spanish sector. In May 1926, caught in this vice-like squeeze, out-numbered and out-gunned, Abd-el-Krim's forces were forced into unconditional surrender.[28] Primo de Rivera had successfully crushed in a few months a colonial rebellion which had been a nightmare since 1909.

The Disintegration of the Dictatorship

If Primo de Rivera had retired in 1925 or 1926, he probably would have gone down in Spain's modern history as one of the most popular statesmen ever. His problem was that he seemed unable to find the moment to go. Ignoring his early pledge of a temporary stay in power, he began moves to perpetuate his rule by adopting a more civilian form of dictatorship. Yet if he had proved successful under the mantle of 'Iron Surgeon', his failure was to be evident as architect of a new political order.

From April 1924 the *Delegados Gubernativos* played a crucial part in the creation of a new party, *Unión Patriótica* (UP), based upon the mobilization of citizens of goodwill and order. At the same time, the Catalan *Somatén*, a kind of bourgeois militia, was expanded to the rest of the country. In December 1925 the Military Directory gave way to a civilian cabinet with the incorporation of technocrats into the government, and the establishment was announced in September 1926 of a National Consultative Assembly, approved by a plebiscite, whose objective was to draft a new constitution that would be the foundation of the regime.

The creation of UP constituted an attempt to turn the military dictatorship into a widely accepted and supported authoritarian regime, based on a mass national movement. Yet it never really succeeded. UP remained an artificial movement which became the perfect protective umbrella for the traditional *caciques* and thousands of careerists thirsty for jobs and official protection, a wide club in which they could share the spoils of power. With the exception of some *Mauristas* and a relative success in mobilizing the rural Castilian bourgeoisie, the new movement failed to draw in the 'new men' sought by the regime. In fact, at a local level there was a remarkable continuity of the traditionally local dominant groups.[29]

Unlike the dynamism and mobilization that characterized Fascism with its all-embracing totalitarian objectives and its brutal persecution and elimination of political opposition, Primo remained a paternalist leader and an improviser in politics, unable or unwilling to annihilate his adversaries. UP was never created with the idea of establishing a 'new order' but to give passive conformity and credibility to the dictatorship. Its ideological stagnation was concealed behind a façade of public involvement and external features borrowed from the Italian model. There were mass parades and ceremonies of homage to Primo, and even ridiculous attempts to establish a personality cult. The dictator, portrayed as an exceptionally talented leader, was hailed as 'the sentinel of the west' always alert to the Bolshevik threat, the saviour of the fatherland and the personification of perfect values of humanism, piety and justice. UP lacked any ideological coherence and could barely conceal its internal differences and contradictions under vague ideas of monarchism, patriotism and anti-Communism. The party lacked any organic vitality, remaining a governmental creation nourished from above.[30] It was thus far from being a valid instrument which could be mobilized to back the regime when this began to show signs of exhaustion. In fact, as the regime began to decline, the numbers of UP members fell dramatically, from 2 million in August 1924 to 600 000 in December 1929.[31]

Equally, the *Somatén* was not even a pale shadow of the Fascist militia. Being organized by the local Captain Generals who often used the local *caciques* as agents of recruitment, it lacked any real independence and always remained under army control. In Cataluña its membership was smaller than it had been in 1923.[32] The National Assembly, the crucial institution commissioned to advise Primo in legislative matters and write a new constitution, was another utter failure. The internal discrepancies in the regime could never be solved. Lacking the visionary zeal or even the ruthlessness of other dictators, Primo de Rivera could never balance, or suppress, the competing interests within the system. In the end, the final draft by the National Assembly favoured a position intermediate between an authoritarian and a liberal formula which did not please anyone. After more than three years of paralysis and disagreements, that institution drew up plans for the creation of a corporative chamber consisting of representatives of the state, and the provinces, and the municipalities, as well as delegates of social classes and of UP. Half of them would be appointed and the other half elected by universal male suffrage. Yet the new parliament would have little more than advisory powers, as the executive was only responsible to the monarch. The project was rubbished by the press and attacked by all the semi-tolerated dissident political voices of the country, and was even criticized by Primo who found it 'too authoritarian'. Faced with widespread contempt, criticism and indifference, the project had to be abandoned.[33]

As political uncertainty mounted, opposition to the dictatorship began to gather momentum. Prominent intellectuals criticized Primo's arbitrary rule, his widespread use of censorship, his close links with the Catholic church, and advocated the return of basic freedoms. In 1924, the famous philosopher and writer Miguel de Unamuno was deported to the small Canary Island of Fuerteventura. Others went into exile where they continued to launch devastating attacks against the dictator and the king.[34] The liberal intelligentsia and the progressive middle classes were outraged by a decree of May 1926 enabling the government to decide on exceptional measures even when these were incompatible

with the law.[35] Thousands began to flood into the Republican movement. The expansion of ecclesiastical orders, the obligatory study of
religion in schools and finally a decree in March 1928 allowing Catholic
colleges to give academic degrees mobilized the academic world against
the regime. Since 1928 universities were closed as professors vacated
their chairs and students fought in the streets and campuses against the
police. Primo had to back down, but it was too late and the damage was
done. Class disruptions and youth protests lasted until his last days in
power.[36]

Cataluña was another stronghold of opposition to the dictatorship.
The centralist and patriotic position of the regime meant the banning
of any language or symbols but those of Castilla for official purposes.
Even the *Mancomunidad* was suppressed in January 1924. The active
support for the military coup offered by leading members of the *Lliga
Regionalista* lost that group its credibility as the main representative
of Catalan Nationalism. Henceforth that role was monopolized by
left-wing Catalan Republicans. Leading them was *Estat Català*, a quasi-
separatist party led by the eccentric Francesc Maciá, a former army
colonel. From his exile in France, his group collaborated with Anarcho-
Syndicalists, mounting joint raids and expeditions across the border.
With the exception of a fierce encounter at the Prats de Molló in
November 1926, Maciá's adventures hardly went beyond symbolic
gestures. Yet they served to rekindle the spirit of defiance and resistance in Cataluña.[37]

More threatening for the regime was the emergence of opposition
within the army. Up to 1925 this had come basically from the *africanistas*.
After the successful campaign in Morocco, Primo was not only reconciled with them but began to promote colonial officers to key positions.
Franco himself was appointed in 1928 to be in charge of the Military
Academy at Zaragoza. However, the regime was faced with growing
unrest from other military sectors. On the one hand, senior generals
with close links with the old political class had been prepared to accept
Primo's *pronunciamiento* as a necessary temporary military intervention
in politics, yet they were furious at the dictator's plan to transform his
provisional government into permanent rule. On the other, Primo's
attempts to cut down the military budget, reduce the inflated officer
corps and deal with the promotion system, were bound to create enemies. While the *junteros* defended the closed scale or strict promotion
by seniority, *africanistas* supported advancement by war merits. By the
decrees of 9 June and 26 July 1926 Primo once more came up with

the intermediate solution of offering promotion by special selection carried out by a *Junta* largely appointed by the dictator and in which senior generals were bypassed.[38] This measure was seen as a possible source for favouritism and arbitrary decisions, and opposed particularly by the aristocratically dominated Artillery Corps, where promotion had always been by seniority.

On 24 of June 1926, veteran Generals Weyler and Aguilera, in close touch with old politicians such as Count Romanones and even with some Republicans and Anarcho-Syndicalists, intended to stage a coup to restore the 1876 Constitution. Such a farcical combination was a total disaster and easily dismantled by the authorities. Primo was happy to fine the conspirators. Those wealthy like Romanones were fined half a million pesetas, and modest Anarcho-Syndicalists just 1000 pesetas.[39] Soon a new conspiracy was organized under the leadership of José Sánchez Guerra, head of the Conservative party since the assassination of Dato in March 1921. Once again it relied on a farcical combination of forces, members of the old governing classes, Anarcho-Syndicalists and army officers. Guerra landed clandestinely in Valencia expecting to lead a military revolt. However, at the last minute most officers involved in the plot hesitated, giving the government time to nip the coup in the bud. The rebellion was only successful among artillery officers and these only gained the upper hand in the small town of Ciudad Real. The uprising was easily put down. Primo dissolved by decree the Artillery Corps, but in a clear show of his fading grip and in open defiance to the dictator, a military court found Sánchez Guerra not guilty. The verdict augured ill for the future of the dictatorship.[40] These revolts, although unsuccessful, were revealing the growing divisions in the army and the shrinking support for the regime.

The final blow came with the onset of the world economic depression. The trade slump of 1929 brought about a sharp drop in exports and rising prices. Regarding the maintenance of the peseta as an indicator of economic prosperity, the state intervened to defend the exchange rate. Speculators helped themselves to juicy pickings of the country's gold and currency reserves and finally the peseta had to be devalued, falling from 29.50 against sterling in July 1928 to 42.10 two years later. The depreciation of the peseta shook the confidence of economic circles and of the whole regime.[41] Years of lavish public spending meant a huge deficit budget and lack of reserves to fall back on.

It was the withdrawal of support from the Right, not the attacks of the Left, which doomed the regime to destruction.[42] Landowners and industrialists rejected a fiscal policy which paved the way for a more progressive taxation and, in a clear vote of non-confidence, refused to contribute the loans and credit that Primo was desperate to raise. They were not prepared to pay for the economic crisis and made it clear that the regime no longer inspired their confidence. The same groups who hitherto had hailed the regime's interventionist and corporatist policies as splendid, now became their most outspoken detractors. Primo was vilified and his paternalism, mainly institutionalized in the arbitration committees, portrayed as a tragic error, a sell-out to the Socialists and of permanent damage to their interests.[43]

Feeling the collapse of the regime, even the Socialists began to distance themselves from it. Opposition to the existing collaboration with the dictatorship had intensified since 1927, but it was not until the summer of 1929 when a majority voted against participating in the National Assembly that Prieto's pro-Republican wing gained the upper hand. By then, even Largo Caballero, ever sensitive to grass-roots sentiment, had come to accept the imminent fall of the regime and wished to avoid the isolation of the Socialist movement as the only significant force in Spain still supporting Primo.[44] Hence the PSOE–UGT gradually moved towards the Republican camp, knowing that they had the advantage of being the strongest organization in the country.

Finally, the king also sought to disassociate himself from his own prime minister. Alfonso was well aware that Primo's growing unpopularity was involving the monarchy. Determined to escape its consequences, he thought that by dismissing the dictator he might appear as a liberator, and might wash himself clean of the responsibilities of 1923.[45] Alfonso had welcomed the dictatorship in 1923, but it was not long before he began to regret the demise of the old order. Unlike the Italian King Victor Emmanuel, Alfonso XIII was reluctant to play second fiddle to a dictator who was more charismatic than him. He had grown tired of a regime in which he played a secondary role. He could no longer dissolve parliament and form and dismiss cabinets, and was upset by Primo's mordant outbursts that he would not be 'bourbonized'.[46] His role was limited to rubber-stamping Primo's arbitrary decisions. The dictator's establishment of the National Assembly and the military decrees of 1926 were particularly resented by the king who found himself in February 1929 aghast at having to sign the decree dissolving the Artillery Corps. Yet there was nothing he could do as long as the regime basked in its economic and military successes. However as soon the dictator's fortune began to fade in 1929, Alfonso could not wait to get rid of him and began to approach members of the old governing elites to find an alternative.[47] He certainly had been informed in the past of the different military conspiracies. Alfonso was aware of a new military intrigue being organized by General Batet, Military Governor at Cádiz, which seemed to have the support of many garrisons in the south and the sympathy of the Captain General of the region, Alfonso's brother-in-law.[48] The king used the existing economic downturn as well as the growing army's discontent to exert pressure on Primo to retire quietly.

In January 1930, the dictator was a very sick man suffering from diabetes and alcoholism. Feeling isolated and abandoned, he secretly resorted to the eccentric measure of writing personally to the Captain General of each military region to find out whether he still could count on their backing. It was a desperate last attempt to cling to power and an open display of disrespect towards Alfonso, the Head of State.[49] When all of them replied evasively, Primo realized that he no longer enjoyed the support of the military, the ultimate source and foundation of his power, and resigned on 28 January 1930. In this way, the rule of one of the most curious and peculiar dictators of this century ended. He died in exile two months later in a small hotel at Paris.

The Departure of the King

By casting his lot with the military in 1923, Alfonso thought he was securing his throne. In fact, he was destroying his constitutional underpinnings and joining his fate with that of the dictatorship. After almost seven years of authoritarian rule, the king was clearly vulnerable to attack and criticism. Moreover, showing a clear divorce from the national will, Alfonso decided to follow a course which increased popular discontent. Instead of moving quickly towards a genuine constitutional and democratic system, he hurriedly entrusted the government to another general, Dámaso Berenguer, with instructions to dismantle gradually Primo's political apparatus and to organize the return to the constitutional normality of the pre-1923 years. This interregnum was known as the *Dictablanda* ('soft dictatorship').[50]

By opting for a 'bayonet with a civilian touch', the king made a colossal error.[51] The appointment of another general confirmed the reluctance of the monarch to undertake a thorough break with the past. Berenguer was a loyal monarchist and the current Head of the Royal

Military Household. Yet Alfonso could not have chosen a more disliked officer. Berenguer had been the High Commissioner of Morocco at the time of the Annual disaster. Hence, regardless of his personal guilt for that catastrophe, his name was forever associated in popular opinion with the slaughter of thousands of Spanish soldiers.[52] Besides, he was a sick man confined most of the time to a wheelchair and thus lacking the energy needed to consolidate the dynasty.

Furthermore, it was ludicrous to expect that the impact and the significance of the previous regime could merely be erased as if nothing had happened. Above all, Alfonso seemed to have forgotten that the dictatorship had basically been established because the oligarchic liberal order could no longer work. Additionally, far from being a parenthesis in which nothing had changed, dramatic economic and social transformations took place during Primo's rule. The obvious consequence was that the old elitist system, moribund in 1923, was an anachronism in the much more modern and advanced Spain of 1930.

It was a fallacy to attempt to turn back the clock of history. The dictatorship's expansionist economic policies unleashed a process of modernization which altered Spain's social fabric. They helped consolidate the upsurge of the middle classes and of the organized labour movement, loosening the grip of electoral *caciquismo* and making it impossible to restore the politics of immobilism. In these years more than a million people migrated from the countryside to large cities such as Barcelona, Madrid, Valencia, Bilbao and Zaragoza. Agriculture was still the largest sector of the economy but fell from 57.3 to 45.51 per cent of the workforce, while employment in the industrial and service sectors grew from 21.9 and 20.81 per cent to 25.61 and 27.98 per cent respectively. Increasing urbanization was accompanied by a similar dramatic fall in illiteracy, more children in primary schools, a spectacular development of the railway and road system, and the production of telephones, radios and other signs of modernity.[53]

The attempt to reconstruct the old dynastic parties was never a viable solution. Fragmented and in crisis before 1923, they were in total disarray in 1930. Banned from public office, their clientelist networks destroyed and constantly denounced in the dictatorship's media as little more than corrupt professional politicians, the former governing elites appeared not only as obsolete and outdated figures from a past era, but also little better than thieves. Moreover, when the king recalled their services to save the throne, many did not respond with enthusiasm. They could neither forgive nor forget that Alfonso had identified himself for years with a regime which denigrated and vilified them. Some, like the former Minister of Economy and leader of one of the Liberal factions, Santiago Alba, refused to return from exile. Others like Sánchez Guerra, nominal head of the Conservative party, initiated in February a campaign attacking this unconstitutional and 'perfidious' monarch. He was joined by many former ministers and prominent personalities of both dynastic parties declaring themselves monarchists without a king. Known as Constitutionalists, they supported the organization of elections to a constituent assembly which would draw up a new constitution, discuss the king's responsibility in the arrival of the dictatorship and debate the kind of regime to follow. Others went even further and joined the Republican camp. Those dynastic politicians still prepared to rally round the Crown were marked by their striking defeatism and pessimism and soon engaged in their traditional petty squabbles and their attempts to return to old clientelist practices. Thus the Liberal notables, Count Romanones and Marquis of Alhucemas, could not conceal their anger when Berenguer filled his administration with members of the old Conservative party. Believing it was their *turno* to manipulate the next elections, they kept plotting to bring down the government. For them nothing had changed and the sooner they returned to power the sooner they could resume business as usual.[54]

By contrast, the republican cause had never seen better days. It is suggested that the dictatorship converted more people to Republicanism than all the historical Republicans together.[55] The former regime's censorship, economic interventionism as well as other arbitrary measures and rules pushed thousands of small entrepreneurs, intellectuals and members of liberal professions towards the Republican camp. The mobilization of these people who previously had not revealed any interest in politics, was a formidable boost for Republicanism. All of them hoped to find a remedy for their grievances by opting for thorough political change and instead of regarding the unknown with apprehension, they considered a change of regime as the best means to leave behind the clerical obscurantism and social backwardness of the old order.[56]

In February 1926 a coalition of Republican groups, *Alianza Republicana*, was created. In this alliance, old Republican parties such as Lerroux's Radical party were joined by new ones led by young and energetic leaders whose reputations were not tarnished by a shady past and whose programmes included social and economic measures which could appeal to the lower classes. Among this new generation stood out Manuel Azaña, President of the Atheneum, Madrid's cultural centre. The alliance sought to minimize differences between its members and collaborate in common goals: bring about the end of the dictatorship, and then organize a successful campaign which could lead to the summoning of a Constituent *Cortes* and the establishment of a modern and progressive Republic.[57]

With the gradual return of civil liberties of expression and association in 1930, the Republicans went on the offensive. Unlike the monarchists clinging to the old clientelist system, they excelled at the new reality of mass politics, attracting thousands of people to rallies and meetings in which the king was continually accused of perjury by violating his own constitution and supporting the dictatorship. The Republican propaganda campaign benefited enormously from the constant defections of former Monarchists who now were eager to join the republican bandwagon. Outstanding were the examples of Niceto Alcalá Zamora, leader of one of the factions of the Liberal party and former minister, and that of Miguel Maura, son of the five times Prime Minister Antonio Maura. Facing the prospect of an obsolete and old-fashioned monarchy slowly crumbling, large sectors of the middle classes, attracted by the prospect of a conservative Republic led by moderates, believed it was worth sacrificing an unreformed king and prevent the situation from degenerating into social catastrophe.[58]

On 17 August 1930 representatives of different Republican groups, including Catalans and, in a private capacity, the Socialists Indalecio Prieto and Fernando de los Ríos, held a crucial meeting at San Sebastian. They agreed to be an alternative power bloc to the ailing monarchist regime and collaborate in an electoral campaign to bring about a Constituent *Cortes* which would lead to the proclamation of a Republic and the granting of autonomy to Cataluña. With the full incorporation of the Socialists into the pact in October, a provisional government was set up in which the latter were given three portfolios and the rest were shared by the different republican groups. In order to dissipate the fear among the middle classes that a Republican take-over would mean a thorough social revolution, the crucial posts of Prime Minister and Minister of the Interior were left for Alcalá Zamora and Miguel Maura respectively. As Miguel Maura described it, the Republican–Socialist pact represented a 'mattress' upon which the new regime would land softly.[59] The Republic would be a system of order and moderation avoiding demagogy, excesses and anarchy, while filling the dangerous power vacuum created by the disintegration of the monarchy.

Nevertheless, feeling the national mood for quick change, the provisional government also engaged in revolutionary activity to accelerate the demise of the old order. They concluded that the Berenguer administration, rocked by growing industrial action and students' protest, would collapse with a mere show of force. Neither did they want to be overtaken by the subversive activities of discontented officers who were in touch with Catalan Republicans and counted on the support of the rapidly expanding, after its legalization in April, CNT. Thus the provisional government tried to give cohesion and bring together all the disparate forces working to bring down the regime. After many hesitations and postponements an insurrection was organized to take place on 15 December 1930. Chastened by the bitter memories of 1917, the labour leaders proceeded cautiously, waiting for military participation before committing their followers to a general strike.[60]

Three days before the accorded date, the impulsive Captain Fermín Galán initiated the rebellion on his own in the isolated northern garrison of Jaca (Huesca), near the French border. Upset by so many vacillations and doubts, the impatient Galán believed that his daring action would force the hand of the irresolute Republicans and would be the spark to ignite an all-embracing revolutionary movement in the country.[61] In freezing temperatures, his small forces were the following day beaten back by troops sent from Zaragoza. After a quick encounter which caused a few casualties, Galán refused to flee abroad and gave himself up. He and his second in command were summarily executed within twenty-four hours. The authorities acted rapidly before the 15th. Most members of the provisional government were arrested or had to go into hiding.[62] Most compromised officers remained passive, with the exception of a minority which took over the airbase of Cuatro Vientos outside Madrid and confined their actions to flying over the capital and dropping some anti-monarchist leaflets before escaping abroad. With the workers failing to come out in large numbers in the main cities, the revolt remained confined to some scattered pockets easily put down by the police.

Following the usual dismal record of Spanish rebellions, the insurrection of 15 December was an utter disaster. Its failure lay in the heterogeneity of forces, ranging from bourgeois republicans to discontented officers and the labour movement, combined in the same enterprise. However, despite its defeat, it delivered a further blow to the regime.

The Republic had now its martyrs and Alfonso could be presented as a bloodthirsty and cruel monarch willing to consolidate his reign by any means. Additionally, the revolt had revealed the determined attitude of different sectors to return to the pre-1923 *status quo*. This included a significant proportion of the armed forces. Many had hesitated at the last minute and refused to act, but they were no longer plotting against the dictatorship but against the dynasty itself.[63]

Berenguer's hopes to restore normality were finally dashed in February, when all the political parties refused to take part in the general elections. Even the liberal notables refused to participate in re-establishing the *turno* charade, especially since the Conservatives were the group to benefit from it. Berenguer had no alternative but to resign.[64]

Realizing that the power vacuum was threatening to bring the regime down, Alfonso approached Sánchez Guerra, hitherto one of his most bitter critics, and entrusted him with the creation of a new cabinet. This measure that might have been appropriate one year earlier was now too little too late. Sánchez Guerra did not waste time and hurried to prison to offer the bewildered members of the provisional government portfolios in his cabinet. It was either an extremely cunning move to incorporate, or at least split the opposition, or the final proof of monarchist desperation. Once they got over their initial surprise, the imprisoned Republican leaders declined to be ministers of the king. By asking for their collaboration, Sánchez Guerra had indicated how precarious the situation of the monarchy was.[65]

Alfonso, as shocked as the Republicans by Sánchez Guerra's behaviour, promptly accepted the latter's resignation. As in the post-1917 years, the solution to the crisis was once more the formation on 18 February of a national government containing rival monarchist factions. A temporary alliance of old politicians had been tried in the past when they still had some charisma left with scarcely positive results, but it could hardly be expected to succeed in 1931. In the new administration there were old characters of the past, from the Liberal Romanones to the ultra-Conservative Cierva, mixed with representatives of the financial, landowning and business elites.[66] They were joined by two groups in open decline: the Catalan *Lliga* and the fragments of *Maurismo*. The latter, a shadow of its past proud movement, and the former a declining force in Catalan politics since its support for the dictatorship in 1923.[67]

Thus an increasingly isolated king, running out of ideas, left the survival of the regime in the hands of a combination of failed and discredited politicians and representatives of the most privileged economic sectors of the country. It proved to be fatal. On the one hand, the old governing elites were gripped from the start by a paralysing mood of defeatism and gloom. Gabriel Maura, one of the ministers, described it later as feeling they were escorting the Crown to its funeral.[68] On the other, they quickly returned to their old habits of mutual distrust, nepotism and spoil-sharing. Indeed, the creation of the new government was marred by a sad squabbling over posts and patronage. It was thus no surprise that Romanones, the professional politician of the old school *par excellence*, was the strong man of the new situation.[69] They agreed that the frustrated and sick Berenguer should remain in the cabinet at the War Office. The two key posts of Prime Minister and Minister of the Interior were given to two irrelevant and non-political persons, the octogenarian Admiral Aznar and the inexpert Marquis of Hoyos respectively, as the competing interests of all factions had to be accommodated and no-one could be seen to have an edge in the amount of power and patronage over the others. Finally, in order to have time to re-organize their old clientelist networks, they decided first to hold municipal elections in April.

At the same time, the prison where the members of the provisional government were held had become a real source of authority. They resembled a shadow cabinet ready to take over control of Spain, receiving thousands of letters and visitors and being treated with extreme courtesy and respect by their jailors. Their trial in March was a farce. The government, eager to be seen as tolerant and merciful, advocated leniency with the distinguished prisoners. However, the military court went beyond that. Its President General Burguete, one of the fiercest repressors of the revolutionary movement of August 1917, revealed how much times had changed. He allowed the accused to travel from prison in private cars and agreed to hold the trial in the largest room so that a large pro-Republican audience, never contained in their cheering, could be present. Lawyers were permitted to turn the defence of their clients into an attack against the regime. The core of the defence was that there could not have been a rebellion against the constitutional order since the king himself had violated it in 1923. The verdict was a virtual acquittal: they received the minimum sentence of six months and one day and were then set free and greeted as heroes by enthusiastic crowds. Burguete even commented that he personally voted for their total absolution.[70]

For the April municipal elections, the Republican–Socialist coalition engaged in a frenzied exercise in popular mobilization, arguing in their programme that the outcome would be a plebiscite on the monarchy. Their activities contrasted with the passivity of the government, whose members, not familiar with the reality of mass politics, just kept busy reconstructing their old clientelist networks. The task of gaining the popular vote was left to 'patriotic' ladies, members of the nobility, some former partisans of the dictatorship, and above all the Catholic Church.[71]

The results of the elections of 12 April stunned the country. The monarchists obtained overwhelming majorities in the countryside but forty-seven out of the fifty-two provincial capitals voted for the Republican–Socialist coalition. In total, more than twenty-two thousand Monarchist councillors were elected, compared to almost six thousand for the opposition. Despite the overall Monarchist majority, clearly where public opinion could be expressed freely it had voted massively against the regime. The rural vote had no serious meaning, being just traditional sheep-like obedience orchestrated by the still omnipotent local *caciques*.[72]

It was not so much Republican strength as Monarchist disarray which proved decisive. During the crucial twenty-four hours following the results, the artificial foundations of the regime simply disintegrated. Unlike previously, there was never even a timid attempt to present the manufactured overall majority delivered in the countryside as a proof of endorsement for the monarchy. On the contrary, the bewildered monarchists, lacking will-power and baffled by the electoral outcome, conceded defeat and deserted *en masse*. The Crown was sunk into oblivion by a group of confused and leaderless politicians overtaken by a mixture of weariness and defeatism.[73] They accepted without resistance the unpalatable truth: the results were a plebiscitary verdict against the monarchy.

The provisional government had little to do with the course of events. They went through natural joy as the results were arriving to fear at their possible arrest and the imposition of martial law, to euphoria at the spectacle of the Monarchist edifice crumbling before their eyes.[74]

The first sign of governmental demoralization was given by the Minister of War, General Berenguer, sending out a circular on the night of 12 April to the regional military authorities urging them to avoid clashing with the people and to accept the expression of the national will. Prime Minister Aznar admitted the following day to an even greater concession of defeat. Asked by journalists if there was a crisis, he retorted honestly and naively that there could be no bigger crisis than that of a country that went to bed Monarchist and woke up Republican. With the exception of the hard-liner Cierva, most ministers in the extraordinary council of 13 April agreed with Romanones that the king had to be advised that the government could not continue, the people had cast their vote against the regime and negotiations with the opposition should begin as soon as possible.[75]

Alfonso did not need much convincing. By then, he was not only aware of the demoralization of his politicians, but also of the desertion of his army. The officers had acted in the past as the dynasty's praetorian guard, saving the throne in 1917 and 1923. However, after their recent experience during the dictatorship, the harmony of the military corps was shattered and thus they were not prepared to intervene again in politics.[76] The army's neutrality was the last nail in the dynasty's coffin. With their abstentionist attitude, popular will prevailed over royal sovereignty for the first time in Spain.

Romanones' visit in the afternoon of 14 April to Alcalá Zamora in order to negotiate a political truce confirmed to the Republicans that victory was theirs. An emboldened Zamora gave the king until sunset to abandon the country. Earlier in the morning, General Sanjurjo, head of the Civil Guard, had gone to the house of Miguel Maura, the Minister of Interior in the provisional government, to assert the loyalty of that institution to the Republic.[77]

Slowly but steadily, enthusiastic crowds, unchallenged by the authorities, began to pack the streets of the main cities. The power vacuum left by the Monarchist stampede was filled by the masses. Throughout 14 April one town after another proclaimed the Republic while no-one tried to defend the still-existing monarchy. Power lay in the streets, the provisional government only had to pick it up.[78]

The Second Republic represented the culmination of a process of mass mobilization and opposition to the old politics of notables. It had been halted but not crushed in 1917. The advent of the dictatorship in 1923 with a project of national renovation from above offered a different alternative but its failure cleared the way for the initiative from below. At the same time that the members of the provisional government were taking possession of official buildings, Alfonso XIII, symbol of a past era out of tune with the new political and socio-economic realities, was on his way to exile, swept away by the tide of history.

4

THE SECOND REPUBLIC: A BRIEF EXERCISE IN DEMOCRACY, 1931–6

La Niña Bonita

The establishment of the Republic was greeted with enormous joy by enthusiastic crowds. It was popularly nicknamed *la niña bonita* ('the pretty girl'). Many seemed to believe that almost magically overnight all the pending and highly conflictive social and economic problems inherited from the monarchy could be solved and a modern, progressive and egalitarian nation created. And yet, the new regime could not have come at a worst moment.

Indeed, in 1931 Spain constituted an exception in Europe. Whereas the Republic represented the first genuine exercise in democracy, elsewhere on the continent the political trend was taking an opposite direction as constitutional regimes were succumbing to dictatorships and Fascism. Furthermore, the entire world was plunged into the most dramatic economic depression ever known. Unemployment soared as incomes and exports fell, international trade plummeted and available capital dried up. Within this context of economic crisis and political extremism, the introduction of a package of reformist measures to improve the appalling conditions of many Spaniards led to dramatic consequences. On the one hand, the wealthy economic classes regarded the Republic as the antechamber of Bolshevism and prepared themselves to destroy a system which threatened their vested privileges. On the other, notwithstanding the reformist zeal of the new ministers, the impossibility of borrowing capital from abroad added to the huge debt inherited from the dictatorship's years of lavish expenditure meant that they lacked the means to carry through many of their projects. Thus when the rising expectations in traditionally aggrieved groups were not matched by reality, popular disenchantment began to replace the previous enthusiasm. The result was that the new legislation was insufficient to satisfy the Left while it inflamed the Right.[1]

In April 1931, for the first time in Spain, the state machinery was in the hands of a coalition of parties committed to the modernization of the country and the introduction of a vast programme of reforms. Their authority was confirmed by the results of the election to Constituent *Cortes* in June which gave an astounding victory to those who had signed the San Sebastián Pact. Out of 470 seats, the PSOE became the largest party with 116, several regional and national left-wing Republican groups returned 180 deputies; among the centre and right-wing Republicans the winners were the Radicals who with 90 deputies became the second largest group in the chamber. Alcalá's party failed to attract the moderate vote obtaining only 22 seats with another 20 going to some minor parties. The Right was utterly defeated as its diverse parties could only muster 45 deputies.[2]

The Republic constituted a resolute attempt to create a viable and accepted framework to solve Spain's fundamental problems by democratic means.[3] The government, first through emergency decrees and then in the Constituent *Cortes*, introduced a programme based on social and political reforms. It included curbing the privileges of Church and army, the drafting of a progressive constitution, the granting of autonomy to Cataluña and legislation to benefit the working classes, particularly the long-awaited agrarian reform.

The reform of the Catholic Church, both a privileged institution and steadfast bulwark of the monarchy, was regarded as a long overdue process necessary to transform Spain into a modern and secular state. Divorce and civil marriage were allowed by law, and religious symbols eradicated from public buildings. A more far-reaching threat to the social and economic status enjoyed by the Church was article twenty-six of the constitution which barred ecclesiastical orders from teaching, ended in two years state subsidies for the clergy and forced the latter to disclose its property and interests which for the first time would be under taxation.[4] At the same time, the War Minister, Manuel Azaña, introduced a package of reforms to modernize the armed services and make them an apolitical institution. The infamous Law of Jurisdictions which gave the military judicial authority over civilians was abrogated and officers had to take an oath of loyalty to the Republic. The question of 'responsibilities' for the disaster in Morocco was re-opened and some of the military arrested and tried. Measures to deal with the inflated officers corps, a traditional burden in the state budget, were approved. The number of divisions was halved, the length of military service reduced to one year, senior officers were encouraged to take voluntary early retirement on full pay, the Military Academy at Zaragoza was closed, and promotion by war merits frozen.[5]

Simultaneously, the Socialists Francisco Largo Caballero and Fernando de los Ríos, Ministers of Labour and Justice respectively, introduced a series of measures aimed at ameliorating the appalling living conditions of ordinary people, in particular those of rural labourers. Salaries were increased and rents frozen. Primo's arbitration committees were now re-named *jurados mixtos* ('mixed juries') and extended to the countryside. The eight-hour working day was introduced to cover all types of labour. Finally, in order to solve unemployment in rural Spain, the Laws of Municipal Boundaries and Obligatory Cultivation were passed. The former meant that employers could not introduce outside labour until those in a given municipality had jobs; the latter that land had to be used for arable purposes or otherwise be expropriated.[6]

The progressive character of these reforms had the effect of frightening the dominant economic classes who initially had believed that the departure of the king was a price worth paying in exchange for a socially conservative Republic. They felt that the implementation of this reformist legislation, particularly in a period of depression, meant a radical redistribution of wealth. Thus having lost political power in 1931, the landowning and financial oligarchy were not prepared to accept any changes which threatened their economic supremacy. Their intransigence was matched by their devastating condemnation of the government, particularly the Socialist ministers, accused of plotting the destruction of the capitalist system.[7]

The Right was in disarray after the fall of the monarchy. With the old dynastic groups disbanded, the badly organized new right-wing parties suffered a heavy defeat at the polls in June 1931.[8] Unlike the dynastic notables, the new political Right in Spain, largely influenced by the emergence of European Fascism, was authoritarian, nationalist and rabidly anti-democratic. Though united in the common goal of destroying the Republic and often co-operating closely, the right-wing parties pursued two different strategies. There were those known as '*catastrofistas*' because they devoted all their energies to overthrow the new regime by violent or catastrophic means. They included the Carlists, whose revival was largely produced by their fierce hostility to a lay and anti-clerical Republic. They quickly developed a paramilitary organization, the *Requeté*. Another group was formed by hard-line Monarchists who had supported and occupied important positions in the dictatorship. They were few in numbers but had great influence due to their individual wealth and connections with powerful interests. Finally, there were small Fascist groups who came together in 1933 to form the Falange under the leadership of Jose Antonio Primo de Rivera, the dictator's eldest son. In addition, there were others known as '*accidentalistas*'. They adopted a more legalist approach believing that the forms of government were 'accidental' and that the essential issue was the socio-economic content of the regime. In fact, the *accidentalistas*' stand was defensive and pragmatic. They were aware of the Right's precarious position in 1931 and of the impossibility of destroying the Republic at the peak of its popularity. Thus their plan was to play the democratic game, build a mass party with which to win elections and then take over the government and destroy the regime from within. Despite the different methods, the identification of objectives of both *catastrofistas* and *accidentalistas* was clearly revealed when they came together under a right-wing umbrella group known as *Acción Nacional*.[9]

The Republic's reformist legislation forced the Right to strike back. In particular, the *accidentalistas* proved to be extremely successful in using their vast financial resources and propaganda network in order to mobilize a formidable coalition of forces with which to launch their offensive against the government.

The upper echelons of the clergy had been among the most eager supporters of the old regime and were vehemently opposed to reform. Yet, though Catholicism had been consistently losing ground in the urban centres and in most of eastern and southern Spain, it still counted on the loyalty of the farmers of Castilla, the Basque Country and Navarra. Thus it can be argued that the anti-clerical zeal adopted by some Left Republicans, instead of a more gradual and cautious approach, was unwise and even self-defeating.[10] It resulted in the alienation of those moderates willing to compromise, such as the Papal Nuncio Monsignor Tedeschini, and strengthened the hand of the extremists within the Catholic hierarchy. Yet the argument of the Church being an innocent victim cannot be sustained. Even before the introduction of new legislation, influential Catholics such as the Cardinal Primate of Spain and

Archbishop of Toledo Segura already had declared war on the Republic with savage pastorals. They could not resign themselves to see the Church, the symbol of old Spain, suffer the modernization that had been undertaken in nearly all the Western world. Rooted aversion to democracy had been long embedded in the Catholic Right and had recently borne conspicuous fruit in its sympathy and active support for the dictatorship.[11]

Indeed, a central role in the creation of an *accidentalista* right-wing mass party was played by leading Catholics such as the highly influential *Asociación Católica Nacional de Propagandistas* (ACNP). Led by Angel Herrera, this organization of mainly former students at Jesuit schools owned the largest and most powerful chain of newspapers and radio stations. Herrera himself was the editor of *El Debate*, the most important Catholic journal.[12] The right-wing media echoed and inflated the vitriolic attacks of the Catholic hierarchy. The Republic was portrayed as the embodiment of anti-Spain: godless, satanic and evil. The expulsion from the country of rabid anti-Republicans such as Cardinal Segura and later of the Jesuits was the proof that the government revelled in crushing the poor and defenceless Catholic religion. That campaign was accompanied by subtle propaganda to win over the armed forces. The concession of autonomy to Cataluña was described as the beginning of the break-up of the fatherland and Azaña's reforms were distorted to make them appear as an attempt to crush the army. Particularly receptive were the *africanistas*, enraged by the re-opening of the responsibilities issue and the freezing of promotions on merit given during the Moroccan wars. These measures just confirmed their instinctive feelings of hostility towards the 'unpatriotic' Republic.[13]

At the same time, the ACNP relied for financial backing on its close links with business and employers' organizations, and for the creation of a mass following on its influence over the Catholic farmers in Castilla in the *Confederación Nacional Católica Agraria* (CNCA). Indeed, although industrialists and businessmen collaborated in the right-wing offensive, boycotting the new order by continuous flight of capital, the fiercest enemy of the Republic was the landowning class.[14]

Industry and business had already endured under the dictatorship wholesale paternalist measures that were never applied in the countryside. It was the rural oligarchy above all that became the main bastion of opposition to the new regime and the pillar on which a movement was organized to restore the religious and social order which had prevailed before 1931.[15] The Republican social legislation, although far from revolutionary, if implemented could have had far-reaching consequences in rural Spain. For the first time the balance of legal rights swung away from the landowners to the rural proletariat. The smooth functioning of the *latifundios* depended on a vast pool of surplus labour working endless hours for miserable wages. Apart from the pending threat of a thorough agrarian reform, the new laws meant that labourers now not only worked fewer hours, but also that their wages were increased since owners were now forced to grant overtime pay whenever they required a longer workday, as they almost inevitably did during harvest. In the context of a world depression with agrarian prices and exports falling, it constituted a challenge to their traditional sources of power and authority. With Socialists dominating the local administration and prominent in the mixed-juries, the working contracts were bound to be favourable to the labourers. Additionally, landowners would no longer be able to keep wages down by bringing cheap labour from outside or carry out rural lock-outs by leaving vast tracks of land uncultivated.[16]

Thus the countryside became the bitterest battleground in the 1930s.[17] It was the place where two opposing views clashed brutally: clerical and traditional against progressive, secular and egalitarian. It was also from here that Spain's underlying social conflicts were transmitted into national politics. On one side, the interests of the landless labourers were taken on board by the Socialists. During the first two years of the Republic, the composition and character of the UGT was altered drastically. With Socialists in the government, in particular Largo Caballero legislating as new Minister of Labour, thousands of unskilled and landless labourers from the south joined the *Federación Nacional de Trabajadores de la Tierra* (FNTT), the landworkers' union affiliated to the UGT. Consequently, the UGT was transformed from a relatively small organization of the labour aristocracy of the capital, and dockers, miners and metalworkers in the north, into a powerful mass movement where nearly 40 per cent were southern and radicalized landless labourers. The UGT not only became the largest movement of the organized working classes, but also displaced the CNT as the main representative of the rural proletariat.[18] On the other hand, the CNCA could mobilize hundreds of thousands of small tenants and farmers from central and northern Spain. Created in 1917, the CNCA represented the most successful Catholic movement in Spain. In 1931 under the leadership of José María Gil Robles, it became the strongest anti-Socialist organization. Despite its inter-class rhetoric, it was a confessional organization controlled by big landowners working closely with bishops and local priests.[19] With their Catholic sensibilities already aroused by the anti-clerical legislation, the Castilian farmers, poor but proud of their ownership status, were easily persuaded by the right-wing propaganda – which described in apocalyptic terms the government's pursuit of the collectivization of the land and therefore their own proletarianization – that they shared the same interests as those of the landowning oligarchy. They were the cannon fodder of the legalist Right. The struggle between these two mass movements, the Socialists and the legalist Right, was the main cause of the breakdown of the Second Republic.[20]

The Republic also had enemies on the Left. Initially the CNT under the leadership of the Syndicalist old guard, mainly Angel Pestaña, was prepared to establish a *modus vivendi* with the new regime. In particular, in their Catalan stronghold, years of common persecution, clandestinity and collaboration between left-wing Catalan Republicans and Anarcho-Syndicalists seemed to herald a period of good relations.[21] Yet for the Anarchists in the FAI there was hardly any difference between Monarchy and Republic. If anything, the new political system was worse since their bitter rivals, the Socialists, now held positions of power. Throughout 1931 an internal struggle was under way between moderates and radicals for control of the CNT. The FAI (Federación Anarquista Ibérica – the Iberian Anarchist Federation) preached a policy of implacable hostility towards the new regime, practising the so-called 'revolutionary gymnastics' or continuous violent urban and rural uprisings in preparation for the final revolutionary offensive. A wave of revolts and wild-cat strikes in different cities throughout 1931 led the government to resort to force and crush them brutally causing numerous casualties.[22] Governmental repression and Socialist control of mixed-juries played into the hands of the FAI. When thirty of their most significant moderate leaders tried to counter-attack with the publication on 1 September of a common statement condemning the reckless activities of the Anarchist hot-heads, they had already lost the battle. Most of them were dismissed from their posts and many even left the CNT to form a new Syndicalist movement, *Sindicatos de Oposición*.[23] With the FAI in full control, their campaign of violence continued unabated. Ironically, they were playing the game of the Right whose media were eager to accuse the Republic of a being a regime of anarchy and disorder.

It was remarkable that during its first months the coalition government remained united despite the mounting attacks from both extremes of the political spectrum. Ministers sought to minimize their differences, find compromises and remain together until the nation had been given a constitution.[24] Despite the heterogeneity of its components, consensus and moderation prevailed. The Socialists excelled in the exercise of caution. Indalecio Prieto was very prudent as Treasury Minister, controlling the budget deficit and tightening spending. Largo's and de los Ríos' decrees were endorsed by all ministers and seen as necessary proposals simply aimed at mitigating the gravity of the economic crisis. A more radical initiative giving workers a measure of control in industry was dropped and the more controversial question of *latifundismo* and agrarian reform was left to parliament to debate. As a concession to the Socialists, Spain was defined as a Republic of workers of different classes. Yet private property was recognized as a fundamental right which could not be expropriated except 'on grounds of public utility'. Catalan Republicans led by Maciá and his lieutenant Lluis Companys who had rushed in April to proclaim the creation of the Catalan Republic within Spain's Federal Republic quickly backtracked. They accepted the advice of the government to wait and recognize the faculty of the Spanish parliament to grant autonomy to Cataluña. Finally, Azaña's reforms were enthusiastically supported as a national necessity to cut the heavy defence budget.

The first cracks in the coalition were caused by the contentious religious question. The Catholic ministers Alcalá Zamora and Miguel Maura were evidently unhappy with the anti-clerical legislation. The burning of convents in Madrid and other cities in May produced dismay and divisions. They were temporarily solved when the Minister of the Interior, Maura, facing the indifference of many Left Republicans unconcerned by the fate of the Church, counted on the support of the Socialists to be given full powers to deal vigorously with those causing disorder and arson. Martial law was declared and the army called out to restore order and protect Church property. It was the very Catholic Maura himself who soon thereafter decreed the expulsion of the vociferous anti-Republican Cardinal Segura and the Bishop of Vitoria Múgica.[25] Yet the two Catholic ministers finally resigned in October when article twenty-six banning religious education was passed. Somehow, the coalition was patched up when with the final approval of the constitution in December Alcalá Zamora was elected first President of the Republic. The new constitution introduced universal suffrage to elect a single chamber and granted the vote for the first time to women.

More threatening in the long-term were the divergences between the two largest parties, the Radicals and the Socialists. The latter had traditionally criticized the opportunism, demagoguery and financial corruption of Lerroux's party. The shady reputation of the Radicals was such that in 1930 all those participants in the San Sebastián Pact agreed that they should not be given any portfolio related to economic matters.[26] In 1931, the Radicals could claim the mantle of being the senior Republican Party, but they had moved dramatically from their former revolutionary position of the early years of the century. Lerroux now presented himself as a moderate and the guarantor of a socially conservative Republic and, indeed, many former monarchists voted for and even joined the Radical Party in order to disguise their past under the cover of the 'republican respectability and historical prestige' of that party.[27] Monarchist infiltration accentuated the rightwards shift of the Radicals and confirmed the Socialists' belief that Lerroux was a power-hungry and opportunist crook. Socialists and Radicals avoided an open clash by both backing the candidacy of Azaña as new Prime Minister in October. However, it was evident that Lerroux believed it to be a temporary measure and that he, as leader of the largest Republican Party, should hold the post of Prime Minister. When in December, Azaña made clear that the *Cortes* would not be dissolved and that he was to stay with Socialist backing, the Radicals abandoned the government. An embittered Lerroux gradually began to move into opposition and to plot his come-back at whatever price.[28]

Agrarian reform and Catalan autonomy were the two main battle-grounds of 1932. They were key issues for the Right: the former was a threat to their economic power and the latter was considered the first step towards the break-up of the fatherland. The *accidentalistas* carried out a well-organized campaign of obstructionism and attrition in the chamber, introducing amendments and complicated technical questions for every clause of the new bills. It was a well-planned strategy whose objective was not only to delay the new legislation, but also to increase the exasperation and weariness of the labouring classes with the government. Ironically, the Azaña administration was rescued from the frustrating parliamentary deadlock by an aborted *pronunciamiento*. On 10 August 1932, General Sanjurjo, rebelled in Seville in order to 'rectify' the extreme revolutionary character that the Republic was adopting.[29]

The coup was quickly put down and the conspirators imprisoned. Its impact was the opposite to what Sanjurjo intended. It served to recycle

Republican enthusiasm and end the legislative paralysis. With right-wing deputies in disarray, and the Radicals momentarily playing up their reformist commitment, the agrarian reform and the Catalan statute were passed in September.[30] On 30 November Maciá's coalition of left wing parties, *Esquerra Republicana*, won a landslide victory in the first elections to the Catalan Parliament and he was elected President of the Catalan government or *Generalitat*.

The Right reached different conclusions from the military fiasco. *Accidentalistas* blamed the *catastrofistas* for the government success. According to them, a reckless action ended in one day all their achievements in stalling reform for months. Thus under the leadership of the parliamentarian for *Acción Nacional* and Secretary of the CNCA, Jose María Gil Robles, the *accidentalistas* formed in February 1933 a mass Catholic party: the CEDA or *Confederación Española de Derechas Autónomas* (Spanish Confederation of Right-Wing Autonomous Groups). It was a vast coalition of right-wing Catholic groups whose objective was to gain power by mobilizing Catholic and conservative Spain and whose slogan was the defence of religion, fatherland, law, order and property. Their refusal to declare their loyalty to the Republic, and their bellicose rhetoric full of admiration for Hitler and Mussolini made their acceptance of the democratic process sound hollow. Closely allied to the CEDA was the so-called Agrarian minority which had already obtained twenty deputies in the elections of June 1931. The hard-line Monarchists set up *Renovación Española*, an elitist and conspiratorial group led by the ex-minister of the dictatorship, José Calvo Sotelo. Nevertheless, both groups never stopped collaborating. It was reasons of tactics not of ideological or political incompatibility that produced the split. The legalist Right preserved its anti-Republican spirit intact, but remained committed to an accidentalist path in the belief that it was the best means to undermine the Republic.[31]

In such a context, agrarian reform was far from successful. While failing to fulfil the expectations of the workers, it terrified the landowners. After many internal divisions within the government and the discarding of several projects, the final law was clearly not a thorough reform. It was a document of extraordinary complexity with many provisions which were either vague or contradictory. It was clearly aimed at southern Spain, where more than one-third of the total land surface and about half of the cultivated area fell into one of the categories of expropriable land, and neglected measures which could have won over the smallholders of the north and centre. The Minister of Agriculture, the Radical–Socialist Marcelino Domingo, was a good-hearted but weak man who knew very little about agrarian matters. Like most Left Republicans he was more concerned with constitutional and political legislation and so failed to act energetically to impose the new law rapidly. Worse of all, the institution established to carry through the law, the Institute of Agrarian Reform (IRA) lacked the technical and economic resources to compensate landowners, resettle peasants and provide them with the minimum means to make their plots produc- tive. In one year, of the planned sixty thousand families who should have obtained land only 10 per cent of them had acquired it. Yet for landowners this was an assault on their sacred rights of property and encouraged them to bide their time to reverse the reform.[32]

Throughout 1932 violent clashes between peasants and authorities increased. Most revolts were Anarchist-inspired but some were sponta- neous acts of despair. In January 1933 the FAI once more organized an uprising against the state. It was rapidly crushed everywhere but in a remote village of Cádiz, Casas Viejas. There the rebels barricaded themselves in the house of the local Anarchist leader and began shoot- ing at the police. They were finally burnt out, put against a wall and shot. The final death toll was nineteen peasants and one policemen. Rural repression was nothing new in Andalucía; the difference was that this time it had not been perpetrated by the hated Civil Guard, but by Assault Guards, a recently created Republican police.[33] A widespread wave of protest swept the nation. It was not only Anarcho-Syndicalists who were enraged, but, in a blatant exercise of hypocrisy, Lerroux joined forces with the Right accusing the government of representing a barbaric regime persecuting innocent peasants.[34]

The Azaña administration never recovered from the Casas Viejas affair. One fatal consequence was that it exacerbated the internal ten- sions which had existed within the Socialist movement since the 1920s. The old leadership under the cautious Julián Besteiro, President of both PSOE and UGT since 1925, believed in a slow, peaceful and grad- ualist progress towards Socialism after going through a stage of bour- geois revolution. They were reluctant to cut links with Primo in 1929 and later opposed the idea of being part of the Republican govern- ment. For them, Socialists should not be involved in the bourgeoisie's historic task and should let the Republicans establish their own system, avoiding any ministerial collaboration. The moderates were outvoted in 1931 by the other two wings of the movement. There were those led by Indalecio Prieto who viewed the consolidation of the Republic as their main objective. Being democrats above all, they resisted co-operation with the dictatorship in the 1920s and were eager to participate with the Left Republicans in creating a progressive and social-reformist Republican order. There was also the trade-unionist sector led by Largo Caballero, which was always concerned with the best way to strengthen the influence of the UGT. Their pragmatism and opportunism led them to support the dictatorship in 1923 and then make an about turn when that regime was clearly crumbling. In 1931 Largo welcomed the Republic and enthusiastically accepted the offer to join the government. He was well aware that as Minister of Labour the state machinery could be used to the advantage of the UGT against the CNT as well as to introduce wide-ranging social legislation. The followers of Prieto and Caballero agreed that the Socialists had to be the major source of consolidation and defence of the Republic, but by 1933 their alliance began to founder. Whereas Prieto saw the continuity of the coalition government as the best formula to prevent the Right from re-gaining political power, Caballero's frustration with his experience in the cabinet increased. Largo loathed the idea of being in a government using repression against the working classes and events such as Casas Viejas made his position more difficult. No less important was his awareness of the growing bitterness in the countryside, the radicalization of the UGT, in particular of the FNTT, and the danger of losing ground to the Anarcho-Syndicalists. Disillusionment with the Republic among part of the Socialist rank-and-file began with the successful delaying tactics of the Right and their massive propaganda campaign equating the reforms with Bolshevism; despair was to follow when they realized that even as legislation was approved in Madrid it remained little more than hope on paper. There was limited machinery to enforce the new decrees and landowners managed to ignore them in the provinces. Socialist frustration was exacerbated by the fact that their militancy was restrained by their leaders in the government. Thus some like Largo began to question the wisdom of remaining in a cabinet unable to enforce its own legislation and which was sacrificing their credibility with the masses. This view took them gradually from being strong supporters of the Republic to their open advocacy of revolution. The unabated rise of Fascism in Europe and their belief that the CEDA was its Spanish variant encouraged even further that radicalization.[35]

To make matters worse for the embattled Azaña administration, Lerroux was now openly leading an offensive to oust the Socialists from government and 'return control of the Republic to the Republicans'.

In April 1933, local elections were held in those places where the results two years earlier had been suspended due to clear Monarchist rigging. The outcome was a victory for the CEDA and the Radicals. Despite being traditional right-wing areas of Navarra and Old Castilla, the Radicals claimed that it was ample proof that the electorate wanted political change. By the summer, Lerroux's plans gained momentum when the Radical–Socialists, one of the main groups in the government, split when its leader, the Minister of Agriculture, Marcelino Domingo, was opposed by a section led by Gordón Ordás who refused to continue the alliance with the PSOE.[36] The Radicals then tabled a motion of confidence that was won by the government with only a narrow majority. The close result was the excuse that Alcalá Zamora was seeking to dismiss Azaña. The Prime Minister was thus overthrown by a President who believed that his authority would be strengthened in a Radical-led administration. Using his presidential power, he mounted a constitutional coup and appointed a Radical cabinet without majority support in the chamber.[37] When the new government was brought down by a vote in parliament, Alcalá dissolved it and ordered new general elections.

During its two years in power the Azaña cabinet had modernized and transformed Spain faster than in the previous two hundred. The reforms had obviously caused deep traumas in society. However, the new laws had not been thorough and embracing enough to satisfy the Left, while fuelling the hostility of the Right and its determination to destroy the Republic.

The Politics of Reprisal

The electoral law had been designed to prevent fragmentation and return strong governments. In each province the party list with the majority of votes received 80 per cent of the seats and the second 20 per cent. It thus called for electoral coalitions since a relatively small difference in votes meant huge swings in terms of seats. Hence, by fighting separately in November 1933 the parties of the Left made a colossal mistake for which they paid dearly. With the *Caballeristas* ousting the followers of Besteiro in 1932 from their dominating positions in both the PSOE and the UGT, the Socialists, in most provinces, decided to fight alone.[38] The result was a catastrophe. The PSOE, although the single most supported party with 1.6 million votes, only returned 58 deputies. The Left Republicans dropped to 36 seats (23 of them belonged to the Catalan *Esquerra*). By contrast, the Right presented a united front and benefited from a well-funded and aggressive campaign. The CEDA and their allies the Agrarians with 115 and 36 deputies respectively became the largest group in parliament. The *catastrofistas* had 56 seats. The other great winners were the Centre and Right Republicans with 168 deputies. The Radicals, particularly, showed no scruples in entering into tactical alliances which, depending on the region, included in many cases the CEDA. Thus with only 800 000 votes, half the number of those obtained by the PSOE, they obtained almost twice as many seats, 102.[39]

Apart from the evident defeat of the former governmental forces, the outcome of the elections was far from clear. Gil Robles could not muster a majority in the chamber even if all the other right-wing parties backed him, nor would Alcalá trust the government of the Republic to someone known for his anti-republican rhetoric. At the same time, Lerroux and other minor Republican groups did not have enough seats to form a government. In December, the deadlock was broken when Lerroux was confirmed Prime Minister in a Radical-dominated cabinet with the support of CEDA votes.

Some have seen Lerroux's deal with the CEDA as a noble attempt to republicanize the *accidentalista* Right.[40] This thesis seems not to be borne out by the events in the following two years. On the contrary, by forsaking all their principles, the Radicals just confirmed their opportunism and shady reputation.[41] Whereas Lerroux was eager to obtain power regardless of the price, Gil Robles appeared as the strong partner in this unwritten alliance. According to their deal, the Radicals were allowed to share the spoils of office, but in return they had to introduce legislation put forward by the CEDA. That eventually amounted to the dismantling of the reforms of the previous period – the so-called 'politics of reprisal'. In this way, the Radicals became the Trojan Horse through which the Right won back the state machinery. In the context of deepening economic crisis and social dislocation, with unemployment soaring especially in agriculture, the building and metal sectors, and the lack of welfare provisions, the polarization of the country and the radicalization of the working classes reached a peak.[42] For the CEDA, the Radicals were mere pawns in its long-term strategy. For the time being, they could be used as a front to reverse the past legislation. Yet Radical administrations were short-lived affairs as they were continually held to ransom, dropping ministers or proposals not to the CEDA's liking. Robles' objective was to foster political instability (there were eleven governmental crises in less than two years), split the Radicals and leave Lerroux more dependent on right-wing votes, until finally the CEDA could rule on its own, destroy the Republican constitution and create an authoritarian corporate state.[43]

In March 1934, the CEDA threatened to withdraw its support unless Diego Martínez Barrios, too soft as Interior Minister for their wishes, was removed. Lerroux complied and in the subsequent reshuffle that portfolio was given to Rafael Salazar Alonso, a hardline landowner from Extremadura. Martínez Barrios, representative of the most Liberal wing of the party, moved to the opposition benches and in May, with twenty-two other deputies, created his own group, *Unión Republicana*.[44] As the Radical Party was shrinking, widespread bitterness and frustration kept increasing. Earlier reforms were flouted or reversed, the anti-clerical legislation abandoned, power swung back to owners who did not waste time in destroying the workers' gains of the past period by means of sackings, evictions and wage-cuts. The seeds of the civil war were thus sown.[45] In April, Robles created a new crisis when he imposed upon a hesitant Lerroux and a reluctant Alcalá, the granting of an amnesty for those involved in the conspiracy of August 1932.

The most conflictive spot remained the southern countryside. There social legislation was not so much destroyed right away as simply not enforced. With Salazar Alonso as Interior Minister, the rural oligarchy felt confident their time had arrived to recover much of the lost ground and reduce the peasantry to submissiveness once more. Socialists were sacked from mixed-juries and replaced by the landowners' representatives, salaries were slashed, working contracts were not fulfilled and land was returned to those expropriated. The exploited labourers were told by their landowners that if they went hungry they should *comed República* ('eat Republic').[46]

Unlike the CNT, the Socialists had discarded insurrectionary tactics and held back its militants until 1933, advising restraint and trust in governmental reform. Their confidence was, however, being gradually eroded by the slowness of the implementation of the agrarian reform. Then disillusion with defeat in the elections was followed by the employers' offensive. Against this background, the growing disappointment with the Republic felt by the FNTT, now led by the *Caballerista* Ricardo Zabalza, was of no surprise.[47] The expected confrontation arrived when the Law of Municipal Boundaries was repealed in May. This meant that, in harvest time, landowners were able to bring cheap labour from outside areas to the detriment of local workers. The FNTT then decided to launch a general strike in June affecting fifteen southern provinces. In such a crucial conflict, the contrast between the two warring sides was glaring. The *Caballerista*-dominated UGT failed to support the landworkers. They revealed with their behaviour how their verbal revolutionarism hardly went beyond mere rhetoric intended to prevent Lerroux from using its majority to reverse Azaña's legislation.[48] In contrast, Salazar Alonso was determined to inflict a deadly blow to Socialist power in the countryside. He rapidly declared the harvest a national utility and treated the strike as a threat to public order, using ruthless violence to put it down. In fierce clashes with the police, thirteen peasants were killed. Hundreds of Socialist militants, including councillors and even four deputies, were arrested and workers' centres and local trade unions closed. As the FNTT suffered a massive setback, the tide was clearly turning in favour of the rural oligarchy who began to feel strong enough to restore the semi-feudal relations of dependence which had prevailed before 1931.[49]

Almost immediately thereafter, the centre of contention shifted to Cataluña, the last stronghold of the Left. There, the *Generalitat* presided over by Lluis Companys introduced in April the Law of Agricultural Contracts.[50] This gave the *rabassaires* ('tenant vine-growers'), the right to purchase the land they had cultivated for eighteen years. This measure brought the *Generalitat* into conflict over legal jurisdiction with the central government when the incensed Catalan landowners backed by the *Lliga* took their case to Madrid on the grounds of unconstitutionality. Companys agreed to withdraw it but then passed the old law in a slightly different form in the summer. The Radical cabinet, now led by the inexperienced Ricardo Samper, intended to avoid a frontal clash and attempted to find a compromise.[51] The CEDA, however, had something different in mind.

On 9 September the CEDA organized a huge rally in Covadongas (Asturias). The chosen spot could not have been more provocative. Covadongas was the place where the mythical *reconquista* had begun. The gathering was reminiscent of Fascist parades. A bellicose Gil Robles, cheered by the green-uniformed members of his party's youth (JAP) and hailed as Chief, launched a rabble-rousing speech against the Republic. Invoking parallels with the legendary past, he threatened to start a new reconquest of Spain, this time against Reds, separatists and freemasons. On 26 September Gil Robles withdrew his support for the government and demanded ministerial participation in any new administration. On 1 October, Samper duly resigned.[52]

Spain's division into two polarized camps had become a reality. Both sides could not help but draw parallels with the European background. The revolutionary rhetoric used by some Socialists in order to halt the revisionist process initiated by Lerroux was perceived by the Right as a Bolshevist threat. Equally, in the light of contemporary events on the continent, left-wing misgivings were understandable. The CEDA did not conceal its admiration for the Fascist regimes, its intention to destroy the organized labour movement, revise the constitution and set up an authoritarian and corporative system. Examples of how Mussolini and Hitler in 1922 and 1933 respectively had accepted a minority of portfolios in coalition governments and then easily destroyed democracy from within gave rise to widespread fear that Spain was heading a similar way. Even more recent and frightening was the Austrian example where Chancellor Engelbert Dollfuss, leader of a Catholic Party ideologically very similar to the CEDA, had staged a coup in February 1934 and established a dictatorship after the brutal repression of Socialists in the so-called 'cleaning-up of Red Vienna'. Making clear that they were not prepared to share the fate of their Austrian and German counterparts, the Socialists threatened an armed rising should the CEDA join a cabinet.[53] Despite intense lobbying by leading Republicans from different groupings, Alcalá finally gave way and on 4 October allowed Lerroux to form a new administration in which the CEDA held three portfolios. This announcement sparked an insurrection the next day.

The October revolution of 1934 was, as usual, a fiasco. Once more, the Socialists had confined themselves to little more than threatening rhetoric with the aim of convincing Lerroux and Alcalá to block the CEDA's access to power.[54] When their bluff was called, they had to lead a revolution for which they were largely unprepared. By contrast, the authorities had carefully planned their response. A state of war was declared throughout Spain and the army was given free rein to put down the rebellion. Thousands of Leftist leaders, including Largo Caballero and Azaña, were rounded up and troops quickly took control of the main cities. With the FNTT severely mauled only a few months earlier, the countryside remained relatively quiet. In Barcelona, Companys proclaimed the existence of a Catalan state within a Spanish Federal Republic, but had to surrender in less than twenty-four hours when the army seized key positions in the city and began bombarding the *Generalitat*. Only in Asturias did the revolution temporarily succeed. There, a real united front of all Leftist groups was established and the miners, armed with dynamite, held out for a fortnight. With the declaration of the state of war, power passed into the hands of the War Minister, the Radical Diego Hidalgo. Yet the real mastermind was General Franco. It was he, appointed technical adviser to the Minister of War, who insisted on the use of troops from Africa, Moors and the Foreign Legion.[55] Ironically, paying lip service to the *reconquista* myth, Moorish mercenaries were shipped to Asturias, the only part of Spain never conquered by the Arabs. All kinds of savage atrocities including widespread use of torture and execution of prisoners, unreported due to the censorship, broke the resistance of the Asturian workers. Their only condition for surrender was to give themselves up to the regular army and not to the African troops.[56] The total toll of the October events was 1355 killed and 2951 wounded, the majority of them in Asturias followed then by Cataluña.[57]

The aftermath of October 1934 seemed to prove right the CEDA's legalist strategy. With the crushing defeat of the Left, a vicious and retaliatory counter-revolution began in earnest. About 40 000 Republican and Socialist militants languished in prisons with many others having to go into hiding or abroad. As unemployment soared and the economic crisis worsened, wages were slashed even further, trade unions disbanded and mixed-juries suspended. Peasants were evicted, town councillors overthrown and replaced by nominees of the local *caciques*, the Church restored to a prominent position, Catalan autonomy suspended and the *Generalitat* replaced by a Governor-General appointed in Madrid. Spain was back to the worst times of the monarchy.

The year 1935 was the peak of CEDA's power. Gil Robles used and abused his position to make and dismiss cabinets and gradually acquire more power.[58] Lerroux and Alcalá were aghast when the CEDA leader insisted on carrying out death sentences on several Asturian miners. Robles could only be dissuaded at the price of an increased presence in the government. At the same time, the hypocrisy of the CEDA's social programme was fully revealed. Manuel Giménez Fernández, one of the three CEDA's ministers whose entry in the government in October had sparked the revolution, turned out to be a moderate Christian-Democrat who as Minister of Agriculture displayed a genuine concern for finding a conciliatory solution in the countryside. Giménez naively believed that landowners could be moved towards a less intransigent position by the appeals of a friendly Catholic minister. When he tried to introduce some measures to forbid evictions and favour small tenants and leaseholders, his own party accused him of being a 'white bolshevik' and he was removed from his post. He was replaced by the

Agrarian Nicasio Velayos who quickly introduced the Law of Reform of the Agrarian Reform that meant sudden death for the remnants of the progressive agrarian legislation from the earlier period.[59]

The CEDA emerged, for the first time, as the single strongest party in the governmental coalition, in the cabinet reshuffle of May 1935 with five portfolios. Gil Robles seized for himself the crucial post of War Minister. In that position, he transformed the army into a counter-revolutionary bulwark. Liberal officers were purged and their places filled by *africanistas* and hard-liners. Franco for his outstanding role in October was rewarded with the appointment of Chief of the General Staff, Martín Baguenas, a former chief of police with the monarchy, became the new Director of Security, other *africanistas* such as the Generals Goded and Mola were also promoted to key positions.[60]

Suddenly in the autumn of 1935 a series of financial scandals involving leading members of the Radical party came to the surface. Their tarnished reputation suffered a deadly blow from which they never recovered and Lerroux and his closest cronies had to leave office.[61] This unexpected twist of fate convinced Robles that his time had arrived. In early December, he caused the fall of the government in order to compel Alcalá to entrust him with the premiership of the new cabinet. To Robles' chagrin, the President of the Republic opted for the other available solution: dissolution of parliament and the appointment of one of his political friends, Portela Valladares, to organize new general elections on 16 February 1936. Gil Robles had overplayed his hand. When Alcalá alleged that his decision had been caused by the inability of the current chamber to sustain stable governments, Robles could hardly reply that he had engineered that instability so as to speed up his claim to power.[62] In a desperate reaction, Robles tried to lobby Franco and other friendly officers to stage a coup. It was in vain as the generals felt they were not ready to act. A frustrated Robles then had to quit his job and devote his energies to the new electoral campaign.[63]

The Slippery Road to War

With Spain polarized into two hostile and warring camps, the electoral campaign of 1936 was conducted in a frenzied mood. Aware of the importance of the outcome, both sides fought the elections as a question of survival. For the Left, their cause represented the defence of democracy and the Republic against the oncoming threat of dictatorship and Fascism. For the Right, it was a struggle to uphold the traditional values of christianity against the peril of revolution and Bolshevism. It was relatively easy for the parties of the Right to enter into tactical coalitions on a regional basis, establishing a National Bloc of the so-called forces of law and order. It was, however, more difficult for the Left to seal an alliance.

In fact, the conclusion of the Popular Front was an arduous task accomplished basically by the resilience of Manuel Azaña with the support of Indalecio Prieto. The electoral defeat of November 1933 and the repression after October 1934 led to the widespread recognition that all left-wing forces should have some form of unity. Hence, throughout 1935 Azaña's main goal was to revive the governmental coalition of 1931. His charisma had been enhanced by his months in prison and persecution by the authorities, who finally had to release him with others such as Largo Caballero because no evidence could be found against them.[64] Banking on his personal record as the man who embodied the original spirit of the Republic, the former prime minister began a frenetic campaign of mobilization and re-organization of the dispersed and demoralized forces of the Left which culminated in a massive rally in Comillas, outside Madrid in October. Before a crowd of about 500 000 people, the largest ever in Spanish history, Azaña outlined his programme as the basis for an electoral alliance. This encompassed immediate amnesty for the thousands of political prisoners and a return to the social reformist legislation of 1931. Soon thereafter he formally invited the Socialists to join him.[65]

Yet the Socialist movement was anything but united in 1935. With the *Besteiristas* in open decline, the struggle for control of the largest political force in Spain was between the followers of Indalecio Prieto and Francisco Largo Caballero. Prieto had always considered it a mistake to have broken the alliance with the Republicans in 1933. His opinion was further confirmed by the failure of the October revolution and its violent aftermath. Aware that the only way to regain power was through a vast electoral coalition, he was eager to co-operate with Azaña. However, he met the obstinate opposition of Largo Caballero. For the veteran trade union leader, his governmental experience had been marked by frustration and his spell in prison had only deepened his distrust of the bourgeois Republic. In 1935 both camps embarked upon a bitter polemic and dialectical war which was to continue unabated during the following years. The *Caballeristas* were dominant in the UGT and the *Prietistas* in the PSOE. They were also geographically divided. The sections in Madrid and the south were behind Caballero. Ironically, those in the north where its rank-and-file had been more successful in October, particularly in Asturias, were Prieto's strongholds. Thus the latter was quick to uphold their past record to remind the *Caballeristas* that their own revolutionary rhetoric never went beyond mere posturing and would only serve to impede the winning of the next elections and avert the danger of a CEDA-dominated cabinet.[66]

Largo's uncompromising position was paradoxically difficult to sustain due to the stance then taken by the Communist Party (PCE – Partido Comunista de España). In order to halt the Fascist tide sweeping over Europe, the Soviet Union abandoned her former intransigence and in the summer of 1935, the VIIth Congress of the Comintern espoused the initiative of seeking broad alliances of all the progressive forces of a country, the so-called Popular Front. Spain, with its own young democratic system on the verge of being overthrown, seemed the appropriate place to put this strategy into practice. Even though small in numbers and in strength, the PCE thus became a passionate defender of a pact with Azaña and the liberal bourgeoisie. It was still necessary for Jacques Duclos, the Comintern agent in France, to meet twice a stubborn Largo Caballero. The veteran trade unionist in the end gave way, but with the condition of no ministerial responsibility. At last, the Popular Front's joint manifesto, basically accepting the moderate goals of the Republicans, was agreed on 15 January 1936 and signed by a vast coalition of groups ranging from Republicans to Socialists, Communists, Angel Pestaña's recently created Syndicalist Party, and the Workers' Party of Marxist Unification (POUM).[67] It also could rely on the support of the CNT–FAI anxious to see thousands of their militants freed from prisons.

The electoral results were very close. The centre was practically wiped out returning 51 deputies (the Radicals only obtained four seats). The Popular Front won by a narrow margin; 4 654 116 to the Right's 4 503 524. Yet due to the electoral system, it meant a huge swing in terms of seats (the Right returned 124 deputies, with 88 belonging to the CEDA; the Popular Front gained 278 deputies, 99 of them Socialists).[68]

Until the last moment, Robles tried to prevent the *fait accompli*. He persuaded some generals, including Franco, that the victory of the Popular Front meant anarchy. They tried then to cajole the Prime Minister into annulling the results and declaring martial law. Yet Portela Valladares refused outright and the only consequence was to accelerate the government's resignation and the handover to Azaña.

Their hopes of frustrating the Leftist return to power were finally dashed by the position of General Pozas, head of the Civil Guard, who was opposed to any coup and even sent out his forces to surround all the suspect garrisons.[69] Between March and July, Spain was on a slippery slope to war. The Left were back in power and committed to hastening the reformist path abandoned in 1933. Yet with the Socialists refusing to compromise their principles for a second time by accepting ministerial responsibility, Azaña had to form an all-Republican administration. An emboldened Caballero hinted that the time for a revolutionary take-over was fast approaching. The new administration rapidly freed all political prisoners and promised to accelerate social and economic reforms. However, in most cases the government soon found itself reacting to events. After two years of repression, the working classes had run out of patience and were not prepared to be cheated again by parliamentary trickery. With their expectations revitalized by the electoral victory, during the following months a wave of industrial strikes, with workers demanding pay increases and better conditions, rocked the cities while thousands of landless peasants, encouraged by a revived FNTT, began to occupy landed estates, particularly in Extremadura. The government had no option but to legalize such seizures *a posteriori*. Between March and July, more land was redistributed than in all the previous years of the Republic.[70]

At the same time, with the CEDA's legalist tactic shattered by the outcome of the polls, the initiative passed to the advocates of violence. The Right began to put all its efforts into mounting an army conspiracy. Having lost the political argument, for them there was no alternative but to resort to military means. The Falange found its numbers swelling dramatically with the continuous inflow of disillusioned members of the JAP. The CEDA itself began to take a secondary role allowing the hardliner Monarchists of *Renovación Española* to take the political lead. On 8 March several leading *africanistas* gathered at the house of the CEDA's unsuccessful candidate for Madrid, the stockbroker José Delgado, to discuss and organize a military coup.[71]

After March 1936 political violence escalated dramatically. Falangist and Carlist gunmen succeeded in sinking the country into an atmosphere of terror and anarchy. Left-wing groups retaliated in kind and the toll of victims kept mounting. Clashes between rival forces became a normal feature in the streets. Up to July, there were 269 political killings. This climate of chaos benefited the Right. Its powerful media magnified and exaggerated every small incident in order to incite the army to put an end to this Republic of lawlessness and disorder. These calls were echoed in parliament by leading right-wing personalities.[72] They always forgot to mention in their vehement statements how much of this violence was the responsibility of their own supporters.

In April, President Alcalá was impeached on the grounds that he had exceeded his authority by dissolving the *Cortes* twice in one term. The old leader had, with his behaviour in 1933 and 1935, antagonized the Left and the Right simultaneously. This initiative was part of a twofold strategy. Its first step was the elevation of Azaña to the Presidency, to be then complemented by the appointment of Prieto in May as new Prime Minister.[73] The first part of the scheme was easily accomplished, but the second met with the total opposition of Largo Caballero. The latter by his behaviour not only confirmed the civil war within his own party but only achieved the worst of two worlds. Largo continued to talk as if revolution was imminent without doing anything to prepare for it. On the contrary, in practical examples such as the building dispute in Madrid, he behaved as a reformist trade unionist advocating conciliation and clashing with the more militant CNT. Yet his words had the effect of terrorizing the middle classes and speeding up preparations for an armed insurrection. Additionally, by blocking any Socialist participation in the cabinet, he neutralized the energetic Prieto and impeded the formation of a strong government which might have averted the coup.[74]

Finally, the Galician Santiago Casares Quiroga was appointed Prime Minister. A weak, indecisive and sick man with tuberculosis, he was definitely not the appropriate leader to defend the Republic at its most crucial moment of need. Indeed, the government proved impotent and unable to curb the violence or the military conspiracy. The idea of sending all the suspect leading generals to distant outposts only worked in their favour, as they could now forge a rebel network all over the country. Plans for a military uprising continued unabated. Sanjurjo, from his exile in Portugal, was the visible head of the movement. The real director in the peninsula was General Mola who had been sent to Navarra, a Carlist stronghold and so the ideal place for a popular reactionary mass following. The *Unión Militar Española* (UME), a semi-clandestine organization which claimed 3500 officers, played a fundamental part in establishing conspiratorial cells in every province. All the right-wing political groups were aware of preparations for the coup and collaborated with their contacts, finances and manpower for its successful accomplishment.

In July, everybody in the country but Casares seemed to be conscious of the military threat. With a confidence stretching sometimes to the borders of insanity, the Prime Minister persisted in dismissing the worrying news as unfounded rumours and even told Prieto that his warnings were 'menopausic outbursts'.[75] On 12 July Jesús Castillo, a prominent left-winger and lieutenant of the Assault Guards, was assassinated by a right-wing hit squad. Following the pattern of tit-for-tat retaliation, his companions decided to avenge him by killing a leading right-winger. That night the Monarchist leader José Calvo Sotelo was arrested and then murdered. That latest killing gave the rebels the pretext to stage their coup. How could the Republic guarantee law and order when its own police forces were murderous villains? On the night of 17 July the military insurrection began in Morocco.

5

A Modern Crusade: The Spanish Tragedy, 1936–9

The International Dimension: The European Civil War

The Republic proved in the summer of 1936 that it was far from a failure. Unlike many other European countries whose constitutional regimes in the interwar years were overthrown without hardly a struggle, Spain fought back. The Republic did not fail but was 'failed' after a vicious conflict which lasted for almost three years.[1] In this context, Spain became the last and fiercest battle in a European civil war which had been under way since the Bolshevik triumph of 1917.[2] International participation and the ideological zeal which surrounded both sides conferred upon the war the character of a crusade. Whereas for the rebels, theirs was a movement to defend the values of traditional and Christian Spain against godless Bolshevism, for the Republic, it was a battle for democracy and Socialism against political immobilism and Fascism.

The insurrection was not prompted by fears of a Communist take-over or by the growing disintegration of public order. It had been carefully planned immediately after the electoral defeat of February 1936 to prevent the new government introducing wide-ranging social and economic reforms. At no time, had the conspirators anticipated massive popular resistance. They were confident that their uprising, in a country with a long tradition of *pronunciamientos*, would lead to a relatively swift take-over, at the most in a few days.

In fact, the coup went completely wrong. After the first three days, the rebels or Nationalists had only succeeded in their strongholds, that third of Spain which voted for the Right in February 1936: the Catholic heartland (Galicia, Old Castilla and Navarra) and Morocco. Exceptions were Oviedo, Zaragoza and a strip of land around Sevilla. Yet here the triumph was far from secure; surrounded by hostile territory, they were only captured through the audacity of officers who, after initially proclaiming their loyalty to the government, switched sides and struck by surprise against the confident authorities. In the main industrial cities (Madrid, Barcelona, Valencia and Bilbao) and the rural south, the uprising was defeated by the swift action of workers and peasants. Furthermore, a majority of senior officers, large sections of the peninsular troops and police forces remained loyal to the Republic. The fleet, the tiny air force and the gold reserves were also in the hands of the government. The African army, the professional force which could decide the outcome of the war, was paralysed by the problem of transport across the Straits of Gibraltar.[3]

It seems reasonable to speculate that the insurrection could have been crushed in a relatively short time. However, the international response proved crucial. Both sides rapidly looked abroad for diplomatic and military support. The reply given by the European chancelleries determined the course and the outcome of the conflict.[4] First, they transformed a failed uprising into a long civil war and, second, they secured victory for the insurgents.

Mexico was the only state that from the beginning supported the Republic wholeheartedly. The revolutionary and strongly anti-clerical regime led by President Lázaro Cárdenas identified itself strongly with Spain. Yet its distance and scarcity of resources hampered Mexico's ability to play a major role. Its contribution was basically that of purchasing weapons from third countries that were then reshipped to Spain, the sending of fuel, food and clothing, and the representation of Republican diplomatic interests in many nations where its overseas foreign office personnel defected to the Nationalists.[5]

Republican hopes rested on the Western democracies, particularly the sister Popular Front in France. When pleas for help to quell the revolt arrived in Paris on 19 July, the French government, led by the Socialist Léon Blum, promptly agreed to help. That decision was not only produced by ideological solidarity but also because it was in France's national interests that a friendly government remain on her southern border. However, the defection of the Spanish Military Attache,

Antonio Barroso, and his subsequent leaks to the press of Blum's plans
to send weapons to Spain, transformed what initially seemed a clear-
cut operation into domestic strife. In fact, France herself was affected
by political polarization. In 1934 the French Republic was rocked by
financial scandals involving its political elites and a right-wing coup was
narrowly averted. In the spring of 1936 with the country divided into
two major blocs, a Popular Front coalition of Communists, Socialists
and Radicals defeated an alliance of right-wing forces. News of intervention in Spain gave the right-wing media, clearly favourable to the
insurgents, the required ammunition to mount a devastating campaign
against involvement in a foreign adventure, branding the government
as treacherous and unfit for office. Within the governmental coalition,
many in the Radical party began to have second thoughts. They
included political heavyweights such as Yvon Delbos, the Foreign
Minister, Edouard Daladier, the War Minister, Edouard Herriot, the
Speaker of the Chamber, and even Albert Lebrun, the President of the
Republic. They feared that intervention in Spain could either lead to
the outbreak of war on the continent or to the spread of the conflict to
France herself. An exception was Pierre Cot, the Radical Air Minister,
who backed fully Blum's decision to aid the Spanish Republic. With a
frenzied domestic atmosphere and the cabinet divided, the position of
Britain, France's vital ally, was therefore crucial. Thus British opposition to intervention tilted the precarious balance in the French administration and on 25 July Blum reversed his initial commitment to
support the Republic.[6]

Seemingly Britain maintained a strict neutrality throughout the
conflict. Yet this position merely served to conceal the fact that
the British administration waged a secret campaign destined to ensure
a Nationalist victory. Among British ruling circles, Communism was
regarded as the enemy. In such an ideological framework, the signing
of a Treaty of Friendship between France and the Soviet Union in May
1934 was not welcomed in London. Even more discouraging were
the Popular Front victories in Spain and France in 1936 which were
compared with the phase of the Kerensky government in Russia in
1917 before it was overwhelmed by revolutionary upheaval. When the
Spanish Civil War broke out, the sympathies of the British administration soon became evident. For reasons of class and upbringing, they
detested what a left-wing Republic stood for, and approved of the anti-
revolutionary objectives of the Spanish insurgents as they had done
with those of Hitler and Mussolini. At the same time, diplomatic and

intelligence reports confirmed this view. The atrocities committed on both sides were very differently interpreted. Whereas those in the Republican zone were portrayed as the consequence of mob-rule, those in Nationalist areas were described as restoring law and order. Additionally, Britain controlled about 40 per cent of the total foreign investment in Spain. This capital was largely concentrated in the iron and pyrite industries, followed by the electricity sector, public utilities, citrus fruits and sherry. Thus ruling economic circles were naturally inclined to favour the victory of a right-wing rebellion, fearing that their huge investments could be seized by the trade unions loyal to the Republican government. With this interpretation and their acute anti-revolutionary prejudice, the British government concluded that in Spain the army was combating a virtual Soviet under the umbrella of a lifeless government, unworthy of either direct or indirect support. General Franco himself was viewed as a good military man, who was prudent, conservative and nationalist, and who had risen only to fight the spectre of social revolution. His victory would lead to the establishment of 'a liberal dictatorship' very favourable to the interests of the United Kingdom. The heart of the problem for British diplomacy was that formal Republican legitimacy was in the same camp as the dreaded social revolution, while the counter-revolution remained formally illegitimate. Consequently, although maintaining for the home audience an image of scrupulous neutrality, the real position of the British administration was perfectly encapsulated by the instructions of the Prime Minister, Stanley Baldwin, to his Foreign Minister, Anthony Eden, on 26 July: 'On no account, French or other, must you bring us into the fight on the side of the Russians!' Britain's attitude proved crucial in the first days of the conflict. On 22 July the British administration accepted Franco's requests to close the ports of Gibraltar and Tangier to the Republican navy which was blockading the straits. Then they restrained their French ally from helping the Republic. Simultaneously, they turned a blind eye to those prepared to intervene in favour of the rebels.[7]

While the Republic was being ostracized in the international arena, the response received by the Nationalists was entirely different. From the start, they could rely on the open support of Portugal. With the sympathy of the dictatorship of Antonio Salazar, the nominal head of the rebellion, General Sanjurjo, and another 15 000 prominent Monarchists established there the headquarters of the conspiracy. During the first weeks of the war, Portugal's proximity to the battleground was of inestimable value to the rebels. She became the perfect spot from which foreign aid could be delivered, and served as the liaison for the divided Nationalist zones. Also ten thousand Portuguese 'volunteers' joined the rebels.[8] Yet Salazar could only offer small military assistance. Much more important contributions came from Germany and Italy.

Before July 1936, Germany had shown no interest in Spain's political developments. With her expansionist plans focused on the east, Spain was a distant land outside her sphere of influence. Furthermore, German economic interests there were relatively small.[9] Consequently, the first requests for aid from General Mola were promptly rebuffed by a German Foreign Office caught by surprise by the coup and fearful of international complications. It was at this vital moment that Franco proved his superior cunning over all the other army leaders. He established contacts on 22 July with two National-Socialist Party members in Morocco, Johannes Bernhardt and Adolf Lagenheim, who agreed to travel to Germany and deliver a plea for military assistance. By using Party channels, Franco bypassed the German bureaucratic machinery and appealed directly to Hitler. Supplied with a personal letter from him, Franco's messengers arrived in Berlin on 25 July and met Rudolf Hess. Understanding the crucial nature of their mission, Hess quickly arranged a meeting that same evening with Hitler then on holiday at Bayreuth where he was attending the Wagner festival. Then and there the German dictator took the personal decision to support the insurrection. With Hitler probably still under the influence of Wagner's music, 'Operation Magic Fire' was immediately set into motion. In a few days, a German vessel, the *Usaramo*, left Germany loaded with *matériel* destined for Franco. This included ten Junkers 52 transport planes, six Heinkel 51 escort fighters, anti-aircraft guns, bombs, ammunition and various other items. Ten more Junkers 52 were on their way. For Hitler, strategic considerations were paramount. He quickly grasped the opportunity presented to him. By sending very little, he could create a friendly state bordering France, Germany's continental enemy, who then would be surrounded by potentially hostile neighbours. For Hitler, betting on a rapid Nationalist victory, it was a limited risk worth taking. His involvement in Spanish affairs was to be surrounded by total secrecy. However, if that failed, Hitler thought he could defuse opposition by playing the anti-Communist card and allege that he was only helping the rebels to rescue Spain from Bolshevism. As the war progressed, other economic and logistical considerations also became important. Spain's raw materials were a blessing to a Germany bent on rearming. Furthermore, the Spanish war represented an ideal opportunity to determine the limits of resolution and tolerance of the Allies. It was also the perfect testing ground for men and equipment and provided the occasion to stir up trouble in the west of Europe while planning to expand eastwards.[10]

Italian intervention was the result of a combination of factors in which political opportunism was very significant. For Mussolini's expansionist dreams, it was important to have a friendly Spain in the Mediterranean. Thus, unlike Germany, Fascist Italy displayed genuine concern for Spanish internal politics. After a period of excellent relations with Primo de Rivera, the establishment of the Republic was greeted with dismay by the *Duce*. Henceforth, Italy supported all anti-Republican activities in Spain. The military conspirators of 1932 were promised weapons. In March 1934 Mussolini received a delegation of Monarchists and Carlists. They obtained money and training facilities. Also, since June 1935, José Antonio, the Falange leader, was granted a monthly contribution of 50 000 lire. Paradoxically, when the prospect of a rebellion in 1936 seemed more serious than ever before Mussolini refused to become embroiled.

The timing of the coup could not have arrived at a worst time. Italy had just come out of her Abyssinian adventure militarily and economically exhausted and diplomatically isolated, and therefore reluctant to embark on a new enterprise. Thus requests for assistance for the forthcoming coup in June and July were rebuffed. After the uprising, Mola and Franco sent their first messengers with pleas for military aid to Italy. Between 21 and 25 July they met Count Ciano, the new Foreign Minister and Mussolini's son-in-law, who although seemingly willing to help also made clear that the decision was not his and had to turn down their requests. Within the following seventy-two hours, the original resolution to stand aloof from Spain was dramatically reversed. Mussolini hesitated during those days. His ego was certainly flattered by being the recipient of pleas for help and he had the opportunity to assist the establishment of a potential ally in the Mediterranean. However, his sudden about-turn in policy was basically the result of a careful exercise in political opportunism. Indeed, it came as the culmination of a complex and anything but spontaneous decision-making process, largely based on the evaluation of different sources of information. Between 25 and 27 July, the *Duce* received a considerable number of diplomatic and intelligence reports which led him to conclude that by supporting the rebellion he held a winning hand. He was aware of

British hostility towards the Spanish government and of their pressure against Blum's involvement who by then had withdrawn his initial offers to help the Republic. Hence he assumed that Britain would not object to discreet intervention in favour of the insurgents. It is unclear if he knew of Hitler's recent decision to send aid but a further consideration was news from the Soviet Union indicating that the Kremlin was deeply disconcerted by the situation in Spain and did not intend to do anything. Final assurances that once the African troops were in the peninsula the war would be over in a matter of weeks convinced Mussolini that covertly supplying a small amount of equipment was a very cheap price for potentially massive rewards. On 29 July, the Italians began to dispatch a dozen Savoia–Marchetti transport and bomber planes, followed by twelve Fiat C.R.32 fighters to Spanish Morocco.[11]

Thus Italian and German intervention added to British acquiescence and French impotence changed in a few days the Spanish contest. Nationalist desperation, well expressed by Mola's confidence to his secretary on 29 July that he was contemplating suicide, was suddenly transformed by the prospect of a quick victory.[12] By early August, the first successful airlift of troops in modern warfare was under way. Thousands of soldiers of the elite African army, the Foreign Legion and the *Regulares* (Moorish mercenaries commanded by Spanish officers), initiated their inexorable advance towards Madrid leaving behind a staggering trail of blood, desolation and carnage. The ill-armed and inexperienced militias were no match in the open field and were either forced to retreat or massacred. On 10 August the two halves of Nationalist Spain were joined. Four days later Badajoz fell. Thousands of Republican defenders were herded into the bullring and slaughtered. At the same time, the Nationalists now had unrestricted access to Portugal, a major conduit for goods and weapons.[13] A secret meeting on 4 August between the heads of the German and Italian intelligence services, Admiral Canaris and Colonel Roatta respectively, sealed the military collaboration of both countries in Spain. They agreed that their activities should continue beyond the airlift supplying weapons and technology as well as allowing their air forces to engage in fighting and bombing missions. Germany confirmed that she had no interests in the area and was prepared to allow Italy a free hand in the Mediterranean in exchange for Italian support for German expansion eastwards.[14] On 3 September Talavera, the last important town before Madrid, was captured. In a month, the African army had completed a successful advance of 300 miles. The war seemed to be reaching its end.

The secrecy surrounding foreign intervention foundered when three Italian Savoia bombers landed by accident in French Morocco. Blum was furious and felt that he should then be free to help the Republic. His decision was followed by stormy cabinet meetings in which he was vehemently opposed by some Radical ministers who feared that intervention could lead to war against Germany and Italy. The latter's position was clearly reinforced when Baldwin, going over the head of Blum, directly contacted President Lebrun to warn him that if war broke out, as a result of their assistance to the Republic, France would be alone.[15] This pressure culminated in an ultimatum delivered by the ambassador, Sir George Clerk. Faced with the break-up of the Entente with Britain and even the demise of the Popular Front in France, Blum gave way. He was persuaded not to resign by leading Spanish Republican diplomats with the argument that a friendly government in France led by him, even with its hands tied, was better than a potentially hostile new administration. Finally, the French came up with an intermediate solution: a Non-Intervention Pact or the introduction of an arms embargo on both sides. If successful, they believed that the Republic would have a good chance of crushing the insurrection. Yet before France unilaterally instituted non-intervention on 8 August, Blum arranged with the Air Minister Cot the dispatch of several planes to Spain, the shipment of weapons to Mexico and a trickle of arms for the hard-pressed Republicans; this he hoped would be enough to put down the rebellion. What Blum had not envisaged was that his ill-advised retreat from intervention was to spell doom for the Republic.[16]

The idea of a Non-Intervention Agreement was enthusiastically endorsed by the British administration. It became the perfect instrument for British foreign policy: a smoke-screen behind which to conceal its hostility towards the Republic and a means to stop the French rushing to help the embattled Republic.[17] Under its tacit neutrality the British administration worked to undermine the Spanish government. Anglo-Spanish trade plummeted when on 13 August the current commercial payment agreement between the two countries was suspended. This measure served to block the disbursement in London of a considerable quantity of sterling earned by Spanish exports to Britain. Also a financial transaction of the Republic via Barclays Bank to purchase arms in America was impeded, while a simultaneous operation carried out by the rebels through the Westminster Bank was permitted.[18]

Twenty-seven nations, including all the major powers, adhered to Non-Intervention and a working committee presided over by Lord Plymouth was set up in London in early September. This scheme was full of loopholes: the committee had no power to act and could hear accusations only from its own members, cutting out both Spanish parties and also independent accounts. It was never more than a sham which actually worked in favour of the insurgents. Under British auspices, Non-Intervention became the ideal means to reconcile the political objectives laid down by the Foreign Office: it prescribed an arms embargo towards the combatants, granting the same status to the legal government as to the rebels; it served to confine the war within Spain, restraining French participation and maintained the semblance of neutrality for the domestic audience, diverting the criticism of the Labour and Liberal opposition, while avoiding confrontation with Germany and Italy. The British government expected the war to be brief. Given that Germany and Italy continued their vital support for the rebels despite their signing of the agreement, the upholding of the embargo, followed under duress by France and others, clearly damaged the Republic, who, shunned by the democracies, had to operate in the open arms market and, in consequence, make do with over-priced and obsolete equipment from private arms dealers.[19]

While the Allies had chosen to ignore the plight of the Republic, Aid Committees began to spring up in their cities and villages with the aim of raising food, money, medicines and clothes to help the beleaguered Spanish people. Soon, many attempted to do more and even go and fight in Spain. All these initiatives were closely monitored with growing embarrassment by the Soviet Union. Indeed, since 1934 Russian foreign policy had been marked by its moderation. The aim was to break diplomatic isolation and seek an understanding with the Western powers, founded on their common fear of German expansionism. Discarding sectarian slogans of class war and world revolution, the support for Popular Fronts was part of that strategy. Henceforth Communist parties were no longer the enemy of the liberal bourgeoisie but their loyal partners against the Fascist threat. The Spanish Civil War presented Stalin with a dilemma. On the one hand, he could not consent to the emergence of another Fascist state which, moreover, encircled his potential ally, France. On the other, a Republican victory could lead to a social revolution in Spain with the result of driving the Allies to side with Germany against the Soviet Union. Hence the Kremlin encouraged humanitarian aid while hesitating to take sterner measures.

Consequently, the Non-Intervention Agreement was initially welcomed as a possible solution, but its continuous flouting by Germany and Italy forced Stalin's hand. Firstly, the Comintern organized the transport of volunteers to Spain, the so-called International Brigades. They came from all parts of the world to fight Fascism, as represented by Franco's forces and their German and Italian allies. For them, Spain constituted the last-ditch battle against what began to appear as the triumphal march of reaction in Europe.[20]

Additionally, since late September small numbers of weapons were sent to the Republic. It was only on 15 October that the first large-scale shipment of Soviet military aid reached Spain, after the Kremlin had warned that if violations of the Non-Intervention Agreement were not immediately stopped the Soviet government would no longer feel bound by it. The goal was to supply the Republic with enough *matériel* to survive hoping to win time until the Allies finally realized that their real enemy was Fascism. Thus he instructed the relatively small number of Soviet personnel, always below 2000, to stay out of range of artillery fire and to encourage political moderation and even restrain revolutionary fervour within the Republican camp. Saving the Republic was thereby instrumental in Russian designs to transform the strategy of domestic Popular Fronts into an alliance between the Western democracies and the Soviet Union against Fascism.[21]

By early October everybody assumed that Madrid was about to fall and that the war would soon be over. General Mola had affirmed that he would be taking coffee in a famous cafeteria on 12 October. A table was kept for him, but he never arrived.[22] Against all odds the Nationalists were held at the gates of the capital. The arrival of Russian military equipment, particularly 'Mosca' fighter planes and T-26 tanks, and the first members of the International Brigades marked a turning-point. The Nationalists lost command of the air and no longer were fighting ill-armed soldiers. Furthermore, the terrain favoured the defenders. Street-fighting and barricades was more suited to the militias than the African army, invincible in the open field. The foreign volunteers were still few in number but their presence gave an enormous boost to popular morale. For the first time, galvanized by famous slogans such as *'No Pasarán!'* ('They shall not pass'), the Republicans felt they were no longer alone. A series of frontal attacks from different points failed to dent the defences. By 23 November Franco had to halt the offensive.[23]

Short of manpower and now facing a better-armed enemy, the Nationalist plans for a swift capture of the capital and the conclusion of the war failed. As in July the insurgents found themselves in dire straits and even contemplated defeat.[24] Franco once more turned for help to his German and Italian friends. They again replied positively and their increasing involvement altered the struggle, transforming a Spanish conflict into a European Civil War.

The foundations of the Non-Intervention Agreement – conceived by Britain and manipulated by the Fascist states as a delaying mechanism to give the rebels time to win the war – had to be re-interpreted. In the light of the new circumstances, Germany and Italy abandoned their previous prudence and decided to commit sufficient forces to facilitate Franco's ultimate victory. The alliance between both dictatorships was formally announced on 1 November with the formation of the Rome–Berlin Axis. Two weeks later they officially recognized the Nationalists as the legitimate government in Spain and soon they were at war in all but name with the Republic. The dictators had burnt their boats, for now their prestige was irrevocably attached to Franco's fortune.

Hitler dispatched the Condor Legion, the finest air force of the period. It consisted of a permanent squadron of about 6000 German troops (in total some 20 000 would serve at different times), anti-aircraft guns, tanks and the most modern bombers and fighter planes in the German arsenal. They would be crucial not only in providing Franco with a decisive air superiority, but also in training a devastating war machine ready for when conflict broke out in Europe. However, Hitler, not yet prepared to frighten the Allies through excessive involvement, let Italy carry the brunt of the effort.[25] Mussolini moved from his initial caution of limited aid towards massive participation. In December the first soldiers of the so-called *Corpo di Truppe Volontarie* (CTV) left Italy. By March 1937 about 50 000 Italian troops organized in mechanized divisions were fighting in Spain (the final total number of Italian troops involved would be 80 000). In turn, the Soviet Union increased dramatically its support for the Republic. Soviet merchant ships laden with military equipment left the Black Sea for Spanish ports. France, first under Blum and then after the reshuffle of June 1937 in which the Radical Camille Chautemps became Premier, continued a policy of 'relaxed non-intervention' conniving in the smuggling of armaments over the Pyrenean frontier. International volunteers continued to arrive until reaching a maximum of about 45 000.

Nevertheless, it was evident that unless the policy of Non-Intervention was either abandoned altogether or genuinely enforced, the Republic

was at a clear disadvantage. Despite the slick strategy of the Axis powers to equate their intervention with that of the Republic's friends,
there was a staggering difference in terms of quality, quantity and regu-
larity. Concerned not to raise major objections in Britain, they camou-
flaged their troops as volunteers fighting Bolshevism. In fact, they were
professional soldiers, constantly re-supplied and equipped with the best
available *matériel*. By contrast, the International Brigades were com-
posed of civilians who had to be armed, trained and fed by a besieged
Republic. The long distance between the Soviet Union and Spain also
meant a more irregular source of supplies which grew more hazardous
as the Italians used any means to detain or sink Republican vessels
along the Mediterranean.[26] Furthermore, Stalin was not prepared to
match the Axis' commitment in Spain. He remained cautious, scrupulously trying to avoid any major incident and insisting on Russian
personnel keeping a low profile. In contrast, the Fascist dictators,
emboldened by the non-interference of the Allies, increased their
audacity and involvement, as well as their hypocrisy, as the war dragged
on in Spain. Finally, while the Nationalists received all this massive support on credit, the Republicans had to pay for theirs by sending abroad
their gold reserves, some to France and the bulk to the Soviet Union in
October 1936.[27] In this respect, Italian aid was extremely generous,
while Hitler sought to secure economic rewards. Nationalist repayment
took the form of raw materials, particularly iron ore, vital for
Germany's re-armament programme. Two companies, Hisma at the
Spanish end and Rowak as its German counterpart, were established to
organize the entire trading relationship between the two countries.[28]

The Nationalist Zone: The Making of a Caudillo

Franco's long career was marked by stunningly constant good fortune.
The series of favourable and unexpected twists of fate which surrounded his meteoric rise to power constituted a perfect example of his
remarkable luck. Franco's reputation was made in the Moroccan wars.
There he gained rapid promotion for his bravery in combat, becoming
a general at the age of 33. Franco's character was enigmatic and secretive. He was considered a good professional soldier with conservative
views, but unlike most other fellow officers, he refused to display any
clear political leanings. On the contrary, he seemed happy to serve
loyally under different regimes. Appointed by Primo de Rivera as

Director of the Military Academy at Zaragoza, he was never an obvious part of the factions for or against the dictator. As with most *africanistas*, he was unhappy with the arrival of a left-wing Republic but he stayed clear of the plotters in 1932. Franco played a leading role in the crushing of the Asturias revolution of 1934 and later was made Chief of the General Staff by Gil Robles. Yet he was too cautious to associate himself too closely with any political group. Thus, with the dissolution of the chamber in December 1935 and the victory of the Popular Front in February 1936, he toyed with the idea of a coup, but caution prevailed. Banished by the new government to the Canary Islands, Franco was kept informed of the developments of the conspiracy but remained uncommitted. The conspirators, annoyed by his vacillations, even nicknamed him 'Miss Canary Islands 1936'. An exasperated Sanjurjo even commented that the plans would go ahead 'with or without Franquito'. Franco only decided to join a few days before the insurrection and did not land in Morocco until the rebellion had succeeded there. He had previously secured not only the safety of his wife and daughter but also that of himself with a letter guaranteeing his loyalty to the government and if that failed a diplomatic passport to flee abroad where he had been guaranteed a secret bank account. Few people could have foreseen then the role played by the Galician general in either the Civil War or its aftermath.[29]

Had the coup then succeeded, he would have been awarded with the post of High Commissioner of Morocco. Paradoxically, the failure of the coup catapulted Franco from hesitant rebel into indisputable leader. Indeed, a series of sinister disasters for the Nationalists cleared his road to absolute power. On 20 July the rebels lost their leader when General Sanjurjo was killed in a plane accident in Portugal. At the same time, two other leading conspirators, Generals Goded and Fanjul, were defeated and executed in Barcelona and Madrid respectively. Simultaneously, the insurrection lacked a charismatic civilian leader: Gil Robles was discredited after his electoral defeat of 1936; Calvo Sotelo, the most outstanding senior Monarchist, had been assassinated a few days before the rebellion; and finally, José Antonio, the Falangist leader, was imprisoned in Alicante and would be executed in November.[30] With the coup faltering, Franco found himself without a serious political or military rival and in charge of the elite African troops, the most important asset in the Nationalist camp.

Uniformity reigned over the areas controlled by the rebels. Wherever the coup succeeded, political activity automatically ceased to exist and authority passed into the hands of the military. Right-wing parties raised militias and joined the army. The officers, most of them *africanistas*, conducted the war as if it was a colonial struggle with the hostile population playing the part of natives. Terror was used consciously as a political instrument by the new authorities. Not only sympathizers of the Popular Front, but even those whose political loyalties were unclear or fellow officers reluctant to join in, were swiftly rounded up and shot in their thousands. Realizing that supporters of the conspiracy were few in numbers in many places, mass repression was the perfect tool to terrorize the working classes into acquiescence and accomplish the necessary *limpieza* ('cleaning up') to rid Spain of atheists, separatists and Reds. In their campaigns, the blood-thirsty Moors were often used as the vanguard troops – looting, pillaging and mutilating enemies in the captured territory so that those not physically eliminated would be broken by fear and seek survival in submission.[31]

Military imperatives indicated the need to establish a unified command and a commander-in-chief to replace Sanjurjo. On 23 July a National Defence Committee was established in Burgos under the presidency of General Cabanellas, the only senior division general who had revolted against the Republic.[32] Yet Cabanellas, reputed to have been a freemason and close to the Radicals, was disliked by the other officers and could exercise little authority over them. General Queipo de Llano in Sevilla was running his area as a private fiefdom. Also in parts of the north, the Carlists with the connivance of General Mola were consolidating their own rump state.[33] Thus in order to prevent the danger of cantonalism, the most important generals gathered in Salamanca on 21 September to choose a single Generalissimo. Franco faced hardly any opposition to fill the post. His two potential rivals, Queipo and Mola, could not match his position. Queipo was considered an eccentric lunatic and was automatically disqualified by his involvement in conspiracies against the monarchy. Mola, although a strong candidate as director of the rebellion, had lost some clout with his failure to organize a successful coup. By contrast, Franco's claim was unassailable. His lack of clear political leanings made him attractive to all different factions. He had the total support of the African army whose successful advances in August had confirmed its vital role in the war effort. Finally, he was the one who had established direct links with Italy and Germany.[34] Before the announcement was made public the generals returned to the front after arranging to resume their discussions a week later. Franco profited from those days to clinch military and political command.

He took a polemical but shrewd decision. Franco decided to divert his advance on Madrid in order to relieve the besieged Alcázar in Toledo, a place that had become the symbol of Nationalist heroism. From the start of the war, with the city in Republican hands, a group of Rightists led by General Moscardó had entrenched themselves in an old fortress or Alcázar refusing to surrender. By opting for rescuing Moscardó's embattled forces, Franco gave Madrid precious time to consolidate its defences. Yet he was aware of the moral and spiritual propaganda at stake. On 28 September the Alcázar was saved and became part of the Nationalist legend.[35] When the other generals met Franco that day, they were greeted by a well-orchestrated campaign deifying the 'saviour of the Alcázar'. Franco maximized his advantage amidst that frenzied atmosphere and obtained from his companions the position of Head of State. Significantly, it was agreed only for the war's duration and yet any reference to the temporary nature of his power had mysteriously disappeared when it was officially published on 1 October.[36]

After this the line between myth and reality was eroded. With the new state lacking intellectuals of any stature, the Catholic Church filled that place and thus acquired a prominent position in the emerging order. But for a few exceptional examples, mainly in the Basque Country, the Catholic hierarchy identified with the Nationalist cause. History was rewritten. The war was no longer a conflict between two opposite sides but a crusade. The insurgents were not rebels against their government, but blessed as the heroes of a new *reconquista*; patriots fighting to liberate Spain from the godless hordes of Moscow. Franco himself was referred to as Caudillo, the name of the medieval warrior chieftains.[37] In this patriotic crusade, the role played by Italy and Germany was carefully toned down. More striking was the ignorance of the vital and murderous part played in this christian crusade by the thousands of 'infidel' Moors.

The Nationalist setback at the gates of Madrid was ironically turned by Franco to his own benefit. He was rapidly saved from the clutches of defeat by massive Italo-German intervention. Furthermore, had the war concluded then, he would have lacked the time to consolidate his personal position. After November 1936, Franco reverted from a war of movement to one of attrition. Germans, Italians and even some Spanish officers often criticized Franco's conduct of the war. They despaired at what they regarded as excessively cautious and slow advances instead of using overwhelming material superiority to smash through the enemy lines and force the Republic to surrender. Yet their objections were misplaced. The Caudillo was not interested in a quick, conclusive and spectacular battle, but pursued a long and weary war to cement his prominence and annihilate gradually but totally the Republicans. Franco's obsession was to purge, through relentless repression, the conquered territory of enemies before resuming his advance. The thorough but obviously painfully slow task of liberating the country meant 'redeeming Spain by blood'.[38]

Slowly but surely Franco consolidated his military and political position in 1937. His battered troops were rescued by the arrival of massive foreign reinforcements. The German Condor Legion was vital in ensuring air supremacy and the thousands of Italian troops helped break the deadlock. They were used in mopping up territory in the south and then seizing the important city of Málaga in February. Confident of their success, the CTV planned to capture Madrid and hoped to end the war by launching in March a striking offensive through Guadalajara to the north-east of the capital. Franco deliberately failed to organize an operation in concert with the Italians who, left on their own, were routed. The Italian disaster at Guadalajara was welcomed by the Caudillo. The last thing he wanted was a quick victory handed to him by Mussolini which would have weakened his claim to have liberated Spain as leader of a patriotic crusade. After the Italian rout, the always arrogant and boastful *Duce* became more committed than ever to the Spanish adventure as he could not pull out his troops until his prestige had been rebuilt on the battlefield.[39] Franco could now run the show without external interference and pursue his slow war of attrition.

In late March, the Nationalists concentrated their forces on the northern front. Surrounded by all sides, this area contained the crucial coal mining industry and explosives factories of Asturias and the steel-making plants and shipyards of the Basque Country. Despite their isolation and overwhelming inferiority in equipment, the Republicans mounted a stiff resistance which was only finally broken by the use of terror bombing as never previously seen in Europe. The Condor Legion, perfecting the technique of mass bombardment of cities, preceded the advance of ground forces. On 26 April, Guernica, the ancient Basque capital, was practically wiped out by German planes. Crowded with refugees, this small town did not present any military incentives, but like Badajoz one year earlier sent a clear message to those who offered resistance to Franco's new order. To add insult to injury, the Nationalists organized a deceptive propaganda campaign alleging that Guernica had been dynamited by retreating Republicans in order to fabricate a false story for propaganda purposes.[40]

The fall of Asturias in October 1937 concluded the northern campaign. With the capture of that vital industrial area, the military balance was swinging clearly in Franco's favour. The Republicans launched a series of well-planned diversionary offensives to halt the Nationalist advances in 1937: Brunete in July, Belchite in August and Teruel in December. Despite their initial tactical surprise, they all ended in bloody stalemates which favoured Franco's overall strategy of gradually bleeding the enemy. Thus Republican break-throughs became long battles of attrition in which both sides paid an appalling cost in lives and *matériel*. The result was that whereas Franco, well supplied by the dictators, could soon make up the losses, the Republic could not. These three offensives revealed that the sheer material superiority of the Nationalists could always prevail over the courage of the Republicans.[41] In Teruel, for instance, the Republic obtained an important victory in January 1938, capturing a provincial capital for the first time. One month later the city was back in Nationalist hands and the Republicans had lost irreplaceable human and *matériel* reserves. Franco was then able to advance with hardly any opposition through Aragón, reaching the Mediterranean in April and cutting the Republic in two. Victory seemed imminent.[42]

Throughout 1937 Franco also consolidated his political supremacy. For the first months of the war, the political nature of Nationalist Spain remained extremely vague. There was a motley coalition of forces involved: Monarchists, Carlists, Catholics, Falangists, CEDA supporters and some conservative Republicans. Franco proved a masterful tactician manipulating all the different groups and imposing his authority over them. That task was rendered easy by two significant factors. Firstly, the already mentioned lack of any rival of outstanding stature. Secondly, despite their tactical differences and nurtured ambition of putting their own stamp on the future, there was more that united than actually divided all the diverse factions. They all had not only collaborated between 1931 and 1936 in the common goal of destroying the Republic, but also during this period they had undergone a process of 'fascistization', sharing a similar anti-democratic, authoritarian, ultra-catholic and corporativist programme. They then participated in the military conspiracy and readily accepted that in order to wage a successful war they had to subordinate their activities to military command.[43]

In December 1936 Manuel Fal Conde, the Carlist leader, was forced into exile after attempting to establish an independent Carlist military academy. By replacing him by the more docile Count Rodezno, Franco thwarted the potential challenge of a semi-autonomous Carlist movement which threatened his total control.[44] Yet Ramón Serrano Suñer, Franco's brother-in-law, was the chief architect of the new regime. An extremely intelligent young lawyer, close friend of José Antonio and a CEDA Deputy for Zaragoza, Serrano had already been instrumental in bringing over a good deal of the JAP to the Falange in the spring of 1936.

After his escape from Republican Spain in February 1937, Serrano was shocked by the lack of a political machinery in the Nationalist camp. Franco and Serrano sought to fill that vacuum by enforcing the unification of all the different groups. In order to do so, the rival political forces were outmanoeuvred, particularly the rapidly expanding Falange. Their plans were facilitated by the internal power struggle produced by the death of José Antonio. The different Falangist factions were played one against the other, leading finally in April to an armed clash giving Franco the excuse to intervene and stage a real political coup. On 19 April a decree announced the merging of all the groups into the so-called Traditionalist Falange (FET), often later merely referred to as 'the Movement'. This amounted to the proclamation overnight of Franco as the Caudillo of the only legal political party.[45] Its name, FET, included the two leading forces, the Carlists or Traditionalists and the Falange. Yet, if apparently the symbolism and external paraphernalia of the Falange, and indeed of the Fascist dictatorships, were readily mimicked, they were basically to serve as a cloak to disguise Franco's personal rule. Many silenced their outrage in the interest of the war effort, but a majority of the Right were willing and satisfied accomplices as the Caudillo's 'new order' fulfilled their expectations. Franco's Falange was a tamed movement in which the more revolutionary elements of the old party were either purged or, like Manuel Hedilla, José Antonio's designated successor, even imprisoned. Opportunists, careerists and Franco's supporters flooded into the new party in which the social and agrarian radicalism of the Falange were swiftly ignored.[46]

On 3 June, General Mola, still Franco's most serious rival, was killed in a plane accident. Yet again Providence smiled on the Caudillo. On 30 January 1938 Franco formed his first cabinet. Serrano Suñer as the Minister of Interior was the dominant figure. In what would be a blue-print for Franco's shrewd balancing act of future years, the posts were carefully distributed. All the Nationalist factions – military, Catholics, Carlists, Monarchists and Falangists – were represented. They were all given enough leeway but never hegemony over the others. Thus they all accepted that only under his rule would their particular interests be safeguarded. Above all it was a personal, authoritarian and conservative dictatorship where the old order was balanced with some modern trappings and rhetoric of Fascism. Franco had accumulated in his hands more power even than medieval monarchs. He was the Generalissimo of the armed forces, head of the government and of the state, Caudillo of the crusade with the enthusiastic blessing of the Church, and chief of the only political party. The hesitant rebel had obtained in eighteen months practically absolute control over every aspect of Spain's political life.[47]

The Republican Zone: Chronicle of a Death Foretold

The military insurrection caught the government by surprise. Amidst widespread confusion and despair, Madrid saw three cabinets in one day. The hapless Casares could not believe the seriousness of the situation. Asked for his impressions on the night of 17 July he pathetically replied: 'If the army is rising in Morocco I am going to bed.' The following morning he awoke to a reality of garrisons revolting across the country and workers demanding weapons. He panicked and was replaced by a moderate, the ex-Radical Martínez Barrios. He tried in vain to talk the rebel commanders out of their coup, particularly Mola, by negotiating a compromise over the telephone. He then gave way to a left-wing Republican, José Giral, close to President Azaña, who finally took the decision to arm the population.[48] If that measure had been taken much earlier, the rebellion might have been crushed at birth. However, the reluctance of bourgeois politicians to take that step was understandable since they were as frightened of revolutionary upheaval as of a military take-over.

The great paradox of the insurrection was that it precipitated the very revolutionary process which the army claimed to be forestalling.[49] However, the legitimacy of the Republican government was not in question. The UGT, despite Largo's rhetoric, never planned to destroy the bourgeois Republic. The CNT did not know how to proceed. Lacking a theory of state and aware of its weakness in many parts of Republican Spain, the Anarcho-Syndicalist leaders after a historical meeting with the Catalan President Companys accepted a compromise and refused to impose their own dictatorship. The CNT, an organization built upon libertarian principles, entered a crisis of identity as it reached its highest moment of power.[50] The abyss between its basic ideological tenets and the harsh necessities imposed by war ultimately contributed more to the erosion of Anarchist faith and doctrine than generations of persecutions and clandestinity.

Yet real power lay in the streets and not in the ministerial offices. The state machinery was swept away by the revolutionary fervour which followed the workers' victory over the insurgents in most parts of Spain. A reality of dual power emerged. The central government and its representatives in the provinces had little authority and were bypassed by a myriad of popular committees, constituted depending on the local balance of power. Large parts of industry, commerce and public services were taken over by the workers and the land was collectivized by the peasants. Equally, soldiers deserted their units as workers' militias took control of re-establishing order in the streets and organized the military operations against the Nationalist-held areas. Naturally, this was far from a uniform process. Where the Socialists were strongest the collapse of the pre-war social and political structures was much less than where the Anarchists were dominant (Cataluña, Aragón and some parts of Andalucía). In the Basque Country, where the right-wing Nationalists sided with the Republic in exchange for the concession of Home Rule, the situation hardly changed.[51]

A consequence of the existing chaos was the large-scale violence which reigned over Republican Spain during the first months. Victims were politicians, employers and landowners. A special target of popular hatred was the Church with about 6000 priests murdered. However, Republican terror, horrific as it was, differed dramatically from that of the Nationalists. It was on a much smaller scale and different in nature. Although figures are very unreliable and open to controversy about 55 000 Rightists were murdered, mostly in the first months of the war, for over 200 000 leftists.[52] Unlike Nationalist repression, a cold-blooded and deliberate policy of its leaders, the summary executions in the Republic were carried out from below as a consequence of the crumbling legal order. The killings were spontaneous and often perpetrated by criminal elements or *incontrolados* settling old personal scores. Yet ministers, trade union leaders and even leading figures of the FAI opposed the atrocities and took an active part in ending them and saving many lives.[53]

A pressing problem for the Republic was the constant domestic squabbles and political infighting. Despite the widespread recognition that collaboration was imperative to victory, the unity achieved with relative ease by the Nationalists eluded the Republicans until the end. Focusing on the dichotomy between those who gave priority to the war effort and those who pushed for greater social revolution is simply to miss the core of the argument. By September 1936, the irresistible advance of Franco's professional troops, well supplied by the Fascist dictators, had already solved the question in favour of the former. Indeed, the Nationalists had forced a total war and the Republic had to fight back in those terms. Hence only the effective centralization, deployment and mobilization of all the human and material resources could stave off imminent defeat. The workers' courage in the first days of street-fighting was crucial in crushing the insurrection in large parts of Spain, but it soon became evident that bravery alone could not win the war. Ill-disciplined and poorly armed militias fared badly in open battle. Despite their overwhelming superiority in numbers they failed to advance in Aragón against thin lines defended by organized troops under the command of seasoned officers. Their performance was even worse against the African army marching towards Madrid. Military operations were hampered by constant disputes between rival political forces, with the militias holding votes before an attack and refusing to obey orders from professional officers. There was besides no single Republican strategy. Military power was chaotically fragmented as the Republican forces lacked war consciousness and focused their resistance in merely local terms.[54]

It was with the purpose of harnessing all the energies of the state and achieving unity that the unrepresentative all-Republican cabinet was replaced on 4 September by a genuine Popular Front administration. The so-called 'government of victory' was presided over by Largo Caballero, recognized as the most popular Leftist leader who could channel revolutionary fervour into a united war effort. It contained six Socialists, two Republicans, one Catalan and one Basque Nationalist, and two Communists. In early November two members of the CNT and two of the FAI also became ministers.[55] It was a self-sacrificing gesture which intensified the tensions within the Anarcho-Syndicalist movement.

Largo laid the foundations for the re-construction of the Republican state. Emphasis was placed on the creation of an effective central staff, the restraint of revolutionary power in the rear in favour of a strong government able to mobilize all classes and all material resources in a concerted war effort, and the conscription of all the unruly militias into a cohesive force, the Popular Army. However, this was an arduous and slow process. An aged Largo lacked the energy and the resilience to carry it through and his star soon began to fade. His insistence on holding the War Ministry proved a mistake. His reputation was tarnished when he abandoned Madrid in early November, leaving the capital to a Defence Council under General Miaja, and basing his government in Valencia.[56] Madrid held on, but Largo reaped no credit for it. The loss of Málaga in February 1937 was a new blow to his falling prestige. By the spring, the Prime Minister was an isolated figure surrounded by powerful enemies.

Above all, many Socialists and Republicans had neither forgotten nor forgiven Largo's dogmatic position before the outbreak of the war. Internal Socialist ill-feelings and divisions escalated during his premiership. He offended the PSOE's National Executive when he accepted his appointment without even consulting them, acting as the UGT's president rather than as a party member. To add insult to injury, Largo soon ignored all his previous revolutionary rhetoric and proceeded as a pragmatic and reformist politician putting all his efforts into re-constructing the bourgeois Republic. The Socialist leadership was furious that he was actually taking over their own programme and so revealing that his previous stance had been mere posturing. By blocking Prieto's access to power in May 1936 he might have indirectly contributed to weakening the government and facilitating the insurrection.[57]

To make matters worse, Largo's initial good relations with the Communist Party soon deteriorated. The Prime Minister seemed not to realize the swift and all-embracing transformation that the PCE had experienced. In less than a year, the PCE became, from a relatively minor force of about 20000 activists, an increasingly powerful movement with half a million members. Indisputably, the popularity of the Soviet Union as the only major power rendering military assistance to the Republic increased Communist prestige. However, there were further reasons to explain the PCE's astonishing growth. Amidst the chaos of other groups, the Communists portrayed an image of competence, discipline and clarity. They also possessed a formidable propaganda machine. After the government's evacuation of Madrid, the Communists filled the vacuum. Their leaders became the heroes of the capital, fighting at the front and galvanizing the masses with rousing slogans. The Communist Fifth Regiment with the superior quality of its cadres, its political commissars and professional officers, became the role model for the Popular Army. Apart from the prestige gained by its efficiency, the moderation of the Communist tactics, championing respect for private property and advocating loyal collaboration between the middle and working classes, appealed to thousands of small tenants, artisans, merchants and white-collar workers who rushed to join the party.[58] Largo resented the increasingly dominant role played by the Communists and instead of using subtle diplomacy soon was engaged in bitter clashes with Russian advisers.

Furthermore, the aim of subordinating the independence of the diverse militias to the authority of the state was hardly successful in Anarchist fiefdoms, particularly in Cataluña. There tension kept mounting. The CNT–FAI, although part of the Catalan government, continued to play a dominant role, keeping their armed patrols and refusing to relinquish vital parts of the economy seized in the first days. The Catalan Nationalists found a ready ally to challenge Anarcho-Syndicalist hegemony in the unified party of Socialists and Communists (PSUC) created in July 1936. More than in other parts of Spain, thousands of members of the Catalan lower middle classes joined the PSUC and the UGT in seeking protection from Anarchist aggression. The situation was aggravated by the existence of the small but fiercely revolutionary party of dissident Communists (POUM) extremely critical of the PCE's moderate political line.[59]

Clashes and reprisals between the two Catalan camps increased in the first months of 1937. When in late April, Roldán Cortada, a prominent UGT leader, was assassinated, allegedly by Anarchists, most reckoned that an armed confrontation was imminent. The dispatch of three truckloads of Assault Guards on 3 May by the PSUC Police Commissioner to seize the central telephone exchange held by the CNT was the spark that ignited the impending conflict. Almost immediately barricades were erected across Barcelona. For four days, members of the CNT–FAI and the POUM fought a mini war against the PSUC and the left-wing Catalan Nationalists, leaving hundreds of casualties. Once again the internal crisis of Anarcho-Syndicalism became glaring. They had the upper hand in the contest and, if necessary, reinforcements could be brought from other parts of Cataluña and Aragón. However, the price of their victory would have been further confrontation with the rest of Republican Spain and inevitable defeat by Franco. Thus the Anarcho-Syndicalist ministers rushed to Barcelona and managed to convince their restive followers to lay down their weapons.[60]

The outcome of these events was a strengthening of those advocating centralization of power and restoration of order at the rearguard. The Catalan government lost much of its autonomy as thousands of Assault Guards were sent to Barcelona to separate the combatants and then in October the central government moved its headquarters there. The CNT, though still a huge force, emerged demoralized after what many in its ranks regarded as the capitulation of their leaders. Finally, it sealed the downfall of Largo Caballero and the fate of the POUM.

The May days provided the alliance of Communists, Socialists and Republicans with the excuse to remove Largo Caballero. Ironically, his bitter rivals of the past, the four Anarcho-Syndicalist ministers, were the only members of the cabinet ready to back him. Largo's downfall was not a sinister Communist conspiracy, but rather the settlement of old scores within the PSOE. Indeed, the Communists only asked for Largo to relinquish his control of the War Ministry. However, for the PSOE's National Executive it was the long-awaited occasion to stage an internal coup and eliminate the influence of the *Caballerista* wing in the party. They launched a concerted assault on Largo's remaining power bases; his supporters were purged from key positions in the party, their journals taken over by force and, finally, Largo himself, although still conserving significant authority in the union, was forced to resign his chairmanship in October and a new executive seized control of the UGT.[61]

The new Prime Minister was Juan Negrín, a moderate Socialist close to Prieto and Treasury Minister in the previous cabinet. His government, formed on 17 May, consisted of three Socialists, two Communists, two Republicans and one Catalan and one Basque Nationalist. In the reshuffle of April 1938, the CNT re-entered the government. It resembled the original Popular Front as conceived by Azaña and Prieto in February 1936 and reaffirmed the authority of political parties over trade unions.[62] He continued vigorously the task initiated by Largo of strengthening the central state in order to maximize all the available resources and mount a consistent war effort, even at the price of diluting the revolutionary fervour of the first days.

Negrín has often been dismissed as a Communist puppet, the Moscow man.[63] In fact, the new Prime Minister, an energetic politician who had gained the backing of Communists and Socialists from his skilful handling of the Republic's finances, was above all Azaña's and Prieto's candidate.[64] After some initial hesitations, even the CNT–FAI rendered its support. Negrín was not a mere front for the PCE, he was a realist whose main goal was the pragmatic pursuit of victory. Negrín was aware that the war could not be won without the Western democracies changing their position. In the meantime, the Republic's most vital task was to concentrate all its efforts on sustaining its long-term defensive capabilities. Thus excellent relations with the Communists were crucial. It was not only that the Soviet Union remained the main provider of military equipment, but also that with Republican parties in disarray and the PSOE torn apart by its internal divisions, the PCE was the only united and disciplined political force in 1937 who could mobilize effectively all the social components of the Popular Front. Indeed, the PCE not only argued for a wide inter-class alliance, but went far down the road to realizing it and appealing across class lines both to workers and significant sectors of the middle classes. Thousands of smallholders and urban white-collar workers whose support was necessary for the rebuilding of the Republican state were attracted by the PCE's moderate discourse. But, at the same time, the Communists retained a proletarian constituency to whom it held out a promise of social and economic reform. Inevitably, the Negrín government had to turn a blind eye to the sectarian and violent policies implemented by the Communists. In particular, as the CNT could not be overcome, the POUM became the scapegoat for the May events and the main target of the PCE's private vendetta. That party, accused of being 'Fascist agents' was suppressed in June. Its entire leadership and hundreds of its members arrested. Some were assassinated, the most infamous case being that of its leader Andreu Nin.[65]

Negrín's slogan, 'resisting is winning', encapsulated his war strategy. He was aware that victory could not be enjoyed with the existing *status quo*. Thus his policy of resistance was based on different alternatives. At best, victory could be achieved by linking the Spanish conflict with a European war, or by persuading the Allies either to enforce the existing Non-Intervention policy or to abandon it altogether and give the Republic the military supplies to defend herself; at worst, by mounting an effective war effort to force Franco to negotiate a compromise peace.[66]

Resistance was thus the order of the day. However, the weakness of that strategy was that it hinged ultimately on the question of winning time. Hopes for a change in the international situation had to be balanced with increasing war-weariness and demoralization. In reality, Negrín's accomplishments, against overwhelming military odds, were extraordinary. From the chaotic rag-tag militias of the first months an efficient popular army emerged with the capability to mount well-planned offensives which often surprised the enemy. Being written-off many times, the Republic still lasted for almost two more years, during which time less ground was surrendered than in the previous period.[67] However, small gains on the battlefields were followed by painful losses of human and *matériel* resources which could not be replaced. As Franco held the agrarian heartland, the population in the Republic suffered from growing food shortages and even hunger. The loss of the northern provinces in 1937 and then the success of Franco's troops in reaching the Mediterranean, splitting the Republic in two in the spring of 1938, filled the Republican camp with pessimism. This air of despondency affected even those who held high positions: President Azaña entered a period of self-indulging contemplative life and even the formerly energetic Prieto became such an embarrassing source of defeatism that in April 1938 he had to be relieved of his post as War Minister, which was then taken over by Negrín himself.[68]

Yet the Republic failed to achieve victory not because its policies were wrong but because of the strength of international forces arrayed against it. Negrín struggled not only to combat the Axis-equipped Nationalist armies, but also a crippling embargo which not only prevented the Republic from ever engaging on an equal military footing, but also in the end undercut the attempts to sustain the physical fabric and morale of the home front, crucial to its war of resistance.[69]

Indeed, Negrín ultimately lost the war on the diplomatic front. It was Hitler, Mussolini and Chamberlain who were responsible for the Nationalist victory and not Stalin's ambiguous policies and Communist ascendancy. As it was, the PCE, for all its crimes and errors, played a major role in keeping Republican resistance alive as long as it did.[70] Non-Intervention not only threw the Republic into the embrace of the only great power willing to help, the Soviet Union, but remained until the end a cruel hoax continually avoiding the real issue, the flagrant violations of the agreement by the Axis powers. The presence of entire Italian divisions on Spanish soil, amply proved by the display of captured Italian soldiers, the brutal bombing of cities by the German and Italian air forces, or even the shelling of Almería in May 1937 by German warships, were all conveniently overlooked. A unique and exceptional instance in the infamous history of the Non-Intervention Committee was the Nyon Conference of September 1937 organized under Anglo-French auspices after thirty merchant vessels of different nationalities were sunk in the summer of 1937 by 'mysterious' attacks in the Mediterranean. The tough stance taken this time by the Allies, ordering their fleet to intercept and destroy those 'pirates', revealed how Fascist aggression could be stopped if matched by force. However, Nyon was the exception and not the rule. The piratical attacks stopped immediately. In fact, British intelligence, which had broken the Italian naval codes, knew that they were caused by Italian submarines but this was never publically revealed. Furthermore, the disruption of merchant shipping by air attacks or other means continued unabated.[71]

France continued her policy of relaxed non-intervention, turning a blind eye to the dispatch of Russian weapons from Murmansk to French Atlantic ports and then to their smuggling into Spain. As the Mediterranean route became increasingly difficult and dangerous, French tolerance became vital to the continued openness of supply lines to the Republic.[72] Yet all French attempts to take positive action against Fascist aggression in Spain had to be abandoned under the risk of straining relations with Britain.

In fact, the unexpected Republican resistance in Madrid at the end of 1936 destroyed the British expectations of a short military conflict. At the British Foreign Office, Anthony Eden became increasingly alarmed by the growing challenge presented by the Axis Pact. Throughout 1937, he changed his attitude towards the Spanish war. After the so-called Gentlemen's Agreement with Italy in January 1937 confirming the *status quo* in the Mediterranean, Eden was shocked by the massive dispatch of Italian troops to Spain while Mussolini was leading his country towards a tight alliance with Germany. Eden favoured taking measures to enforce real non-intervention. When that failed, he began to prefer a Republican victory to the alternative of a militarist regime close to the Axis.[73]

However, Eden was an isolated voice in the cabinet. His fears were not shared by the other ministers still bent on a policy of appeasing the dictators and with the accession of Neville Chamberlain to the Premiership in May 1937, his post at the Foreign Office became increasingly untenable. By late 1937 the opposing views in the British cabinet could no longer be reconciled. Italy's joining the Anti-Comintern Pact with Germany and Japan in November 1937 and her departure from the League of Nations one month later confirmed Eden's view that a tough stand should be taken and that Spain should become the test of Mussolini's good faith. For the Prime Minister, on the other hand, Spain was a 'distraction' which should not obstruct the completion of a treaty of friendship with Italy. The cabinet sided with

Chamberlain and Eden resigned in February 1938, to be replaced by the arch-appeaser Lord Halifax. In April a treaty was signed with Italy which recognized *de jure* the latter's conquest of Abyssinia in return for Italian promises of withdrawing her troops from Spain 'once the war was over'.[74]

Nevertheless, the escalation of German expansionism gave the Republic a glimmer of hope in 1938. In March Germany annexed Austria and laid plans for her next prize, the Sudetenland in Czechoslovakia. These events coincided with the formation of the second Blum cabinet in France. Blum was determined not to repeat the indecisive policies of 1936 and to stand up to Fascist aggression. As public outcry mounted after the indiscriminate Italian bombardment of Barcelona, Blum met the Permanent Defence National Committee. The French premier wanted to send an ultimatum to Franco demanding the withdrawal of foreign troops. He also suggested the dispatch of arms to the Republic. Yet Blum's plans were met with reluctance and hesitation. The French generals, well aware of British hostility, advised against taking measures which could endanger peace in Europe and leave France isolated. They also stated that in the current situation France could not spare any military equipment. In the end, Blum had to settle for a half-hearted formula: the total opening of her border to the delivery of Russian weapons.[75] The Blum administration lasted only one month and was replaced by a more right-wing government led by Daladier. The British exerted all sorts of pressure on the new French government to reverse Blum's decision and close the 'hellish' border. According to them it was the French attitude, not the blatant Axis display of force in Spain, which flouted the principles of Non-Intervention and was leading Europe to the verge of war. Spain was thus worth sacrificing on the altar of appeasement. On 5 June the secretary of Lord Halifax wrote: 'the government is praying for Franco's victory and pressing France to stop the supplies reaching the Republic'. After relentless coercion, Daladier finally gave way and the border was closed on 13 June cutting off the last and only safe channel of arms to the beleaguered Republic.[76]

Undeterred by the constant set-backs, Negrín launched a parallel diplomatic and military offensive in 1938. Hoping to enlist the support of the Western democracies, he stated in May his thirteen points to reach a compromise peace based on Spain free from foreign interference, with free elections and full civil rights.[77] At the same time, in order to show that the Republic was far from beaten, a daring offensive was launched on 24 July. The Catalan army, profiting from the military reserves accumulated before the closing of the French border, crossed the river Ebro with the ultimate objective of restoring communications with the rest of Republican Spain. The operation was initially a success, taking the Nationalists by surprise and establishing a bridgehead forty kilometres from their starting point. By early August, Franco had dispatched massive reinforcements to the front and, as in early operations, the Republicans were bogged down in a long war of attrition which would last four months.[78] However, as the battle raged on, the eyes of the combatants were focused on events on the continent.

For a brief time the Republic was jubilant, believing that the tide was turning. Diplomatic relations were deteriorating dramatically. During the spring Nationalist air attacks on neutral merchant vessels, 70 per cent of them British, increased. In total, twenty ships were attacked, eleven of them being sunk or seriously damaged. Chamberlain and Halifax were embarrassed by the popular outcry following their impotence in the face of aggression. Franco only called off the raids in July following Italo-German advice not to antagonize a 'friendly' Chamberlain.[79] Simultaneously, German intransigence regarding their claim to the Sudetenland threatened to plunge Europe into war. Negrín intensified his propaganda campaign, announcing the unilateral withdrawal of foreign troops (the last 12 000 members of the International Brigades left Spain in November). As soon as hostilities broke out, the Republic would declare war on Germany and link its fortune to that of the Allies. Franco was horrified and perplexed. Under heavy stress, for the first time in years, he was unwell, confined to his headquarters for days. On 27 September he let France and Britain know of his intentions to adopt a position of strict neutrality. Yet as the Nationalist Ambassador in Berlin revealed: 'A European war was a nightmare since regardless of our actions, the Republic would automatically declare war on the Axis and thus become allies of those whose neutrality we wished to preserve.'[80]

In the event, the international and domestic situation could not have evolved more favourably for Franco. Rather than risk war with Hitler, the Allies by signing the Munich Pact effectively acceded to the break-up of Czechoslovakia. After the cession of the Sudetenland the Republic's fate was sealed. At once, all hopes of being rescued by the Western democracies were shattered. Additionally, Stalin learnt the lessons of appeasement. The abandonment of Czechoslovakia at Munich signified the end of Soviet hopes that Spain would awaken

Britain and France to the dangers of Fascism. Thus the Soviet Union's interest in the Republic waned as she began to seek an accommodation with Hitler which culminated in the Non-Aggression Pact of August 1939.[81] Furthermore, the Ebro campaign became the sort of war of annihilation always pursued by Franco. On 16 November, the battle ended. It had taken the Nationalists almost four months to push the Republicans out of the territory captured in July. The toll was the heaviest of the entire war: each side suffering over 50 000 casualties.[82] Both armies were exhausted. However, whereas the Republic used up some of its best troops and *matériel* which could never be replaced, Franco could afford the appalling losses. On 18 November Hitler agreed to requests for massive deliveries of equipment in return for more mining concessions. In fact, by the end of the year, eager to see off the Spanish problem, Germany surpassed Italy, for the first time, in the scale of involvement.[83]

On 23 December 1938 Franco initiated his final push against Cataluña. Starved of supplies and heavily outgunned, the Republican defences collapsed. When a hesitant France re-opened the border in January it was too late to prevent a military rout. With the British cabinet still bent on making friends with the dictators, there was little that France could do. A buoyant Ciano even warned that French intervention would unleash a European war. On 26 January Barcelona fell with hardly any resistance. By early February, the frontier was a scene of tragedy. The remnants of the Catalan army, the Republican government and about half a million refugees crossed the Pyrenees. On 10 February the border was reached by the Nationalists.[84]

The official recognition of Franco's regime on 27 February by Britain and France, anxious to extricate Spain's master from his Axis partners, dealt a final deathblow to the Republic.[85] A despairing Azaña resigned from office the following day.

Negrín still refused to accept defeat and returned to Spain. The Republic still controlled the centre-south zone, over 30 per cent of the country, including the cities of Madrid and Valencia. He planned to make a last-ditch stand and hopefully hold out until war broke out in Europe. Although resistance, against overwhelming military odds, seemed uncertain, Negrín knew there was no alternative. Through diplomatic channels he had attempted a peace settlement in February based on three proposals: independence from foreign control; the people's freedom to choose their own form of government; and the promise of no reprisals. The last of these was actually the minimum condition that the Prime Minister expected to clinch before accepting defeat.[86] Yet the Caudillo made starkly clear that there could be no thought of amnesty or reconciliation for the defeated Republicans, who he referred to as 'criminals'. On 13 February Franco introduced the Law of Political Responsibilities, by which supporters of the Republic were declared guilty of siding with an 'illegitimate' political system. The law was retroactive to October 1934. It was the first step towards the institutionalization of Franco's peace: draconian repression in which mass executions, labour camps and persecution would be the fate for the vanquished.[87]

Although Negrín was aware that the Republic had to fight on, his views were not shared by many in the Republican camp. After thirty months of combat, he found the centre-south zone plagued by war-weariness, defeatism and low morale. After the Sudeten set-back and the loss of Cataluña, his calls for continued resistance seemed futile. Moreover, this zone, although surrounded by the enemy and cut off from the Republican leadership since the spring of 1938, had been spared the major military operations. Growing food and armament shortages intensified feelings of isolation and fed political intrigues. Moreover, the PCE's ascendancy under Negrín, hitherto accepted as vital to the survival of the Republic, was now considered the stumbling block to a negotiated settlement. The heart of the conspiracy against all-out resistance was in Madrid under Colonel Casado, commander of the centre army. His belief that the war was already lost and that the slaughter should be stopped was shared by many disillusioned Republican officers, Anarchists and Socialists, all bound together by their common grudge against the Communists. The most prominent among them was Julián Besteiro, the veteran Socialist leader, who had remained in Madrid throughout the war, refusing numerous opportunities to seek safe exile, and had become a fierce exponent of defeatism and anti-Communism. It seems difficult to believe that they were unaware of the scale of Nationalist repression. Yet their illusions of reaching a 'honourable peace' with Franco once Negrín and the Communists were deposed had certainly been fostered by contacts maintained by Casado, Besteiro and other officers with Nationalist agents.[88]

Spurred by a combination of irresponsibility, delusion and naivety, Casado, Besteiro and other minor political and military figures created a Council of National Defence that on 5 March staged a coup against the Negrín government. It was a tragic irony that the Republic succumbed to another *pronunciamiento* which concluded the task that the Nationalist had failed to fulfil in July 1936. For days, Franco happily watched while pro- and anti-Negrín forces fought their own civil war in and around Madrid. Anarchist intervention in favour of the new rebels determined the outcome of the struggle. On 6 March Negrín and his supporters fled. The bankruptcy of Casado's plans was brutally exposed when Franco insisted that he would only accept unconditional surrender. By his action, Casado had ruined definitively the possibility of further resistance and rendered pointless the bloodshed and sacrifices of the previous three years. On 26 March the Nationalists resumed the offensive virtually unopposed. Republican troops deserted *en masse* as many fled towards the coast in a final attempt to escape abroad.[89] On 1 April 1939, the Caudillo announced the end of the war. For half of Spain, long years of reprisals and persecution lay ahead.

6

FRANCO, REGENT FOR LIFE, 1939–75

The Myth of Neutrality

In the spring of 1939 Spain resembled a country occupied by a victorious foreign army.[1] After almost three years of vicious war the economy was in tatters, the transport system had collapsed and there were critical shortages of food and fuel. These appalling conditions did not deter the triumphant Nationalists from embarking upon an unprecedented programme of economic and political reaction. For most of the population, the period until the early 1950s was known as *los años de hambre* ('the hunger years'): worsening living standards, widespread misery and rationing of basic staples. Yet protection for the interests of the social elites whose privileges had been threatened by the Republic's reforms was a priority. Wages were slashed, strikes treated as sabotage and made punishable by long prison sentences and the labour movement regimented under Falangist control.

Reconstruction was pursued with the tools of a war economy. It was a political as much as an economic choice. The two key concepts were autarky and state interventionism. A huge apparatus was erected in order to control wages, prices, agricultural yields and the exchange rate. The National Wheat Service fixed the production of wheat and marketed it, and the National Institute of Industry (INI), a state holding company created in 1941, undertook the development of industries related to defence and to supplement private investment. The objective was to aim at self-sufficiency by drastically cutting imports and encouraging national production. In fact, it served to consolidate the wealth

126

of the large landowners and industrialists protected from foreign competition by high tariff barriers and administrative controls. Autarky proved an utter disaster. As traditional structures and technology remained unchanged, Spain failed to become self-sufficient and production fell drastically. The suffering was exacerbated by the disastrous decision to maintain the peseta at a ridiculous overvalued rate. The result was a flourishing black market which allowed those with money, influence and property to make formidable profits by hoarding basic commodities and selling them at several times the official price.[2]

Politically, there would be no forgiving or forgetting in the new order. April 1939 was not the beginning of reconciliation but rather heralded the institutionalization of full-scale vengeance. Society was divided between the patriots of 'Real Spain' and the hordes who had supported 'Godless anti-Spain'. Retaliation was officially sanctioned by the Law of Political Responsibilities of February 1939 and the Law of Repression of Masonry and Communism of May 1940. Hundreds of thousands of Spaniards fled into exile, but those who stayed and whose political reliability was suspected were rounded up and crammed into overcrowded prisons. Military courts worked full-time delivering vindictive sentences. Even Himmler was shocked by the bloodbath he saw when he visited Spain in 1940.[3] After almost forty years in power, the Nationalists ensured they left few traces of their 'justice'. A reliable estimate for the peak of the post-war retaliation, between 1939 and 1945, would be more than 100 000 executions. About 250 000 people were given long prison sentences during which time their sins had to be redeemed through work. Labour battalions undertaking public works were formed. The biggest aberration of all was the construction, between 1940 and 1959, by 20 000 political prisoners, many of whom died or were badly injured, of the so-called *Valle de los Caidos* ('Valley of the Fallen'), a gigantic mausoleum to the north east of Madrid to commemorate those who had died for 'God's cause'.[4]

The Caudillo built a successful governing class which was to rule the nation for almost forty years. He was the supreme arbiter of a coalition of factions competing for his favour and spheres of influence. Franco was careful enough never to antagonize any of them and ensure that they were all represented all of the time. These groups, popularly known as 'families', were bound together by the so-called 'Pact of Blood' as well as by their shared authoritarian values born from the uprising of 1936 and their obvious fear of a Republican return. Franco cemented his personal rule by perpetuating the memories of the

Civil War. Every effort went to maintain the division between the victors and the vanquished. While he remained in charge, the former could enjoy power and the spoils of victory. Official propaganda fed the idea that he was the bulwark who guaranteed the continuity of the new order. Thus Franco was not just indispensable to political stability, he was consubstantial to it.[5]

Discrimination affected every aspect of people's lives. In order to obtain such vital things as a ration card or a job it was necessary to provide evidence of loyalty to the new system by means of an official certificate or a letter signed by a person who was accredited by the regime. Fear and terror ensured political apathy and discouraged mobilization while the Falange became the main source for jobs, patronage and safety. The public sector was thoroughly purged. Those engaged in education and teaching were particularly affected. History had to be re-written and the task was left in the safe hands of those who shared the spirit of the crusade. Sycophants and apologists orchestrated official propaganda which had little to do with reality. Children were not taught until the 1970s that Spain had been devastated by a cruel Civil War. Instead, they learnt that a national and patriotic movement had saved the country from the clutches of a Communist-inspired conspiracy. The Caudillo as leader of this holy crusade was linked with the noble medieval knights of *la reconquista*. He was the annihilator of Communism, a source of generosity and intelligence who had earned with his bravery the blind trust of every Spaniard.[6]

The most successful of Franco's myths was that of his neutrality during the Second World War. Official biographies depicting the Caudillo as a far-sighted statesman who resisted the pressures of the Axis and thus saved Spain from the ordeals of war were believed long after his death.[7] In fact, nothing could be further from the truth. Franco was not neutral during the European conflict. He wished for a German victory, helped the Axis as much as he could and even tried to enter the war. Spain's final non-involvement was due to a combination of circumstances in which luck as well as external factors beyond Franco's control were crucial.

In 1939 the Caudillo saw himself as a natural partner and comrade in arms of Hitler and Mussolini. On 27 March Spain adhered to the Anti-Comintern pact and on the 31st a five-year treaty of friendship was signed with Germany. A similar agreement with Italy had existed since November 1936. In May, Spain abandoned the League of Nations. However, the German invasion of Poland caught Franco by surprise. Both he and Mussolini, whose mutual affection and excellent relations had grown after three years of collaboration, clearly wanted a German victory but both were aware that hostilities had broken out too soon. Thus they agreed to sit on the fence waiting for the evolution of events. Yet their feelings were clear. Mussolini even invented a new term, 'non-belligerence', to show his preference for the Third Reich without actual participation in the conflict. Spain's neutrality was just a step behind that of Italy. There was no desire to be impartial, but economic and military weakness precluded any other option at this stage.[8] Ideologically, Franco felt close to the Fascist regimes and despised the Western powers. While the Axis had provided crucial aid during the Civil War, France had taken a pro-Republican stand. Finally, there were territorial claims ranging from Gibraltar to chunks of Africa which could only be obtained if the Allies were defeated.[9] Franco even temporarily forgot his obsessive anti-Communism. As Germany and Russia signed the Non-Aggression Pact in August 1939, which one month later led to their division of Poland, he commented to Serrano Suñer: 'It is odd that now we are allies of the Russians.'[10]

Mussolini and Franco were astonished when country after country fell to the ruthless German war machine in the spring of 1940. Timing was the main problem. Anxious to share the spoils of victory, they had to join before the conflict was over. However, aware of their military deficiencies they had to be careful not to be caught in a long war for which they were ill-prepared. The sudden collapse of France in June seemed to indicate that the moment to make their move had finally arrived. The *Duce* informed Franco that he would no longer remain a spectator and on 10 June entered the conflict.[11]

Franco was more cautious than the ever-zealous Italian dictator. As an army officer himself, he was aware of the chaotic state of his troops. Widespread food shortages and economic bankruptcy had also to be considered. But, above all, the Caudillo wanted to extract a 'fair' price for his support. Impressed by the German *Blitzkrieg*, he tried hard for the next months to clinch a good deal before joining the Axis. Britain's skilful diplomacy coupled with Germany's contemptuous attitude prevented that.

With Britain facing defeat, the Iberian peninsula became strategically vital. In particular, the safety of the naval base of Gibraltar was of the utmost importance for her Mediterranean commerce and communications with the empire. Samuel Hoare, an influential ex-minister, was sent on 1 June as ambassador with the special mission of ensuring that country's neutrality. Soon after his arrival he discovered that Spain was almost a German satellite. Under Serrano Suñer's control, as Minister of the Interior and President of the Falange's National Executive, the media was saturated with German propaganda. While the German ambassador, Von Stohrer, was on intimate terms with Franco and his entourage, Hoare had to put up with constant discourtesies, pro-Axis speeches of ministers and Falangist mobs demanding the return of Gibraltar. The Caudillo always met him in his office flanked by signed photographs of Mussolini and Hitler. For fear of being kidnapped, Hoare had to go everywhere escorted. Some of his servants were arrested, interrogated and beaten up and several British consulates attacked. German submarines received unrestricted aid, the Gestapo collaborated with the Spanish police and Nazi intelligence services operated at will. Hoare's strategy was to ignore these provocations. Instead, he played down the German victories as temporary set-backs, exacerbated internal disputes between the Nationalist groups, if necessary by lavish bribery of some generals, and, above all, used the economic weapon. Realizing the precarious situation of the Spanish economy, Britain, with the collaboration of the United States, performed a nerve-racking balancing act, providing just enough credit and vital supplies of food and oil to prevent Franco from going over completely to the Axis, but not so much as to enable him to become strong enough to dispense with maintaining relations with them.[12]

In the summer of 1940, Franco wanted to take part in the war. The apparent collapse of the Allies persuaded him that Spain could finally fulfil its imperial dreams in the slip-stream of Nazi conquests. On 12 June, Spain adopted the previous Italian position of non-belligerency and then two days later seized the internationally administered city of Tangier in Morocco. On 17 June a delighted Franco communicated to Germany the French desire to arrange an armistice.[13]

In early June, Franco wrote to Hitler expressing his warmest admiration and congratulations for his great victories and offering his constant friendship. Flattery was matched by cold calculation. The letter was delivered by his Chief of Staff, General Vigón, sent to negotiate the terms for Spain's joining the Axis. The territorial claims included Gibraltar, French Morocco, part of Algeria and the enlargement of Spanish Guinea. Huge economic and military aid was also requested. In September, Serrano Suñer visited Berlin in order to insist on Spain's readiness to enter the war in return for her colonial demands. He was shocked when the Germans did not treat him as a valued ally but as the representative of a satellite state. Moreover, they were not only vague about the Spanish claims but even replied by asking for the cession of one of the Canary Islands and enclaves in Morocco. In turn, Serrano's procrastination disappointed his hosts. Hitler told Ciano that he was opposed to Spanish intervention because 'it would cost more than it is worth'.[14]

It is no wonder that Hitler considered the Spanish demands preposterous. With Europe under his boot, and in the aftermath of Mussolini's attack on France, he did not need more unwanted volunteers for a war which was already won.[15] From his point of view, Spain should be begging to join the triumphant Axis instead of requesting a ridiculous prize in exchange for a more than doubtful contribution to the war effort. There was additionally the complication that Franco's territorial ambitions were in conflict with those of Mussolini and the territories in question were still under the control of collaborationist French Vichy who Germany did not want to antagonize. Considerable forces in the French colonial army were still capable of defending territory against any Spanish or Italian aggression. The last thing Hitler had in mind was to push these troops behind the emergent French Free Army of De Gaulle. Vichy's value was confirmed by its successful defense of Dakar (Senegal) in September against an Anglo-Gaullist attack.[16]

Still, Franco was undeterred. He blamed the German rebuff on Hitler's underlings and insisted on personally negotiating with the German leader. The meeting between the two dictators took place in the French border town of Hendaye on 23 October. He was accompanied by Serrano who a few days earlier had been appointed Foreign Minister. For Franco's propagandists, Hendaye was the turning point, the place where he outwitted Hitler. There, the Caudillo had fought mightily against ferocious German pressure to join the Axis. His master plan was to ask for the impossible and thus keep Spain out of the war.

In fact, reality could not be more different. Franco's train was late, but it was not, as his followers would later claim, a ploy to unnerve Hitler. The delay was a product of the deficient state of the Spanish railways and left Franco feeling diminished in the eyes of the powerful German leader.[17] Indeed, Spain's fate was in Hitler's hands and there was nothing Franco could do. Unlike the myth, the Caudillo was determined to join the Axis as long as he could secure his precious empire. However, the Nazi leader did not accede to his territorial ambitions, neither seeking to mount a credible deceit nor give an ultimatum. Both dictators simply got bogged down in obliquely opposing monologues.

Hitler thought it was Franco's duty to be on his side in thanks for German aid during the Civil War. The question of distribution of the spoils was a secondary matter which should be left until victory day. He did not even attempt to give any territorial promise since, as he had confided to Ribbentrop, 'With these chattering Latins, the French will hear something about it sooner or later.'[18] The result was that while Hitler kept making triumphalist speeches Franco continued to insist on his territorial demands. It is not surprising that when the former hinted that Vichy had to be accommodated the latter's initial bellicose rhetoric was dramatically toned down and replaced by a recital stressing Spain's appalling military and economic conditions. In the end, both were furious. For the Germans, Franco was an ungrateful coward who had missed his chance to join victorious Germany. Hitler declared, 'With these fellows, there is nothing to be done' and 'Rather than go through that again, I would have four teeth extracted'; remarks which clearly showed not a threatening attitude, but impotence and frustration. Simultaneously, the Caudillo, far from exuding satisfaction after heading off 'unbearable' German pressure, appeared dismayed. He told Serrano, 'These people are intolerable. They will not give us what is ours by right.' He had expected to obtain an empire and was leaving with his hands empty. He could not know then that it was his good fortune that Hitler was unable to meet his imperial ambitions.[19]

At Hendaye Franco found himself on the receiving end of a lesson in the realities of power. His naive hopes of massive territorial gain, courtesy of the Third Reich, were shattered before his eyes. It was thus German intransigence and not Spanish cunning which confirmed the latter's non-belligerence. Yet Franco, still anxious to be at the victor's side, put his signature to a secret protocol committing himself to join the Axis and participate in the attack on Gibraltar, the so-called 'Operation Felix'. However, it left the precise date of Spanish entry in Franco's hands until military preparations were completed.[20] For the Caudillo, this meant waiting until almost the last shot had been fired.

Unexpected British resistance in the autumn of 1940 made it difficult for Franco to predict the moment to make his move. With the attempted invasion of Britain faltering, Hitler considered initiating 'Operation Felix' in February 1941. Serrano travelled again to Germany in November and Admiral Canaris visited Spain in December. Yet with the Germans remaining vague about Spain's imperial demands, Franco alleged the country was still not prepared. In fact, there was never any danger that Hitler would consider invading Spain given the level of valuable co-operation from Franco. Additionally, as German reports from Spain confirmed the appalling transport and food conditions, Hitler decided that preparations for the assault on Gibraltar should be discontinued.[21] Furthermore, even if Hitler intended forcing the issue, the disastrous Italian campaigns in the Balkans and North Africa turned the German military machine to the south-east. By then the German dictator, with his eyes fixed on his next big enterprise, Russia, had already concluded that it was better to have a benevolent friend than another costly and inefficient ally.

It is astonishing and highly revealing of Franco's complacent character and egotistical drive for greatness that in the winter of 1940–1 while Europe was being destroyed by war and Spain by starvation, he wrote a work of fiction. Entitled *Raza* ('Race'), it was an account of the experiences of a Galician family, totally identifiable with Franco's own, from the colonial collapse to the Civil War. The romanticized hero embodied the essence of the Spanish race and so was able to save Spain from the foreign poisons of Liberalism and Communism. The book was soon turned into a film and created a past worthy of the providential Caudillo.[22]

Raza revealed the Caudillo's obsession with the Communist threat. Consequently, the German invasion of the Soviet Union in June 1941 marked the culminant moment of his identification with the Third Reich. The 'anti-Soviet crusade' not only fired his pro-Axis enthusiasm but also offered the opportunity to gain a place at the victory table. In July, non-belligerence was replaced by 'moral belligerence' and the first contingent of 47 000 volunteers, known as the Blue Division, was sent to the eastern front to fight beside the German army. Also an agreement was signed to provide 100 000 workers for the increasingly strained German industrial force. During his annual commemoration of the outbreak of the Civil War the Caudillo gave free rein to his pro-Fascist rhetoric. Linking his regime to the Axis, he argued that the first battles of the war had been won in Spain and passionately hailed Germany for 'leading the battle for which Christianity has for so many years longed, and in which the blood of our youth will now mingle with that of the Axis as a living expression of our solidarity'. Even Serrano, taken aback by the Caudillo's reckless speech, confided to the German ambassador that Franco with his imprudence was opening the Allies eyes to the 'true position of Spain'. Previously they had kept on believing that only he, the Foreign Minister, was pushing for war while the 'wise' Caudillo was preserving neutrality unconditionally. Again in

February 1942 a careless Franco declared that one million Spaniards were ready to go and defend Berlin against the Russians.[23]

The Caudillo's impetuous statements were little more than embarrassing. His good luck was that both sides preferred the existing *status quo* and were not prepared to interfere in Spain's internal affairs. While for the Axis he was a loyal friend, the Allies chose to ignore his provocative rhetoric. Britain continued its policy of the carrot, granting with US approval credits of 2 500 000 sterling in April 1941 and avoiding any action which could give Germany the excuse to invade Spain. In fact, Franco was immensely fortunate that Stalin did not choose to respond to the sending of the Blue Division with a declaration of war.[24]

From 1942 the evolution of events, abroad and at home, favoured caution. The successful defence of Moscow and the entry of the United States into the war indicated a protracted conflict. Spain's economic and military position would not sustain a long war effort and the grudging price offered by Hitler did not make the risk worth contemplating. At the same time, internal disputes in the ruling Nationalist coalition were reaching boiling point. Initially, all the groups shared a common sympathy for the Axis. However, as the war dragged on, whereas Falangist enthusiasm for Germany remained undiminished, many senior generals began to show increasing scepticism towards an ultimate German victory and reluctance to embark on a war for which the country was not prepared and which would only strength the Falange's influence in the regime. Furthermore, in the internal struggle for power, officers, mostly with Monarchist sympathies, became weary of Falangist thuggery and rhetoric. In particular, they were concerned with the concentration of power and influence in the hands of Serrano Suñer.[25]

Rivalries exploded on 16 August at the end of a religious ceremony celebrated in Begoña (Bilbao). A group of Falangists threw a bomb at a Carlist gathering presided over by General Varela, the War Minister and an outspoken critic of the Falange, and Serrano, causing about one hundred wounded among the bystanders. In this moment of high tension threatening the break-up of the Nationalist coalition, Franco proved a master manipulator, balancing and appeasing the rival factions. On the one hand, Varela and Galarza, his ally at the Home Office, were sacked and replaced by the pro-Axis hard-liners General Asensio and Blas Pérez respectively. On the other, one Falangist was executed, and Serrano Suñer, the main target of the army's hatred was dismissed. Franco himself replaced him as President of the Falange's National Executive and General Jordana, a moderate and neutralist, became Foreign Minister.[26]

Years later Serrano's dismissal would be portrayed as proof that the Caudillo, aware of the forthcoming Allied victory, had begun to shift towards that camp and sacked the man who personified the Axis cause. In fact, Serrano Suñer cannot be made a scapegoat for pro-German policies. They were very much those of Franco himself.[27] His downfall was, above all, a product of domestic policies. Serrano's sacrifice was the price to appease the army. Moreover, Franco was not sorry to dismiss a powerful, intelligent and ambitious politician who had been hogging the limelight. Suspicions that his brother-in-law might be building his own independent power base had been growing. Franco's distrust was intensified by the disingenuous dinner table questions of his young daughter Carmen, 'Who is in charge here? Papa or Uncle Ramón?'[28] Rather than dynamic personalities, he preferred to surround himself with sycophants and nonentities. While the Falange was left in the hands of a docile section of loyalists such as the Secretary-General José Luis de Arrese, Serrano's leading position in the regime was gradually filled by Admiral Luis Carrero Blanco. Elevated in May 1941 to Undersecretary of the Presidency, unlike the independent Serrano, Carrero was utterly devoted to Franco. A staunch Catholic, he was to become the ideal committed assistant, carefully attuned to Franco's wishes and extremely discreet in proffering his own advice.[29]

It was war developments that marked Franco's shift towards a more balanced neutrality. Nevertheless, the presence of the prudent Jordana at the Foreign Office definitely facilitated relations with the Allies. The most difficult test arrived in November 1942 during 'Operation Torch', the Anglo-American landings in French North Africa. At this crucial stage, most ministers, fearing that Spain was a target of the Allies, advocated letting the German army into the peninsula, but they met Jordana's obstinate opposition. Actually, some in the American administration, including Vice-President Wallace, doubtful of Spanish neutrality, had proposed an assault on Spanish Morocco ('Operation Backbone'). However, British pressure and the advice of the US Ambassador in Spain, Carlton Hayes, won the day and those plans were abandoned. Franco received personal guarantees from President Roosevelt on the territorial integrity of Spain and her colonies, while Germany had simply warned him to remain vigilant. The spectacularly swift success of the Allied offensive in North Africa, occupying territories he himself had coveted, inhibited any thoughts of Spanish action.[30]

Dramatic changes on the battlefield (the German retreat in Russia and defeat in Africa) encouraged a movement away from the Axis orbit. Yet it was a long and exasperating process hindered by the attitude of the Caudillo and leading figures of the regime. Franco himself did not contemplate a German defeat until the summer of 1944. The fall of Mussolini in July 1943 was received with alarm. There was a news black-out and an increase in the number of arrests and executions to terrorize into submission those in Spain who sought to capitalize on the collapse of Italian Fascism.[31] Henceforth, Franco began to seek a middle ground which could please both sides. His attacks upon the decadent liberal systems continued, but now he also stressed that the Francoist order was a new model different from Fascism. Being supremely confident of his own leadership, the Spanish Generalissimo even toyed with the idea of appearing as a honest peace broker. He put forward to Western diplomats his contentions that there were two separate wars. One in the east against Communism in which Spain was directly involved, and one in the west in which she was neutral. Also, after constant complaints by the British ambassador, instructions were given to restrict German sabotage and spy activities, and the press adopted a less partisan tone, but all sorts of subterfuges were used in order to obstruct or delay implementation.[32] The Republic of Saló, Mussolini's new regime in northern Italy, was not officially recognized but Morreale, its representative in Spain, continued his diplomatic duties without restrictions.[33] In October, Franco, for the first time, used the term 'watchful neutrality' instead of 'belligerence'. That month the Blue Division was withdrawn from Russia.

Even though the tide was clearly turning in favour of the Allies, tactless diplomatic incidents thwarted the prospect of establishing friendlier relations. In particular, the note in October 1943 congratulating José Laurel, head of the Japanese puppet government in the Philippines, incensed the Americans. The US administration responded by threatening an oil embargo unless Spanish deliveries of wolfram (tungsten ore) to Germany were stopped. Hitherto Spain had encouraged competition between both camps for the purchase of wolfram, a crucial mineral for arms production. The so-called 'wolfram war' began in February 1944 when the US stopped oil shipments. The British, more inclined to find a compromise, devised a face-saving option which brought the crisis to an end in late April: the oil embargo would be suspended in return for the drastic reduction of wolfram exports to Germany, the withdrawal of the volunteers still remaining in Russia and the introduction of more effective measures against German spies and saboteurs.[34]

Although the outcome of the wolfram war represented a Spanish capitulation, it was officially presented as a personal triumph of the Caudillo, determined to maintain neutrality at any price. It also marked the beginning of a gradual about-turn in foreign policy. The incident seemed to demonstrate that despite all provocations, the Allies preferred negotiation to force. Franco correctly concluded that in a future peace settlement, they would not take direct action to remove him from power. Confidence increased when Churchill, in a speech in the Commons on 24 May, praised Spain for not having joined the Axis in the grimmest period of war. Far from genuine admiration for the Francoist regime, the British Prime Minister's aim was to neutralize Spain during the forthcoming Normandy landings. However, his words were rapidly twisted in Spain into a full-scale endorsement of Franco's foreign policy and of his political order.[35]

The sudden death of Jordana in August 1944 and his replacement at the Foreign Office by José Félix Lequerica, the fiercely pro-Axis ambassador to Vichy, was regarded as the Caudillo's inability to extricate himself from his embarrassing German sympathies. In fact, the appointment was more due to Franco's duplicitous strategies at home and abroad. While it was bound to be welcomed by the Axis, it was also a subtle way to distance himself from collaborationist France by failing to replace the Spanish ambassador there. Above all, Lequerica was chosen for his total loyalty to the regime. With the Allies advancing on all fronts, it was imperative to have in charge of diplomacy someone subservient to the wishes of his master.[36]

Hopes existed until the end that the Axis might avoid total defeat and even that Hitler indeed possessed secret weapons which could reverse the trend of war. Spain did not break diplomatic relations with Germany until the day of her surrender, 8 May 1945. Yet the inexorable advance of the Red Army into central Europe and the success of the invasion of France persuaded even the most outspoken *Germanophiles* in Spain that the Allies were on the march to victory. With the main concern being his own survival, Franco began courting the Anglo-Americans. His previous pro-Axis leanings were justified as a subtle game to outmanoeuvre Hitler. He reiterated that the common enemy was Communism and that his regime was based on Catholic principles and thus averse to Fascism. By July the pictures of Mussolini and Hitler were suddenly replaced by those of the Portuguese President and the Pope.[37]

Measures favourable to the Allies were introduced. They were allowed to evacuate their casualties from France through Barcelona and granted overflight rights in Spanish air space. In October Franco personally sent to Churchill an astonishing letter. The Caudillo's thesis was that with the destruction of most European powers, Spain and England, the last two virile nations in the continent, should form an alliance against Russia. The startling conclusion was that the only obstacle to the deal was the sordid machinations of the British secret services. It took three months for a bewildered Churchill to reply, strongly rebuffing Franco's suggestions. Nevertheless, the Caudillo was relieved when the text made it clear that London would like to see his regime removed but regarded as undesirable any attempt to do so by force.[38] As the war drew to a close, it was time for the official rewriting of history. In April 1945, diplomatic relations with Japan were broken. Germany's surrender was announced as 'Franco's Victory'. The most extreme eulogies hailed the Caudillo, 'a leader chosen by the benevolence of God to bestow the gift of peace upon Spain'.[39] The myth of Franco's neutrality during the Second World War was thus born.

The Struggle for Respectability

Attempts to court the friendship of the Allies came too late and amounted to too little. The Francoist regime remained in 1945 the only state whose origins in the Civil War and then its position during the Second World War were closely associated with the defeated Axis. Consequently, it was considered by the international community as a political anomaly and a product of a past era of Fascist hegemony.[40] The motion presented by the Mexican delegation on 19 June 1945 in San Francisco barring Spain from United Nations membership was unanimously approved and endorsed by the great powers the following month in Potsdam. The Francoist regime became a pariah state when the United Nations on 12 December 1946 recommended its members to withdraw its ambassadors in Madrid and excluded Spanish participation from all UN specialized agencies. In 1947 Spain was not allowed to form part of the European Recovery Programme (Marshall Plan) and excluded from the Western defensive alliance, NATO, in 1949.

Many believed that international ostracism would herald the demise of the Spanish dictatorship. However, they had not considered the resilience and determination of the Caudillo to cling to power. Even when the situation was tense his 'blind faith' and optimism never deserted him. His mentality was revealed when he told General Martínez Campos that,

'I will not make the same mistake as Primo de Rivera. I do not resign. For me it is straight from here to the cemetery'.[41] Furthermore, his normal complacency was boosted by an extensive report drawn up by Carrero Blanco in August of 1945 which concluded that ultimately the Anglo-Saxon countries would never allow the introduction of sanctions which could lead to the destabilization of the country and favour the Soviet cause. His predictions proved correct. Menacing though all the measures seemed to be, they were not accompanied by threats of an all-out economic embargo or military intervention.[42]

At Potsdam Churchill opposed the implementation of forcible proposals alleging that the internal political problems in Spain were a matter for the Spanish themselves. British foreign policy remained unaltered after the Labour victory of July 1945. Ernest Bevin, in his first statement as Foreign Minister in the Commons on 20 August remarked that he would like to see Franco and the Falange, an 'unfortunate anomaly', removed but also regarded any attempt to accomplish this by force as undesirable. It was a policy which found ready support among the Conservative opposition but was greeted with dismay by many of his own backbenchers. Against a background of waning power throughout the empire and involvement in the political conflict raging in Greece, the Labour government shared with its predecessors the fear that ousting Franco could lead to a power vacuum or even to a new civil war which could only benefit the interests of the Soviet Union. Ironically, British misgivings were unfounded. Although Franco's obsessive anti-Soviet rhetoric and the deployment of the Blue Division gave the Soviets more than enough motive to seek the end of the Spanish regime, the Kremlin made clear that Spain fell into the Western 'sphere of influence'. Yet Bevin seemed more concerned with the unsubstantiated threat from the Soviet Union than the already proven close links of Franco with the Axis. More importantly, British reluctance to undertake any forceful measure was influenced by the premise of not endangering its immense material interests in Spain which included important financial investments and crucial cheap imports of pyrites, iron ore and potash.[43]

With an economy close to collapse, Franco would have fallen if the great powers had backed with concrete actions their openly proclaimed hatred of his regime. Yet as in the Civil War, British non-intervention ensured the Caudillo's political survival. The idea that Franco could be forced out of power peacefully by international condemnation and replaced by a democratic government was ludicrous. While there was

no doubt that the British government longed for the end of the
Francoist regime, it was unwilling to take the kind of actions that could
realize its objective.[44]

In fact, Britain restrained the French and the Americans from taking
hasty actions. France, aware of the close relations between Vichy and
Franco and grateful to the 30 000 Spanish Republicans who had fought
with the Resistance, was the Western power most inclined to replace
rhetoric with practical measures. When in February 1946 Cristino
García, a Republican who had reached the rank of Lieutenant-General
in the French Resistance was executed in Barcelona, France closed its
southern border and proposed that the situation in Spain be discussed
by the UN Security Council. Initially welcomed by the US, the proposal
was opposed by Bevin. The French, whose administration was a patchy
coalition of Christian Democrats and left-wing groups and who feared
splitting the Western alliance, gave way. As a compromise, Britain,
France and the United States issued a joint note in March expressing their rejection of the Francoist regime, but also confirming their
intention of not intervening to bring about the political change they
advocated.[45]

International pressure would not go beyond the withdrawing of
ambassadors. This was only a symbolic act and never considered the
first instalment in a sustained and vigorous campaign to unseat Franco.
The scheme devised by the Americans in the spring of 1947 to extend
political and economic support to the opposition and give Franco an
ultimatum was also quickly rejected by the British as useless and
counter-effective. Instead, Bevin organized a meeting in October 1947
between leading and rival figures of the opposition, the Conservative
and Monarchist Gil Robles and the Socialist Prieto. It was by then too
late and nothing significant came out of it.[46]

All invitations to the Caudillo to vacate power voluntarily were obviously rejected. Unlike some panicking members of his entourage, he
understood clearly that the moment of gravest danger for his regime
had passed by 1945. Spain was for the great powers not a fundamental
question but just an irritant marginal issue.[47] Thus their actions would
never go beyond mere verbal condemnation. His strategy was to hold
on in the belief that sooner or later the Second World War alliance
would break up and that international ostracism could work to his
own advantage. Official propaganda feverishly played the Nationalist
card, portraying Spain as a besieged state in which the enemies of the
regime were no more than foreign puppets.

It was as inconceivable to expect the physically and spiritually deprived Spaniards in a police state to overthrow the dictatorship as for the opposition to mount an effective campaign without consistent international support. The Republicans, the fiercest enemies of the regime, never represented a serious challenge. The history of Republican exiles was marked by bitter recriminations and internal bickering which lasted until the 1970s. The Anarcho-Syndicalists split over the issue of collaboration with other groups, while the Socialist movement was for years paralysed by its opposing attitude towards the Communists and the disputes between the Negrín and anti-Negrín factions. Scattered and divided, they failed to form a united government which could be recognized by the Allies during the war. A semblance of government in exile excluding Communists appeared in August 1945 under the Republican José Giral in Mexico. Once it became clear that the great powers would not take action to unseat Franco, their initial euphoria became frustration and despair.[48] Only recognized by the Mexican administration, Republican politicians remained there in their little world totally disconnected from events in Spain.

Military tactics were no more successful. As the German occupying forces were retreating in the summer of 1944, thousands of Spaniards who had fought in the French resistance began to congregate on the Franco-Spanish border. In October, some 15 000, mostly Communist, launched a full-scale attack through the Val d'Aran in the Pyrenees. Lacking heavy weapons and the support of the Allies' military might, they were no match for the much larger and better armed Spanish army. For the following years, guerrillas kept the fight alive in different areas of the peninsula. The Civil Guards' effective repressive tactics as well as the impossibility of arousing an exhausted countryside ensured their isolation and eventual liquidation. By 1951, the Communists, recognizing the futility of this strategy, abandoned the armed struggle, although some Anarchists continued fighting until the early 1960s.[49]

The Monarchist challenge seemed more threatening. Significant groups, including many senior officers, had fought the Civil War with the hope of restoring the monarchy and thus regarded Franco's personal rule as a necessary but temporary measure. In March 1943 Don Juan, Alfonso XIII's son and heir, felt confident that the time had arrived to replace the existing pro-Axis order with a Liberal monarchy which would be welcomed by the Allies and be the ideal instrument for national reconciliation. Thus he wrote to Franco demanding a peaceful transition of power. In June twenty-five leading members of the regime's social and political elite signed a collective letter calling for the return of the Crown. In September, after the fall of Fascism in Italy, a group of generals handed a letter to the Caudillo urging him 'with loyalty, respect and affection' to consider if the time had come for a monarchical restoration. The Spanish dictator responded with a mixture of delaying tactics, bribery and patience. His confidence was reaffirmed by the total loyalty of the middle-rank officers who did not regard him merely as 'first among equals' and by the very respectful tone of the generals' appeal, more a plea than an ultimatum. Loyal officers were appointed to key positions and the critics were met separately. Franco calmly explained to them that while he did not discount a future return to a monarchy, the time was not yet ripe. Their challenge vanished when skilfully met by Franco's appeals to *esprit de corps*, patriotism and rewards in the form of promotions, decorations and even titles of nobility.[50]

As the war in Europe was dragging to an end, the Monarchist cause seemed to gather momentum. Don Juan issued his Laussane Manifesto on 19 March 1945 denouncing the Axis connections of the Francoist regime and calling upon the Caudillo to make way for his return. The manifesto was followed by instructions to prominent Monarchists to resign from their posts and form a *Junta* to oversee the expected transition.[51] Ingenuously, Don Juan was hoping that the Caudillo would quietly withdraw with a spirit of decency and good sense. Yet vacating his office was never in the Generalissimo's mind.

Ironically, the frenzied international atmosphere served to consolidate the regime. Increasing guerrilla activities came as a godsend to Franco posing as the champion against the Communist threat. They made possible the revival of the Civil War mentality and reunited the officer corps around him. The return of a Liberal monarchy advocating reconciliation at this critical moment was just such a back door through which the vanquished could again win power. The Nationalist coalition, despite its rivalries, when confronted with a choice between the *status quo* and the risk of 'the Reds' returning, all opted for the former. Simultaneously, the diplomatic ostracism was manipulated by official propaganda to show that Franco was their heroic leader in yet another foreign attempt to destroy Spain. The state-produced cinema newsreel, No-Do, and the media worked frenetically to present the Caudillo as the bulwark against foreign malice defending Spain from an international siege. Without him the country would descend into anarchy and the horrors of another civil war.[52]

At the same time, the Francoist state underwent a masterful exercise in public relations. The objective was to give an appearance of popular and constitutional legitimacy to counter the activities of Don Juan and deflect the hostilities of the Allies for a regime organized along Fascist lines. Changes were basically cosmetic and did not affect the regime's repressive and authoritarian nature. Yet if in the short term they failed to impress the Western democracies, they succeeded in winning over the bulk of the Monarchist camp.

The *Fuero de los Españoles* ('Spaniards' Charter') was drawn up in June 1945. In theory, it defined the rights of all Spaniards. Yet there were no judicial mechanisms to guarantee them and, of course, dissent and freedom of expression were not included. In July the cabinet was reshuffled with the Falangist presence greatly diminished. The Falange, losing the battle for control of the state to the Church, became more than ever before a docile organization used to regiment the labour movement, organize shows of popular support and as a source of patronage. The Francoist order could be defined after 1945 as National–Catholic, as its strong Catholic identity was exploited to distinguish it from Fascism. Leading positions were occupied by Catholics from the ACNP and the Church rose to a prominent position, unparalleled in a long history of influence, having absolute control over education, propaganda and censorship, with religion affecting all public affairs and institutions.[53] Alberto Martín Artajo, President of Catholic Action, was appointed Foreign Minister. He was the ideal man to portray the new image of the regime, one founded on Catholic and anti-Communist beliefs. Yet as with his predecessors, Artajo was chosen for his total subservience and loyalty to the Caudillo who remained the real maker of diplomacy. It was even said that Artajo was merely a short-hand writer, who in his daily telephone conversations with Franco, had to use headphones in order to have his hands free to take down instructions.[54]

As Falangists were being displaced by Catholics, Franco also initiated a skilful ploy to lure Monarchists. Since 1936 the form of the Nationalist state had remained ambiguous. A few days after Don Juan's Laussane Manifesto, the Caudillo alleged, with bare-faced cheek, that it had taken his own efforts to put the Monarchist restoration on the agenda. This was followed by an announcement that Spain would adopt a monarchical form of government and that a Council of the Realm would determine the succession. Eventually, a plebiscite was held in July 1947 to vote the Law of Succession and confirm Spain as a kingdom. Manipulated and controlled by the authorities, the result was an overwhelming endorsement: 14 145 163 or 93 per cent of the vote for and 1 074 500 against.[55]

Transforming Spain into a monarchy was never intended as a first step towards monarchical restoration, but to legitimize Franco's personal rule. Although it enshrined the idea that Spain would one day be ruled by a king, no date was specified. What was indicated was that Franco would remain Head of State with all powers and that he would designate his own successor, becoming thus a 'Regent for Life'. Now he could claim that in the referendum the whole of Spain had ratified his special status.[56]

Most Monarchists were satisfied with the outcome. Their anti-democratic values attracted them to an authoritarian monarchy based on the principles of the uprising of 1936 rather than on the liberal model preached by Don Juan. After much hesitation, Don Juan, fearful that his succession could be displaced by any dynastic rival, agreed to meet Franco in August 1948 on board the latter's yacht, the *Azor*, off the coast of San Sebastián. There the Pretender accepted Franco's suggestion that his son Juan Carlos, then ten years old, would be educated in Spain. With Don Juan's son under his control, the Caudillo had a hostage to justify his indefinite assumption of the role of Regent and an instrument to supervise the political direction of any future monarchical restoration. Furthermore, the publicity given to the meeting was handled in such a way as to give the impression that the monarchy was subordinate to the dictator.[57]

As Franco had expected, the deterioration of East–West relations began to alter international attitudes, particularly those of the United States, towards his regime. The so-called Cold War became a reality between 1947 and 1950. In March 1947 the Truman Doctrine took shape when the US President declared his intention to defend the free world from the Communist threat. Tensions between both camps continued to rise: the Soviet Union seized effective control of those eastern European countries occupied by Soviet forces and in June 1948 initiated the blockade of West Berlin. In the far east, the Chinese Civil War concluded in October 1949 with a Communist victory and in June 1950 war broke out when Communist North Korea invaded South Korea.

In such a context, the calls by right-wing politicians, particularly in the United States where the Spanish lobby was highly active in pressing for the normalization of relations with Spain, became more frequent and vocal. They alleged that Spain had the same right of membership of the United Nations and the enjoyment of full diplomatic relations as Communist dictatorships. From the second half of 1947, the US State Department came under increasing pressure. Franco was praised for his anti-Communist zeal and his close collaboration with the Axis ignored. The House of Representatives even voted to include Spain in the Marshall Plan in 1947 and approved the granting of loans in 1948 and 1949. Truman, vehemently opposed to the Francoist regime, managed to veto these measures. However, particularly after the outbreak of the Korean war, he could no longer ignore public opinion and that of his own legislature and finally agreed to the loan of $62 500 000 approved in August 1950.[58]

US aid arrived providentially when the Spanish economy, beleaguered by bad harvests and short of hard currency, was teetering on the brink of collapse. Much political capital was made out of the West's diplomatic U-turn. A euphoric José Antonio Girón, the Falangist Labour Minister, claimed in the summer of 1950, 'the world is coming to our way of thinking'.[59] Official propaganda spared no effort to demonstrate that at last the international community had recognized the rightness of Franco's principles, or to extol what they called the enormous political skill of the man who had foreseen the Cold War years before it became reality. If in 1941 the Spanish Civil War had been hailed as the first battle against the decadent plutocracies, now it was described as the first victory against Soviet aggression. The Caudillo, the successful warrior against the Communist threat, was lauded as the 'Sentry of the West'.[60]

Notwithstanding all the exaggerations of the propaganda machine, the winds of change brewing in the West certainly served to rehabilitate the Francoist regime. His position seemed fully vindicated when on 4 November 1950 the UN General Assembly voted to rescind the resolution of December 1946.[61] The ambassadors gradually began to return to Madrid. Subsequently, months of arduous negotiations culminated in two diplomatic successes in 1953. A Concordat was signed with the Vatican in August. It represented for Franco, a man who had declared himself 'responsible before God', a personal triumph bolstering his image as the leader of a Catholic monarchy. The Concordat officially endorsed the National–Catholic ideology of the regime, ratifying the central role of the Church in a confessional state. All laws were to be measured against the yardstick of Catholic orthodoxy and no other religion was allowed in public. Canon marriage became part of the civil code, all education had to conform to Catholic dogma and religious instruction was imposed at all levels in schools.[62] In real terms, even more important was the agreement signed with the United States in September. In return for the possession of nuclear military bases, the Americans would pay a certain sum annually in the form of development grants and provide *matériel* for the Spanish armed forces. Crucially, this event confirmed the return of Spain into the Western orbit under the protection and approval of the most powerful nation in the world. Aware of this, Franco had even instructed his negotiators 'to sign anything they put in front of you'. The reward was US backing for his survival. He finally could declare, 'Now I have won the Civil War.' International ostracism was left behind when Spain was finally re-admitted to the United Nations in 1955, and in 1959 when President Eisenhower visited Madrid.[63]

By the mid-1950s the dictatorship entered a period of normalization and political stability. The Caudillo retained all his posts and remained the ultimate arbiter when situations demanded his personal intervention. In February 1956, rivalries between Catholic and Falangist students degenerated into open clashes in which a Falangist was severely injured, probably by the accidental discharge of the gun of one of his comrades. In order to defuse the building tension, Franco adopted once more a Solomonic solution, sacking from the cabinet both the Secretary of the Movement, Raimundo Fernández Cuesta, and the liberal Catholic Minister of Education, Joaquín Ruíz Giménez. A few months later, after France had announced the concession of independence to Morocco, he showed enough realism to relinquish control of the Spanish part of the Protectorate.[64] Yet in general, Franco gradually withdrew from the daily business of politics and began to assume the distant air of a royal personage. The wedding of his daughter Carmen to an aristocratic playboy, Cristóbal Martínez Bordiu, the Marquis of Villaverde, broadened the family network with a close entourage of relatives known as *El Clan del Pardo* ('El Pardo Clique'). Franco would regularly be portrayed in the No-Do as the tireless leader, receiving foreign dignitaries, opening dams or factories, and ensuring the welfare and peace of all Spaniards. In reality, he now could relax and devote increasing amounts of time to his favourite hobbies: hunting, fishing, golf, watching westerns in the private cinema at his residence of El Pardo and even growing potatoes and tobacco. Some of the hunting parties arranged for him in the best private estates often became strenuous three or four days affairs in which jobs, influence and government backing for business deals were negotiated.[65]

Luis Carrero Blanco, appointed Minister to the Presidency in 1951 and then deputy Prime Minister in 1967, took charge of decision-making. Carrero was pragmatic enough to realize that the Francoist order should adapt to the new economic imperatives of the Western world. Under his protection, the Falangist old guard and the ACNP's Catholics were gradually displaced in the government by a new group, the Opus Dei, a powerful and secretive Catholic secular order whose members stood out for their wealth and excellent connections in the business world.[66]

It was the cabinet re-shuffle of February 1957 which initiated the hegemony of the Opus Dei. For the first time, all portfolios relating to economic matters were in the hands of technocrats and experts belonging to that group. In the early 1950s, US aid and the normalization of diplomatic relations had averted the collapse of the economy. There was a great expansion in the industrial sector and an increase in foreign trade, which in turn allowed for vital imports of foodstuffs, raw materials and capital goods. Yet industrial output did not make the breakthrough into sustained growth while traditional structures and technology remained unchanged. The short-comings of autarky, still vehemently supported by Falangists and the ACNP, became increasingly evident. Economic modernization was impossible enclosed in a domestic market with a limited purchasing power, incapable of importing or producing raw materials and capital goods to supply and modernize the economy. By the autumn of 1956 inflation was spiralling out of control and the deficit in the balance of payments sharpened. Protection to sustain an inefficient and backward agriculture brought increasing returns to landowners but also stagnation to a sector starved of investment, and misery to the landless peasants. Simultaneously, rising prices and static wages sparked off, despite heavy state repression, constant strikes for higher pay in the main industrial centres.[67]

The Opus ministers pursued economic modernization and growth. Being liberal and modernizers in economics, they shared, however, the authoritarian values of the other Nationalist families. Their goal was not to open and reform the political system. On the contrary, they believed that the continuity and strengthening of the regime could be secured by delivering prosperity and affluence.

With Carrero's backing, the Opus team led by Laureano López Rodó, appointed in December 1956 Technical General Secretary to the Ministry of the Presidency, embraced economic liberalism and abandoned autarky. They set up an Office of Co-ordination and Planning to organize and fundamentally to change the course of economic policy-making. In 1958 Spain joined the Organization for European Economic Co-operation (OECD) and the International Monetary Fund (IMF). The so-called Stabilization Plan was then introduced in the summer of 1959. Essentially, the plan had two main objectives: to restore financial stability by controlling inflation and to liberalize external trade and encourage foreign investment. The reforms envisaged a reduction in public expenditure, the rationalization of government controls, a drastic devaluation of the peseta to a competitive level of 60 pesetas to the dollar and incentives to facilitate the liberalization of trade and foreign investment. Different Development Plans, borrowed from the French example of economic planning, were introduced in 1964.[68]

The result was an era of unprecedented economic growth which in little more than a decade placed Spain among the most developed nations. There was a spectacular upsurge in the level of foreign trade. Gross domestic product (GDP) expanded at an annual average of 7.5 per cent between 1961 and 1973, second only to Japan in the world, and national income rose by 156 per cent. The country ceased to be primarily an agricultural economy and became a modern industrialized society. The active labour force in the countryside fell sharply from 41.9 per cent in 1959 to 25.3 per cent in 1973 while industrial employment rose from 31.8 to 36.8 per cent and in the service sector from 26.5 to 40 per cent. As agriculture itself was modernized and industrialized, about 3 000 000 people left the rural areas seeking jobs either abroad or in the nation's big urban conurbations: Barcelona, Madrid, Valencia and Bilbao. Likewise, the weight of agriculture in the economy declined dramatically to only 15 per cent of the GDP. Its place was taken by the development of new industries: automobile, chemicals, metallurgy and the sensational expansion of consumer production (washing machines, refrigerators, television sets, etc.).[69]

Spain's successful economic miracle was possible without balance of payment problems – that in most underdeveloped economies normally bring modernization to a halt – owing to three main factors: a huge increase in earnings from foreign tourism; emigrant remittances; and a renewal of overseas investment. With the dismantling of autarky, foreign capital flowed into the country attracted by the prospects of cheap labour, state incentives and potential markets. Foreign investment rose from $40 million in 1960 to $697 million by 1970, 40 per cent of it coming from the United States. Injections of fresh capital provided a boost to the undercapitalized Spanish industry, brought vital advanced technology and contributed to the creation of modern industrial and service sectors. At the same time, Spain took advantage of the demand for manpower from Western countries, particularly France, Germany and Switzerland. It was an easy way to get rid of excess labour at home, exporting unemployment as well as earning large amounts of foreign currency earned by the emigrants. Finally, tourism, a sector hardly developed before 1960, became a leading industry. From a total of 4 194 000 foreigners visiting Spain in 1959, numbers rose to 34 559 000 in 1973. More significantly, their receipts escalated over the same period from $125.6 million to $3091.2 million. Earnings from tourism almost wiped out Spain's trade deficit as well as generating jobs in southern areas traditionally plagued by unemployment, and stimulated ambitious and much-needed infrastructural developments in coastal regions.[70]

During these years, Falangists finally lost the battle to control Spain's political and economic fate. The Falange suffered a severe political blow when the Law of Fundamental Principles of the Movement, a definition of the doctrines of the state, was promulgated in May 1958. Falangists failed to influence the final text that described the National Movement as the communion of all Spaniards who accepted the principles of the crusade. It defined Spain as a Catholic and Social monarchy. This was finally confirmed by a popular plebiscite which in December 1966 endorsed overwhelmingly the so-called Organic Law of the State, a semblance of a constitution which combined all the laws and principles of the regime. In the 1960s, veteran Falangists such as Arrese and Girón were by-passed by a new generation of more gullible and docile elements such as the new FET Secretary José Solís, but public order remained in the hands of hard-liners.[71]

Notwithstanding the fact that the dictatorship by clinging on for so long to autarky had postponed material progress for almost fifteen years, Franco in the late 1960s was fast at taking the credit for the economic miracle. The legitimacy of his rule was not just based on victory and war but also as the guarantor of the peace and stability which enabled Spain to flourish economically and individuals to enjoy improved living standards. He was now an ailing old man affected by Parkinson's disease. When he left a cabinet meeting prematurely for the first time on 6 December 1968, it was taken as a serious indication of his deteriorating health. Confronted by the reality of his own mortality and under Carrero's advice, the Caudillo formally ended years of uncertainty about the succession when on 22 July 1969 he nominated

Prince Juan Carlos as his heir. It was believed that an authoritarian monarchy built on economic prosperity and guided by Carrero Blanco would ensure the continuity of Francoism without Franco. The Caudillo in his nominating speech noted in regard to future times that '*todo está atado y bien atado*' ('all is tied down and well tied down').[72]

The Twilight of the Regime

By the late 1960s Spain was closing the economic and social gap with her neighbours. Yet the successful creation of a modern consumer society was taking place without any fundamental change to the political premise on which the regime was based. The central creed of the Opus technocrats was that growing prosperity and economic development could be a sufficient surrogate for ideological politics and validate the survival of Francoism. Yet it was the economic progress on which the regime prided itself which engendered growing contradictions between the new society and the old state. The opening up of frontiers and markets meant the arrival of modern ideas and values through cinema, literature and tourism. Spaniards, learned from, imitated, and identified with the people of western Europe, their institutions and their way of life.[73] In the late 1960s and early 1970s, the gap between a modern society and an obsolete state still anchored on the principles of the crusade widened to the point of no return. An unstoppable movement gathered momentum in which sectors from without and even within the regime coincided in regarding the dictatorship as an anachronism and a hindrance to progress.

From the late 1950s, the regime began to lose its ability to control and regiment the labour movement. Mass industrialization and emigration to the big towns dramatically increased the strength of the industrial force. Neglected by the technocrats' planning, more daring than their repressed ancestors and radicalized by the poor health and housing conditions they found in the cities, they began to organize themselves in order to obtain a fairer share of the economic boom. Unrepresented by the official syndicates, they first found support and encouragement among Catholic associations, the HOAC, *Hermandades Obreras de Acción Católica* (Workers' Brotherhood of Catholic Action) and the JOC, *Juventud Obrera Católica* (Catholic Workers' Youth Movement). These Catholic groups became a genuinely grassroots phenomenon, profoundly involved in such labour concerns as wages and working conditions. In a dictatorship, they were the only relatively safe channel for discussing labour issues and airing grievances. By supporting strike action and criticizing the social effects of the government's economic measures, many young Catholics found themselves at odds with the Church hierarchy, who sided unequivocally with the regime. These worker-priests played a great part in the first strikes of the late 1950s and early 1960s and contributed to the development of the CC.OO., *Comisiones Obreras* (Workers' Commissions).[74]

The expansion and hegemony of the Commissions within the organized labour movement was the greatest Communist success. Unlike, the UGT and CNT whose clandestine organizations were constantly suppressed by the authorities, the PCE adopted the strategy of 'entryism' or infiltration within the official unions. Taking advantage of the legalization of collective bargaining in 1958, CC.OO. first became active as *ad hoc* committees, negotiating grievances and wages with representatives of the employers, appearing and dissolving once the conflict had been solved. Designated by their fellow workers to represent them in negotiations at factory level, they attracted many Catholics and even disenchanted Falangists. Their success gained them the respect and following of the proletariat and even, at first, the tolerance of the official unions overwhelmed by the fast growth of the labour movement. They filled the vacuum between clandestine and official unions at a moment in which the obsolete syndicalism preached by the Falange was being rejected by the workers.

It was not until 1966, when CC.OO. had already expanded into regional networks and become an entrenched force at the shop-floor, that the state discovered their Communist links and moved to destroy them. It was too late. Repressive measures and arrests only served to spark labour unrest. Hitherto, most industrial action had focused on economic demands, but now there were solidarity strikes throughout Spain with the ultimate political objective of overthrowing the regime. In 1969 the government declared martial law in the country. Ten leading trade-unionists were tried in December 1973 and given a total of 162 years of imprisonment. Labour conflicts and social unrest escalated as CC.OO. became the main symbol of working-class opposition. Despite being punished by law, Spain in the 1970s was the country in the Western world with the highest level of industrial action and labour militancy.[75]

The modernizing trends of the 1960s were also reflected in social and generational changes. Sectors which previously had supported or at least consented to the dictatorship began to desert it. Prosperity brought new values. Thus the relatively small, austere and Catholic middle classes of the 1930s and 1940s became a large progressive section formed by engineers, doctors, teachers and white-collar workers. They increasingly abandoned an authoritarian system in which they had no political voice and lacked the basic freedoms which were naturally enjoyed in all modern Western societies. For the new industrial and commercial elites which had replaced in economic power the old landed oligarchy, Francoism was no longer the guarantor of social order and economic prosperity. On the contrary, it was an obstacle to further economic expansion and social harmony and an irksome anachronism. Its survival both impeded Spain's accession to the European Economic Community (EEC) and increased the likelihood of social unrest. Accordingly, to safeguard their interests the new ruling economic classes were in agreement with the opposition in their quest for change.[76]

More violent and visible was the so-called 'university problem'. The first serious student clashes of 1956 gave way to mass confrontation in the following two decades. The economic boom of the 1960s produced an explosion in the numbers of those in higher education. Campuses became centres of rejection of old Francoist values. There students, often encouraged by their tutors, sought and absorbed forbidden Marxist and revolutionary texts, and embraced, like their European counterparts, pop music and all the rebellious fashions of the age. Free assemblies, sit-ins and demonstrations ended in ritual clashes with the police. By the 1970s the regime, incapable of winning the loyalty of the new generations, treated their dissent as a problem of public order and resorted to violence.[77]

The 1960s also saw a resurgence of nationalism in the Catalan and Basque regions. Yet the two models developed very differently. The revival of Catalan Nationalism was an easy and natural phenomenon. Despite all the attempts by the regime to eliminate symbols of national distinctiveness, the Catalan language and culture had survived intact at a private level. With the liberalization of the 1960s there was mass mobilization against the stiff centralization of the state. Musicians, writers and intellectuals led the campaign to restore and defend Catalan identity. The movement spread to the other Catalan speaking areas of Valencia and the Balearic Islands. Folk songs, poetry and even Barcelona Football Club emerged as rallying points of a population who rejected the regime's claim to the indivisiveness and homogeneity of Spain. Cataluña was the only place where the opposition established a common and united political front. The Assembly of Cataluña of November 1971 brought together representatives of all Catalan groups from Catholics to Communists, from professional associations to delegates of working-class neighbourhoods. It demanded the re-establishment of the Catalan Statute of 1932, political freedom and the return of democracy. The subsequent arrest of some of its members could not halt its activities. A united Cataluña had rejected the dictatorship.[78]

Basque Nationalism, lacking the secure cultural roots of the Catalans, developed into a less political and more violent phenomenon. Radical youths revolted against what they considered the passivity of the PNV's elders and founded ETA, *Euzkadi Ta Askatasuna* (Basque Nation and Liberty) in 1959. They initially concentrated on propaganda, printing pamphlets and distributing leaflets. The resort to armed struggle began with a shooting exchange in June 1968 in which one *Etarra* and a Civil Guard were killed. The ETA leadership saw Euskadi as a nation occupied by a foreign army and so identified its cause with anti-colonial movements then engaged in war in Third-World countries. They pursued a guerrilla strategy based on action/repression/action to draw the population away from their apathy and bring about the independence of their homeland. In August 1968 Melitón Manzanas, the police chief of Guipúzcoa, was shot dead. This killing was followed by a wave of shootings, bombing and robberies. The repressive brutality of the Francoist regime played into ETA's hands. A state of emergency was declared in Euskadi and the police were given a free hand, arresting and torturing hundreds of innocents. Then in December 1970 sixteen members of ETA were tried in Burgos by a military court and four of them sentenced to death, later commuted by Franco to 30 years in prison. Violent and indiscriminate repression in Euskadi and the notoriously unfair manipulation of the Burgos trial gave ETA enormous popularity and elevated them to the status of freedom fighters. In a remarkably short period of time a flood of young Basques, seduced by the romantic appeal of the armed struggle, joined what hitherto had been a tiny revolutionary group. With a friendly milieu and the facility to reach a safe haven in France, ETA escalated its military operations which gradually revealed the vulnerability of the dictatorship to this type of guerrilla warfare. In turn, the disproportionate repressive measures adopted by the security services only enhanced and consolidated the prestige of ETA among the Basques.[79]

The most perplexing of all the transformations which Spain underwent during these years was that of the Church. From its initial obsessive support of the dictatorship, it adopted a position of guarded criticism and finally one of total opposition. For Franco, the changing attitude of the Church was more than a set-back, it was a betrayal and a display of ingratitude he could never comprehend.

From the outbreak of the war in 1936 to the Concordat of 1953, the Church remained solidly behind the regime and obtained in return huge subsidies, political appointments and control over censorship and education. Dissent began from below in the 1950s when Catholic militants and worker-priests from HOAC and JOC lent their support to the oppressed labour movement. These initiatives obviously clashed with the rigid position of the hierarchy. Yet they soon received an unexpected and spectacular boost from the Vatican. Indeed, the arrival of a progressive Pope, John XXIII, and the issue of his encyclicals, *Mater et Magistra* and *Pacem in terris*, defending social justice, civil rights and political pluralism, represented a frontal attack upon the Francoist regime. At the Second Vatican Council (1962–5), the Spanish bishops, firmly embracing the principles of National–Catholicism, found themselves isolated. With the papacy extolling the advantages of dialogue and tolerance, many of the distinguishing features of the Spanish Catholic tradition, purity and integrism, became suddenly obsolete. Confronted and criticized from above, the Spanish ecclesiastical hierarchy entered a period of disorientation and self-examination. The liberal clergy found the enthusiastic support of Paul VI, John XXIII's successor. When Franco refused to relinquish his right granted by the Concordat to nominate bishops, the new pope began to name auxiliary bishops to replace the ageing pro-Francoist old guard and finally appointed the liberal Enrique Tarancón as Cardinal Primate in February 1969. Churches and parishes became sheltering centres for the opposition and Catholic journals vehicles for criticism of the regime. By the early 1970s, the integrist prelates were a minority and the ecclesiastical culture of national nostalgia and exclusivist intolerance was in retreat. Henceforth the Church confirmed its new role as a leading centre of opposition. In September 1971, a joint assembly of bishops and priests formally repudiated the old underpinnings of the crusade when it issued a historical letter preaching reconciliation and begging for the forgiveness of the Spanish people for its partisanship in the Civil War. Shortly afterwards, in January 1973, bishops voted three to one in favour of formal separation from the state and the surrender of all their political prerogatives.[80]

Losing ground in all spheres of civil society, the crisis of identity and legitimacy of the dictatorship was a glaring fact by the late 1960s.

Claims to guarantee public order were undermined by terrorism, labour unrest and student protest. It could no longer claim to deliver social peace when it was rejected by the working and middle classes. Above all, its profession of being a Catholic state sounded ludicrous when it was not only criticized by the Church but was the only nation in western Europe that had since 1968 possessed a special prison for militant priests.[81] For a majority of Spaniards, Francoism had become a political anachronism which had no place in modern society. However, the loyalty of the armed and police forces would ensure that the regime would exist as long as Franco lived.

Tensions in society began to permeate the governing class. The cohesion of the ruling coalition in power slowly disintegrated as the struggle for power between so-called *aperturistas* and *inmobilistas* gathered momentum. *Aperturistas* were those who believed that the regime should be opened and evolve according to the changing times. Different to the early party zealots, they were young pragmatists whose technical expertise and educational record, not their ideological enthusiasm, had gained them entry into the administration. A good example was Manuel Fraga Iribarne, Minister of Information and Tourism since 1962 and author of the Press Law of 1966 which, although still far from allowing freedom of speech, represented a notable relaxation of censorship. Well-connected with the business world and European-minded after years of studies abroad, the *aperturistas* were closely in touch with national and international reality. They reached the conclusion that clinging to an obsolete political system was an irresponsible and ultimately suicidal attempt to postpone the inevitable. Thus they sought to pursue reform from within in order to avoid a more violent revolution from without. A significant number of *aperturistas* formed a group collectively known as 'Tácito' in May 1973. Most of them, junior members of the Francoist political class, put forward their plans in the Catholic press. Their programme was conceived as an attempt to provide a valid formula after Franco's death. They believed that opposition to political liberalization could only increase the likelihood of a sharp, possibly violent, break with the past. Instead, they proposed gradual change by dialogue and compromise with the opposition.[82]

The opposite view was held by the *inmobilistas* also known as the 'Bunker' for the Hitlerian discourse of fighting to the end in the rubble of the Chancellery. They were old-guard Falangists and National Catholics who had as visible heads former FET leaders such as Girón or Fernández Cuesta and the leader of the Neo-Fascist political organization

and editor of its journal *Fuerza Nueva*, Blas Piñar. They were not prepared to accept even minimum reform. Their strength did not lie in
their numbers, a tiny minority of diehards, but in their ability to control and finance commandos of right-wing thugs, and their excellent
connections with top people in the security services, the armed forces
and, above all, with Franco's inner circle, *El Clan del Pardo*.[83]

By the late 1960s Admiral Carrero Blanco, the strong man of the
regime, was the only person who seemed capable of maintaining
the ruling coalition intact. In 1969, his central position was reinforced.
In July, Franco endorsed his *continuista* plan: a monarchical solution in
the person of Juan Carlos closely invigilated by Carrero which would
ensure that Francoism could outlive Franco. *Continuismo* could even be
presented as a middle of the road position between the *inmobilismo* of
the right-wing ultras and the reformism of the *aperturistas*. Carrero's
tight control of power was bolstered soon thereafter. In the summer the
so-called MATESA scandal erupted.[84] In the internal jockeying for
influence, Fraga and Solís gave full publicity to this affair in order to
tarnish the reputation of the Opus Dei as some of its members were
deeply involved. Yet Carrero and López Rodó came out strengthened.
Once again, Franco adopted a Solomonic decision. The three Opus
ministers most connected with the scandal were dismissed, but so were
Fraga and Solís and MATESA was buried. In the reshuffle of October
1969, the admiral, with the Caudillo's total backing, formed a cabinet
which contained an even larger number of Opus technocrats.[85]

Carrero sanctioned the presence of *aperturistas* in government. As
long as they accepted the regime, they could be presented as a proof
of tolerance for internal dissent and broaden the base of recruitment.
In reality, his political position was closer to that of the *inmobilistas*, the
only differences being his strong monarchism and his more temperate
rhetoric. As social unrest, student dissent and terrorism increased in
the early 1970s, Carrero responded with unrestrained brutality. A state
of emergency was often declared and the police and security services
allowed to engage in orgies of arrests, torture and violence. The government encouraged and condoned the activities of the ultras. Different
Neo-Fascist groups emerged and carried out with absolute impunity a
campaign of bombings and attacks against left-wing bookshops, art gal-
leries and even banking institutions. They were used as strike-breakers,
attacking labour leaders and even storming churches beating up 'Red'
priests and their congregations. These thugs not only did the dirty
jobs of the regime, but also by establishing a fanatical right-wing front,

allowed the government to present itself as if by magic in a moderate centre position.[86] The return to terrorist methods only revealed the growing anxiety and despair of a system whose health was deteriorating as fast as that of its leader, the Caudillo. Carrero Blanco reached the peak of his career in June 1973 when a very old and ill Franco made him Prime Minister. It was thus left to his closest adviser to supervise the continuity of the regime after his death.

However, the *continuista* solution suffered two devastating blows from which it would never recover. On 20 December 1973, an ETA commando performed its most daring military feat, '*Operación Ogro*'. Shortly after leaving the Jesuit church where he attended daily mass before going to work, Carrero was assassinated. A huge amount of explosives was buried in a tunnel dug under the street on which his car passed. The explosion was such that the vehicle was blown sky-high, coming to rest in the inner courtyard of a five storey building behind the church Carrero had just left. His death left Francoists in total disarray. A desolated Caudillo commented: 'They have cut my last link with the world.'[87] Then in April 1974, after forty-six years in power, the Portuguese dictatorship was overthrown. This event not only left Spain as the last authoritarian regime in Western Europe, but also demonstrated the fragility of regimes hitherto believed impregnable.

On 28 December, the election of Carlos Arias Navarro for Prime Minister seemed an astonishing choice. As Minister of the Interior, he had ostensibly failed to protect Carrero's life. In fact, his appointment was decided at the last minute by a senile Franco under pressure from his inner circle and the personal lobbying of his wife. Known as 'the butcher of Málaga' for his activities there as public prosecutor during the Civil War and years later as Director of Security, he had a reputation as a hard-liner.[88] His overriding task was to keep the governing class together and ensure the continuity of the essential foundations of Francoism after the transition of power to Juan Carlos. However, Arias lacked the authority of the former Prime Minister. While he was aware of the need to introduce some moderate reforms in order to broaden the appeal of the government, his personal feelings were closer to his erstwhile comrades of the Bunker. The result was continued irresolution which succeeded in satisfying neither camp.

In a televised address to the Francoist *Cortes* on 12 February 1974, the new premier seemed to side with the *aperturistas* when he announced a programme of limited reform which included the election of local officials by popular elections and the right of association for political groups. Although his speech was encouraging, Arias was cautious to placate the *inmobilistas*, stressing that these groups would have to operate within the framework of the fundamental laws of the state.[89] Against a background of worsening public order, Franco's increasing frailty and a vicious press campaign orchestrated by the Bunker, Arias' initial reformism vanished. He ordered the arrest and exile of the Bishop of Bilbao, Antonio Añoveros, for preaching a sermon on the rights of ethnic minorities. The Prime Minister backed down under Franco's orders when Tarancón, supported by the Vatican, threatened to excommunicate the government. However, in March, Franco endorsed the execution of two Anarchists. In June the moderate Chief of the General Staff Manuel Díaz Alegría was dismissed and replaced by the hard-line General Carlos Fernández Vallespín. On 9 July Franco, gravely ill, was taken to hospital with phlebitis and Juan Carlos reluctantly took over as acting head of the state. By early September Franco had miraculously recovered and resumed office. The following month Pío Cabanillas, the Minister of Information, and the most reformist member of the cabinet was removed. His departure was followed by a flood of *aperturistas* resigning their positions in the administration. By the end of the year, Arias' precarious balancing act had collapsed and the ultras held the upper hand. He offered a pathetic image on television when in December he asked the country for confidence and faith in the future while he presented his final Law of Associations in which the Movement's National Council held veto powers. Earlier promises of constitutional reform were effectively dashed.[90]

During 1975 the rapid deterioration of Franco's health was matched by the dramatic crumbling of his regime. A dour and subdued Arias was overwhelmed by the unfolding of events. With inflation rocketing in the wake of the energy crisis, industrial militancy intensified, universities became daily battlefields and worse of all, terrorism continued unabated. In the twenty months following Carrero's assassination, ETA killed a further forty people (mostly policemen and Civil Guards) while other revolutionary left-wing groups such as the Maoist FRAP, *Frente Revolucionario Antifascista Patriótico* ('Patriotic and Revolutionary Antifascist Front'), claimed victims as well.[91] In turn, with the break-up of the regime discernible, die-hard Francoists reverted to the nostalgic rhetoric and brutal repressive methods of the 1940s in a last desperate attempt to quell dissent. Police often opened fire and killed striking workers. Protesters and activists were rounded up in their hundreds, beaten and tortured. Right-wing squads escalated their violent campaign.

In Euskadi alone there were eighty-five terrorist operations committed by Fascist groups. In July, nine young officers were arrested. Encouraged by the Portuguese example, they had joined a clandestine military organization, the so-called *Unión Militar Democrática* (UMD), whose objective was to turn the army into an apolitical institution instead of the guardian of the system against the increasingly vocal nationwide drive towards democracy. The fear of many in the regime was understandable as the army was its last and crucial pillar.[92]

On 27 September, Franco confirmed his determination to fight to the end. Despite worldwide pleas for clemency, including three personal appeals from Pope Paul VI, three militants of FRAP and two of ETA were executed. The event caused consternation in the country and massive demonstrations abroad and even attacks on Spanish embassy buildings. Fifteen European governments recalled their ambassadors. The international atmosphere seemed to return to the post-war years of isolation.

On 1 October, four policemen were killed by a new revolutionary group, believed to be infiltrated by the security services, the so-called GRAPO, *Grupos de Resistencia Antifascista Primero de Octubre* ('Groups of Anti-Fascist Resistance First of October'). That day, the Caudillo reacted in his usual manner. With complacency and undisturbed by mounting national and international opposition, before a crowd of enthusiastic supporters, he revealed how much he was still entrenched in the world of the 1930s. For him, Spain's recent problems were 'all part of a masonic leftist conspiracy of the political class in collusion with Communist-terrorist subversion in the social sphere'.[93]

This was his last public speech. On 15 October, he suffered a heart attack. Two days later, proving his amazing constitution, he still insisted on chairing a council of ministers. In the following days, his condition worsened and he had to be rushed to hospital. The serious risk of confrontation with Morocco over the Western Sahara, the last Spanish colony in Africa, was kept secret from him. Taking advantage of the critical moment, King Hassan of Morocco coveting a territory rich in phosphates and minerals, ordered thousands of unarmed civilians to invade ('The Green March'). The cowardly opportunism of the Moroccan sovereign corresponded with the indecision of a panic-stricken Arias cabinet. An armed clash was finally avoided when, despite earlier promises of self-determination for the Western Sahara, the Spanish government gave way and initiated negotiations which led to the cession of that nation to its neighbours, Morocco and Mauritania. In the meantime, Franco was undergoing the terrible agony of three major operations. He was kept alive only by a massive array of life-support machines.[94] When a tearful Arias finally confirmed the Caudillo's demise on 20 November, millions in Spain, even the many who had opposed his policies, were gripped by uncertainty and even fear of the future. An era had just ended, with the majority of Spaniards having known no other leader.

7

THE TRIUMPH OF DEMOCRACY, 1975–98

Walking on a Tightrope: The Democratic Transition

After Franco's death, Spaniards were gripped by a mixture of uncertainty, great expectations and fear. Although an overwhelming majority hoped that a passage to a modern democratic regime might be managed peacefully, very few dared to predict the country's political development. Everyone was aware that there existed powerful elements at the extremes of the spectrum who were unlikely to relinquish their maximalist positions. In such a context, the skill, determination and goodwill of both the main opposition leaders and the king and his government were to be crucial in accomplishing a negotiated and relatively tranquil transition. Yet the dismantling of the old Francoist apparatus and the building of a democratic system cannot be seen as purely a piece of engineering from above based on the negotiations between political elites. Important though these factors were, it was the radical cultural and economic transformations of the last fifteen years of the dictatorship which were vital.

During this period, a more complex and plural civil society emerged which effectively rendered the continuity of an authoritarian regime obsolete. Political reform was put on the agenda by popular mobilization which confronted the old regime's heirs with the need to establish a dialogue with the opposition. Thus the political elites were successful not because they were able to lead the people but rather because they were able to learn from and follow the public mood.[1] Simultaneously, the traumatic memories of the Civil War facilitated the establishment of a cross-class and cross-party consensus which sought to avoid the mistakes of the past. It was thus a modern consumer and civil society which permitted the construction of a new order based on reconciliation and compromise. In turn, the political elites abandoned old passions in an exercise of collective amnesia that would be known as *Pacto del Olvido* ('Pact of Forgetfulness').[2]

Certainly, the king and his government played a pivotal role guiding the process through the murky waters of the Francoist establishment. Initially, Juan Carlos, duly crowned King of Spain on 22 November, remained a political enigma. Brought up under Franco's tutelage, he seemed to have been groomed to ensure the continuity of the existing order. Consequently, it was not surprising that the opposition rejected Juan Carlos' appointment outright as the ultimate attempt of the regime to perpetuate itself. Santiago Carrillo, the Communist leader, even dubbed him 'Juan Carlos the Brief', predicting that his reign would not last a year. In the event, the young monarch had long before reached the conclusion that his only hope for legitimacy was by becoming King of all Spaniards. The fate of his grandfather and the recent example of the overthrow of his brother-in-law Constantine, King of Greece, made him aware that the dynasty could only survive by endorsing thorough and rapid reform from above. Advised by his father and mentors, in particular his friend and former teacher Torcuato Fernández Miranda, Juan Carlos sought to build a constitutional and parliamentary monarchy as a guarantee of peace and stability.[3]

In order to become 'the motor of change', Juan Carlos had on his side a vital asset: both the international and domestic atmospheres were completely different to those of the 1930s when the Second Republic was established. The Western world was dominated by democratic values. Thus in his numerous trips abroad when still a prince, he sought and obtained the support of European leaders to his cause. In striking contrast to the poor foreign representation at Franco's funeral, Chile's General Pinochet was the only Head of State present, prominent international dignitaries attended Juan Carlos' coronation.[4] Even more important was the domestic situation in Spain. Unlike the 1930s, there existed a modern and Europeanized society no longer polarized by the intense ideological conflicts of the past. A primary example of the evolving times was the Catholic Church, no longer inclined to preach a holy crusade but instead willing to embrace an accommodation with secular forces.

Politicians from both Right and Left were also radically different to their predecessors during the Second Republic. Except for the Francoist diehards, a majority of the governing class accepted the need to open up the system. In a similar way, the PCE, the best organized of all the anti-Francoist forces, had gradually moderated its principles moving away from Soviet influence to embrace, in the 1970s, Eurocommunism or the acceptance of a Western style of parliamentary democracy. In the summer of 1974 the Communists formed with other groups, the most important being the *Partido Socialista Popular* (PSP) led by Professor Tierno Galván, the so-called *Junta Democrática* which demanded the formation of a provisional government to supervise free elections to a constituent assembly, political amnesty, trade union and press freedom and the recognition of the historical rights of Catalans and Basques. The *Junta* proposed Don Juan to lead the coalition. After consulting his son, he declined.[5]

One year after the formation of the *Junta Democrática*, the rest of the political opposition formed a rival alliance known as *Plataforma de Convergencia Democrática*. Even in the final hours of the Franco regime, the opposition could not form a united front. The *Plataforma* was dominated by the Socialists allied with small Christian and Social Democratic groups. In fact, the PSOE had become by the late 1960s a declining force of exiled old men led by Rodolfo Llopis, a faithful lieutenant of Francisco Largo Caballero. Locked in the past and unaware of the reality in Spain, the PSOE was an almost spent force surrounded by nostalgia and passivity. From 1970, the long-established leadership began to be challenged by a renovating group of young Socialists. Unlike the exiled leaders, veteran members of the working classes, the new group were mainly middle class professionals with university degrees and resident in Spain. They defeated the old leadership at the XII Party Congress in Toulouse in August 1972. The renovators' victory was confirmed at the XIII Congress at Suresnes in October 1974 when it obtained the formal endorsement of the Socialist International. The election of Felipe González as new Secretary and Alfonso Guerra to a leading position in the National Executive represented both a dramatic generational change and the shift of strength from a party historically dominated by its Madrid and northern sections to those based in the south.[6]

Despite the less visceral anti-Communism of the new Socialist leadership and the remarkable similarity of the programmes, the *Plataforma* and the *Junta* did not join forces until March 1976, then forming the *Coordinadora Democrática*. The entire opposition agreed upon a democratic break or *ruptura* with the past entailing total political amnesty and free elections to a constituent parliament which would decide upon the form of the new state. The opposition's problem was that despite its ability to mobilize public opinion they lacked the strength to overthrow the system by violent means.[7]

The disappointing first steps adopted by the monarchy reinforced their mistrust that the system could not be reformed from within. Juan Carlos, trapped between democratic opposition demanding rupture and the still intact Francoist apparatus, was treading carefully. In his first speech to the Francoist *Cortes* hints of change were still cautiously balanced with his promise to uphold the principles he had sworn when he accepted the succession. A welcome novelty was when in his visit to Cataluña in February 1976 he broke with tradition and for the first time a Head of State addressed his audience in Catalan.[8]

The king ensured the appointment of Fernández Miranda, an intelligent and 'behind-the-scenes' figure, to the key position of President of the *Cortes* and of the Council of the Realm of Torcuato. Despite his irreproachable Francoist past, he was at the vanguard of the reformist tendency and the ideal candidate to accomplish the dismantling of the existing apparatus.[9] Yet, in this carefully balanced exercise Juan Carlos had to confirm Arias Navarro as Prime Minister.

Arias was unlikely to bring about reform he himself did not believe in. He formed a balanced cabinet of unrepentant hard-liners and some *aperturistas* such as Manuel Fraga at the Home Office and the outspoken advocate for reform Jose María de Areilza in charge of Foreign Affairs. During the first half of 1976, all the achievements of Areilza and Juan Carlos abroad were undone by the Prime Minister's actions in Spain. Arias' speeches were dominated by ambiguity and nostalgic references to the past. On 28 January 1976 when he explained his political programme he insisted on the different nature of Spanish democracy. He contemplated the eventual legalization of political parties, with the exception of Communists and separatists, and the regulation of the rights of assembly. However, he refused to grant a political amnesty, ignored crucial issues such as regional autonomy or trade union freedom, never mentioned when or whether there would be free elections and his language was still full of allusions to the Movement and Franco's fundamental principles. Then in a televised address in April he mentioned the Caudillo seven times by name and resorted to the old cliches of Spain being threatened by a foreign conspiracy orchestrated by international Communism. By then with a government divided and its democratic credibility destroyed, Juan Carlos declared to the US journal *Newsweek* that his Prime Minister was an 'unmitigated disaster'.[10]

Ironically, Fraga, with a reputation of *aperturista*, became the main victim of the unpopularity of the government. Confronted with a formidable wave of strikes and an unabated terrorist campaign, he as Minister of the Interior was blamed for the brutal police response which in Vitoria alone caused the death of five workers. His authoritarian style did not help. He supervised the arrest of five leaders of *Coordinación Democrática* whom he referred to as 'his prisoners' and when confronted with the people's right to demonstrate emphatically claimed that 'the streets are mine'.[11] These unrestrained actions were to haunt him for years to come.

The *Cortes* passed the new Law of Political Association which effectively recognized political parties in June after an impressive speech by the young Minister Secretary of the Movement, Adolfo Suárez. Yet in a bizarre twist they simultaneously rejected the reform of the articles of the Penal Code which penalized party activities.[12] It was a flagrant contradiction which forced Arias' resignation. A jubilant Juan Carlos promptly accepted.

It was popularly expected that Areilza, the most conspicuous reformist in the cabinet, would be the next Prime Minister. Yet Juan Carlos surprised everyone when on 3 July he instead appointed the relatively unknown Suárez. Although not appreciated at the time, Suárez's rise to the premiership was successfully engineered by Fernández Miranda. Though in theory the king could back his own candidate, his choice had to be endorsed by the Council of the Realm where the Bunker was well represented. Thus the appointment of an obvious *aperturista* like Areilza would have encountered serious opposition and endangered the possibility of Francoists embracing reform. Yet the backing of Suárez, a former television director and current Minister Secretary of the Movement, although initially greeted with dismay by the opposition, appeased even the strongest diehards in the regime.[13]

In the event, Suárez's appointment proved an inspired choice. Despite his impeccable Falangist record, he was a young pragmatic politician with few ideological principles. Unlike Arias, still anchored to the nostalgic values of the crusade, Suárez was a man of the times who grasped the public mood for reform. Yet his task was far from easy. He was walking a tightrope between the clamours of the opposition for a democratic break and the resistance of the Francoist establishment. He knew that too brief a transition could create a political vacuum and even a right-wing backlash, but one too slow would lead to popular unrest and frustration. In the event, he opted for a daring strategy which required all his consummate skills. Suárez hastened political reform in order to force the opposition to enter negotiations in which demands for a constituent process would be dropped. Simultaneously, the transition was carried out through the legal channels of the Francoist establishment with the ruling class dismantling itself voluntarily. In this context, Miranda's machiavellian back-door dealings, and the king, as Commander-in-Chief of the armed forces, appeasing the military, made an invaluable contribution to the coming of democracy.[14]

Speed and determination were the keys to Suárez's success. He formed a cabinet of *Tácitos* and young apparatchiks like himself. In contrast to the ambiguity of the previous administration, the new government hastened to show its reformist commitment. Channels of communication were opened with opposition leaders and the Prime Minister himself announced on television in July his plans for political reform, legalization of parties and free elections in June 1977.

In September Suárez presented his programme to the army. He promised never to legalize the PCE or consent to the break-up of the fatherland and in return obtained its support.[15] In October, the political reform was debated in the Francoist *Cortes*. Its acceptance was in effect asking the governing class to commit political suicide. Yet in the heated atmosphere of 1976, only a minority of *inmobilistas* still believed in the survival of an unreformed regime. Deputies were offered lucrative jobs and influential positions in the administration and warned that a negative vote might lead to renewed civil war. At the same time, the debates, skilfully manipulated by Miranda, had men closely connected with the old order such as López Rodó and Miguel Primo de Rivera speaking on behalf of political reform. The final vote in November was a stunning victory for the government: 425 voted in favour, 13 abstained and only 59 voted against. On 15 December, a national referendum provided overwhelming backing for the government, with 94.2 per cent for and only 2.6 per cent against.[16]

By the end of the year Suárez had imposed his agenda. The opposition who had hitherto remained distrustful could no longer fail to recognize the reformist sincerity of the government nor overlook the popular support demonstrated in the referendum. Their demands for *ruptura* were thus quietly abandoned and replaced by negotiations with the government.[17] In December, the PSOE celebrated in Madrid its first congress in Spain for forty years. From February, political parties were formally legalized after only requesting registration at the Ministry of Interior. While unreformed Francoists grouped around Blas Piñar's *Fuerza Nueva*, the two more important formations emanating from the old regime were *Alianza Popular* (AP) and *Unión de Centro Democrático* (UCD). Headed by Manuel Fraga, AP was full of prominent figures of the past including Arias Navarro and López Rodó. Calling themselves the civilized Right, Fraga's party was a model of modernized Francoism seeking to capture the vote of those who had prospered under the previous regime. While accepting democratic reform, AP's rhetoric was still strongly Catholic, centralist and anti-Communist. By contrast, UCD, rather than a party with a clear ideological programme, represented a coalition of heterogeneous interests created in order to bask in the prestige of Suárez. It was formed by a combination of Catholics, Suárez's own team of apparatchiks together with small Liberal and Social-Democrat groups. However, unlike AP, UCD presented an image of modernity and progress while its centrist character enhanced its appeal as buffer between the past and the future.[18]

The transition could not be completed until the PCE, with its deep historical and social roots, was legalized. Carrillo himself, feeling that he could miss the boat, and aware that other opposition parties including the Socialists were happy to forsake Communist claims for their own benefit, returned to Madrid in December. By then leading Communists were openly pursuing their activities in a situation of semi-legality. Yet by organizing a conference in public, Carrillo practically forced his own arrest and kept the issue of legalization alive. He was released one week later. In January 1977 five Communist lawyers were massacred at their offices in Atocha (Madrid) by an ultra commando. To what was one of the worst outrages of the transition days, PCE and CC.OO. responded with admirable restraint. In February, Suárez and Carrillo entered into formal negotiations. The Communist Secretary proved an extremely easy interlocutor. In return for legalization, Carrillo recognized the monarchy, the national flag and promised support for a social contract. In April and despite the earlier promise to the army, the PCE was legalized by royal decree.[19]

On 15 June 1977 the first free elections since 1936 were held. People voted for closed party lists under the so-called D'Hont system of proportional representation, a method which favours the over-representation of the larger parties and prevents too much fragmentation. The results were a particular triumph for the government, and in more general terms, for moderation. Out of 370 seats, UCD and PSOE obtained

166 and 118 respectively. The PCE with twenty deputies and AP with sixteen fared worse than expected. Despite their acceptance of liberal democracy, both PCE and AP paid the price for their old leadership which inevitably evoked memories of the past. Moderate centrist groups also emerged as the hegemonic nationalist forces in Cataluña and Euskadi. The coalition soon to be known as *Convergéncia i Unió* (CiU) led by the astute Jordi Pujol returned eleven deputies and the PNV six. Parties associated with the unreformed past such as *Fuerza Nueva* were wiped out. The people had voted for change and endorsed the 'Pact of Forgetfulness'.[20]

The following two years constituted the peak of Suárez's career. Now relying on the legitimacy of his popular mandate, he was largely successful in consolidating the constitutional foundations of the democracy. An initial success was the signing of a social contract, known as the *Pactos de la Moncloa*, in October 1977. With the economic recession worsening, inflation rising and unemployment soaring, the government summoned the main opposition parties, the two leading trade unions CC.OO. and UGT, and the employers' organization (CEOE). Agreement was made possible by Carrillo's eagerness to collaborate and the fact that the CC.OO. had practically replaced a declining CNT as the hegemonic force of the Spanish proletariat. Communist flexibility made it difficult for the PSOE to reject the plans. In real terms, the left-wing parties were prepared to make sacrifices in order to consolidate democracy. Indeed, the working classes would effectively bear the brunt of the economic crisis. A wage-ceiling of 20 per cent was accepted at a time when inflation was 29 per cent, and a series of monetarist measures to restrict credit and public spending was introduced. In return, the government made promises, which eventually went largely unfulfilled, of major structural reforms including higher pensions and unemployment benefit, improvements in education, the health service and housing programmes, and the adoption of a more progressive income tax. The *Pactos de la Moncloa* represented a significant departure from the politics of confrontation of the 1930s and offered the labour movement a role in economic decision-making.[21]

A more pressing problem was the need to find a solution to the sensitive question of regional autonomy. Ironically, in Cataluña, a historical bulwark of confrontation against centralism, negotiations were remarkably smooth. Suárez followed an audacious strategy bypassing the elected Catalan representatives and negotiating directly with Josep Tarradellas, a former Companys' lieutenant and minister of the Catalan government who, still in exile, was widely recognized as the legitimate embodiment of Catalanism. Thus the government avoided potential party in-fighting and found a respectable interlocutor. Tarradellas flew to Madrid in June 1977 and agreed to recognize the monarchy in return for the restoration of the statute of 1932. In a nostalgic atmosphere, he landed in Barcelona on 23 October and was installed as President of the *Generalitat*. On 25 October 1979, the Statute of Autonomy was endorsed in a referendum by the Catalan people.[22]

In starkest possible contrast, the route in Euskadi was slower and more painful. Unlike Catalan Nationalism, a deeply rooted phenomenon which counted on the overwhelming support of all classes and parties, the question proved to be more divisive amongst the Basques whose experience of autonomy was limited to a very brief period during the Civil War. The problem was compounded by the relatively recent appearance of violence in an area which had been peaceful until the 1960s. Euskadi suffered the worst excesses of police brutality and repression of late Francoism. The result was the radicalization of Basque Nationalism as ETA acquired an aura of legitimacy among significant sectors of the population. Consumed by the problems of placating both the Bunker and the opposition, Suárez, like previous politicians in Madrid, simply did not understand the Basque problem and instead of adopting far-reaching political conciliatory gestures which might have deprived ETA of its mass support, he continued regarding the issue as one of public order.

Euskadi remained thus the black spot of the democratic transition. Whereas in the rest of Spain, Suárez's negotiating skills ensured a relatively peaceful process, for the Basques little had changed since the dictatorship. The same old Francoist police dispersed demonstrations with acts of unrestrained brutality often causing deaths, while right-wing squads continued unhindered in their murderous activities. A total amnesty and the immediate legalization of the Basque flag, the *ikurriña*, were the Basques' minimum demands. However, the government, extremely cautious not to alienate the army, was found wanting in undertaking bold conciliatory steps. Ironically, in October 1974 ETA itself had undergone a tactical and ideological split. A majority of its members initially remained in the so-called political–military branch of that organization (ETA–PM). They sought to collaborate with other left-wing parties in Spain, and although not yet ready to give up the armed struggle, they contemplated its gradual abandonment in exchange for genuine political concessions. Only a few extreme

Nationalist hard-liners for whom the terror campaign to achieve independence had primacy stayed in the ETA military front (ETA–M). The government in Euskadi did not control the agenda but seemed to react to events. Concessions were yielded only after many delays and contradictions. This fuelled popular discontent and eroded its reformist credibility. A full amnesty was granted only to avert a boycott of the June 1977 election. Yet many concluded that Euskadi was still a country occupied by the centralist forces now masked under the trappings of a fraudulent democracy. In September 1977 a large section of ETA–PM joined ETA–M. The wave of assassinations and bombings escalated.[23]

There was no Tarradellas in Euskadi who could embody the aspirations of all the Basque political forces. The PNV and the PSOE, with approximately one-third of the vote each, were the two leading parties. Yet by opting for negotiations with the Socialists, Nationalists in the PNV felt alienated from the process. Furthermore, the PNV found itself in a difficult position. As a party of law and order which embraced Christian-Democratic principles, it rejected violence. However, conserving strong xenophobic components from the past, it competed with the more radical Nationalists for the same electoral space. The result was that under the leadership of the former Jesuit Javier Arzallus, the PNV adopted an ambiguous rhetoric attacking ETA as much as the Spanish state. Thus the drawing of the Statute of Autonomy was bitter and complex. Progress did not start until after new elections in 1979 which gave the PNV a greater majority. Only then did Suárez begin to deal directly with Carlos Garaikoetxea, the PNV's provisional *Lehendakari* or Basque President, reaching an agreement in July. Finally, the so-called Statute of Autonomy was endorsed in a referendum by a clear majority in October 1979. Among the supporters of the 'yes' vote was the so-called Basque Left or *Euzkadiko Ezkerra* (EE), the political front for ETA–PM. However, it was by then too late to pacify the region. Too much blood had been spilt and a significant sector of the population was fully behind ETA–M for whom anything short of full independence was a betrayal. They formed an electoral coalition, *Herri Batasuna* or People's Unity (HB) to promote an alliance of all the radical Nationalist groups in Euskadi. Unlike EE, pursuing collaboration with other Basque left-wing parties, for HB the national struggle had primacy over the social one. For them, the concession of the Statute of Autonomy not only failed to represent the real interests of the Basque people but was also considered a set-back as it could delude part of the population into accepting a settlement with Madrid.[24]

Suárez's crowning success was the production of a constitution designed to avoid the pitfalls of the past. It was the result of the bargaining process of a commission representing all main parties appointed in August 1977. Catalan Nationalists and particularly the Communists proved extremely willing to find a consensus with UCD. Disagreements between the government and the PSOE were solved in a spirit of goodwill during late-night sessions often held in restaurants or in private apartments. Only the hard-line sector of AP and the PNV, simultaneously involved in the battle for Basque autonomy, felt excluded in what they regarded as a UCD–PSOE private pact. In the end, however, when the Constitution was presented to parliament in October 1978, the overwhelming majority of deputies were prepared to endorse it. In fact, its prime virtue lie in its ambiguity so that every significant sector of public opinion could find common ground and not feel alienated.[25]

The final text defines Spain as a social and democratic state ruled by law. Its political form is a parliamentary monarchy with the king as Head of State and Commander-in-Chief of the armed forces but whose authority is reduced to that of a constitutional monarch. National sovereignty resides with the people and Prime Ministers are responsible to parliament and not to the Crown. The voting age was lowered to 18 and the death penalty abolished. In an important departure from the past, the state no longer has an official religion although it recognizes the historical role played by the Catholic Church. Finally, a delicate balance determines the sensitive question of regional autonomy. Traditional rigid centralism is replaced by the recognition of a form of semi-federal state formed by seventeen autonomous regions plus the African enclaves of Ceuta and Melilla. However, while acknowledging different nationalities, it denies the right of secession to any of them confirming Spain as the common and indivisible country of all Spaniards. The text was approved with only six votes against and fourteen abstentions. The abstentionist camp was the PNV and negative votes mainly from AP. Yet Fraga and half of his parliamentary group voted for it. Finally, a public referendum held on 6 December found 87.9 per cent of the electorate in favour with only 7.8 per cent against. Of great significance was, however, the high abstention rate registered in the Basque Country.[26]

After the approval of the constitution, parliament was dissolved and new elections announced for 1 March 1979. The popular vote confirmed the trend initiated in 1977 with UCD and PSOE as the two leading options with 168 and 121 seats respectively. The Communists with 23 deputies experienced a slight improvement and AP saw its representation reduced to nine. The extreme Right returned a single deputy, that of its leader Blas Piñar. Yet in Euskadi the sizeable support achieved by ETA was fully demonstrated when *Euzkadiko Ezkerra* obtained one seat, and even more startling were the three deputies of *Herri Batasuna*.[27]

The electoral triumph of March 1979 marked the high point of Suárez's career. After that, everything went wrong. The boldness and inspiration of his previous years in office deserted him. As in 1931, many people had believed that democracy would solve all of Spain's problems overnight. With expectations unfulfilled, the press alluded to the widespread *desencanto* ('disenchantment') which contrasted with the enthusiasm and optimism of the transition's first years. This phenomenon was more conspicuous amongst the young. Faced with an uncertain future and taking advantage of the dismantlement of Francoist repression, many abandoned their earlier political activism and retreated into their own subculture of drugs, abstentionism and alienation known as *pasotismo* (coming from the poker game 'pass').[28]

Indeed, confronted by the perennial problems of economic recession and worsening public order, the Suárez administration failed to give leadership so that soon references were made to UCD *misgobierno* ('ungovernment'). The economy, long neglected for the sake of political expediency, failed to recover. Hopes that the situation would improve were dashed with the announcement of oil price increases in 1979. The result was a drop in domestic demand, a spate of company bankruptcies and factory closures. Unemployment soared to 12.60 per cent of the labour force in 1980. One year later the figure had reached 15.37 per cent.[29]

The widespread climate of gloom was exacerbated by the glaring failure of the government to halt the escalation of terrorist activities. In a sense, both ETA and the Bunker seemed, for different purposes, to be combining forces to destroy the new regime after the approval of the Constitution.[30] Ultra squads continued their terror campaign, often undeterred by a police still headed by Francoist elements. Infamous Italian and Latin American Fascists who had found refuge in Franco's Spain took an active role in this strategy of tension. Left-wing activists were attacked, cinemas, journals and book-shops bombed and universities assaulted. So-called 'national' zones or areas under ultra control were created in every major city. There, persons regarded as Leftist were abused and beaten up. In the Basque Country, terrorist groups targeted and often murdered well-known leaders and sympathizers of the separatist cause while patriotic mobs were allowed to rampage freely. Between 1977 and 1980, some 40 people, including Argala, the historical leader of ETA–M, lost their lives in ultra actions.[31]

In turn, ETA increased its number of bombings and assassinations. Whereas only 74 people had lost their lives to ETA attacks during the period between 1968 and 1977, 60 deaths were registered during the first six months of 1979 alone.[32] While ETA–PM sought to extract political concessions from the government, ETA–M began to target senior army officers in order to provoke massive repression and break any prospect of negotiated settlement.

That tactic played straight into the hands of the Bunker. The Rightist press made simplistic comparisons with the prosperity and tranquility of the previous regime to conclude that 'we lived better under Franco'. The funerals of policemen or officers became rallying points for right-wing demonstrations inciting the army to take power.[33] In fact, ever since Suárez broke his promise and legalized the PCE, golpismo ('military plotting') in the higher echelons of the armed forces had been intensifying. The propensity of anti-democratic conspiracies was facilitated by the government's absurd policy of treating army discontent and even openly rebellious attitudes with kid gloves. Thus continuous diatribes against Suárez and his Minister of Defence, Gutiérrez Mellado, went unpunished. A flagrant example of this irresponsible leniency was the handling of the so-called 'Galaxia Operation'. It took its name from the Madrid cafeteria where some army officers had plotted to kidnap the entire cabinet while in session. Discovered by the intelligence services, the main conspirator, the Lieutenant Colonel of the Civil Guard Antonio Tejero, was sentenced to a token seven months imprisonment and then returned to his post where he continued plotting. Amidst constant blood letting by ETA and governmental lethargy in stamping out military subversion, golpismo flourished. By late 1980 the rumours of an imminent coup had become deafening.[34]

To further aggravate matters, the governing coalition began to disintegrate. UCD had never been a proper party, but a broad church of disparate interests whose single rationale was to maintain some hold over the levers of power. Its members were bound together by the common goal of presiding over a peaceful and negotiated transition. Yet once the foundations of the new regime had been laid, it lost the basic purpose of its existence. Suárez could not govern with both his cabinet and his parliamentary group divided into antagonistic factions and holding opposite views about any basic legislation. Infighting and dissent were exacerbated by the steep decline in electoral fortunes. The municipal elections of April 1979 gave a massive victory to the Left. Then the first autonomic elections in March 1980 in Cataluña and Euskadi delivered a victory for Nationalist options. The PNV emerged as the leading Basque force, and even more stunning was the overall majority achieved by the CiU in Cataluña. While other Spanish parties held most of their vote, UCD was relegated to a humiliating minor presence.[35]

By 1979 Adolfo Suárez was no longer the energetic leader of the transition. Living basically on coffee, cigarettes and pills, he withdrew to his office in the Moncloa Palace surrounded by his small loyal team of apparatchiks.[36] As Suárez's star was waning, the contrary was the case for the Socialist leader, Felipe González. From the almost skeleton party he inherited in 1974, the PSOE under his leadership emerged in 1977 as the main opposition force. Massive aid from the Socialist International, especially the German SPD, and the youthful image of his party helped relegate the PCE to second place. As in the old times, the PSOE based its appeal on a combination of maximalist rhetoric and moderate practices. The party's hegemony of the Left was increased by the absorption of other rival Socialist groups, the most important being that of the influential Tierno Galván's PSP in 1978. González's next step was to shift to the centre in order to expand the party's constituency, gain ground from a declining UCD and win the next elections. Consequently, he proposed at the XVIII PSOE's Congress to abandon Marxism and embrace Social Democracy. When a majority voted against it, he and the entire executive resigned. His gamble paid off. Aware that the main electoral asset of the party was its leader's personal charisma, none of his Leftist rivals were ready to take over. In the subsequent interregnum, Alfonso Guerra, in charge of running the party apparatus, masterminded internal organizational changes which reduced the number of delegates and introduced a form of block vote which gave greater control to the largest section, Andalucía. In the extraordinary Congress held in September, Felipe González was returned in triumph as Secretary and his thesis approved by a party more centralized and dominated by the leadership than ever before.[37]

In May 1980, the PSOE presented a motion of censure against the government. Suárez narrowly avoided defeat owing to the abstention of some groups. Yet he performed poorly in the televised debates, while González emerged from them reinforced as a real alternative to power. On 29 January 1981, the Prime Minister stunned the nation when he announced his resignation. Tired and embittered by internal bickering, savaged by the press and vilified by the army, he had had enough. He was to be replaced by Leopoldo Calvo Sotelo, the dull Minister of Economy, who was the candidate most widely tolerated by all the UCD's factions.[38]

On 23 February 1981, parliament was in full session to vote on the investiture of the new Prime Minister. At 6.20 p.m. the long-feared military conspiracy struck. Lieutenant Colonel Tejero, pistol in hand, followed by 200 Civil Guards, stormed the chamber. At the same time, units of the crack Brunete armed division took control of key points in the capital and Captain General Jaime Miláns del Bosch declared martial law in Valencia, the third largest city, and ordered tanks into the streets. With the entire political class sequestrated, it appeared as if the democratic system had been successfully overthrown. However, if anything, democracy came out reinvigorated from this lethal attack.

The plotters, still anchored in the mentality of the 1930s, were unaware of how much the international context and Spanish society had evolved. Unlike 1936, there was no sign of civilian support for the insurrection. For most Spaniards glued to their televisions, the image of a Civil Guard with an enormous moustache whipping his gun and shouting abuse at politicians was a sad and pathetic remainder of a past they wanted forgotten. Furthermore, the army *coup d'état* was a harried combination of two different conspiracies. There was a Chilean-type plot pursued by a group of colonels who envisaged the imposition of military rule followed by a draconian policy of repression. Simultaneously, there was another softer plot headed by General Alfonso Armada, the former head of Juan Carlos' military household. This represented a 'De Gaulle' kind of solution, seeking not the destruction but the rectification of democracy by the formation of a strong executive. General Miláns was the link between both plots. The sudden resignation of Suárez had precipitated the events without solving the plotters' different goals. Yet Miláns, a staunch Monarchist, proceeded with the belief, fed by the involvement of Armada, that they had the king's backing. Their assumptions proved completely wrong. Juan Carlos had never intended to play Alfonso XIII to a new Primo de Rivera. The turning point was the king's appearance on television at 1.15 a.m. on 24 February. Dressed in his uniform of Commander-in-Chief, he delared that the Crown would not tolerate any movement against the legal democratic process. From then, the coup unravelled fast. Many Captain Generals had little sympathy for the democratic order, but they all stood by their oath of allegiance to the monarchy. Miláns himself after talking to the king called his soldiers back to barracks. Amidst the confusion, Armada appeared in parliament and attempted to implement his plan. Tejero could not believe it. Seeing himself as a patriotic saviour, he was now offered a flight into exile so that Armada could preside over a government of national unity with some of the politicians he held hostage. He threw Armada out. By noon it was all over. A frustrated and isolated Tejero gave himself up.[39]

The aftermath of the aborted coup saw a re-awakening of mass enthusiasm for democracy. Hundreds of thousands of Spaniards marched in the streets showing their support for the new order. The king won adulation and respect for his decisive role. Even the most recalcitrant Republicans declared themselves to be *Juancarlistas*.[40] Only thirty amongst the most compromised plotters were brought to trial. Tejero and Miláns were sentenced to thirty years imprisonment and Armada to six. Yet UCD could not bask for long in the national euphoria. Calvo Sotelo successfully negotiated the slowing down of the autonomic process for the non-historical regions with the opposition, but infuriated them when with hardly any debate he negotiated the entry of Spain into NATO. Both measures were designed to curry military favour. Yet the premiership of the hapless Calvo Sotelo was dominated by the spectacle of UCD disintegration. Throughout 1982, UCD's diverse constituents broke apart. The Social Democrats went over to the PSOE and the Christian Democrats joined Fraga's party. Even Suárez himself formed his own group, the *Centro Democrático y Social* (CDS).[41]

UCD's crumbling process shared headlines with the internecine struggles raging in the PCE. Despite its embrace of Eurocommunism, the Communists were still controlled by Carrillo's old guard with an iron fist. Failure to emerge as the leading left-wing force intensified internal dissent. By 1981 the leadership came under attack from different tendencies. There were the orthodox pro-Soviet elements in the party who regretted the adoption of Eurocommunism. The Catalan PSUC, the electorally most successful organization, demanded more autonomy from the centre while the Basque Communists, against the instructions of the Central Committee, initiated a dialogue to merge with *Euzkadiko Ezkerra*. Finally, well-known Communists began to demand the revision of the party statutes to permit greater internal democracy. In the PCE's X Congress of July 1981 the leadership defeated all the opposing tendencies. During the following year, Carrillo tightened his control in the best Stalinist manner. Those dissidents who did not leave were suspended, purged or expelled. The Basque Central Committee was expelled and replaced by one imposed by Madrid and the Catalan Communists split into two rival groups.[42]

Calvo Sotelo decided to call new general elections for 28 October 1982. The disarray of his party was such that he even refused to lead UCD in the forthcoming electoral contest. The results were a foregone conclusion. Nobody could match the attractive personality and appeal of the Socialist leader. In contrast to the other older statesmen, he was normally referred to by his christian name, Felipe. The final vote surpassed the most optimistic predictions. The PSOE obtained an overall majority with a record 202 seats. Fraga's coalition emerged with 106 as the new main opposition group. Nationalists increased slightly their representation, CiU returned eleven deputies and the PNV six. The centre practically collapsed. UCD had twelve deputies and the CDS two. The PCE with only four seats disappeared as a major force in Spanish politics.[43]

Between Felipe and Aznar: Democracy at Work

The election of October 1982 marked the critical threshold when democracy was finally endorsed. It also initiated an unprecedented era of Socialist hegemony. The PSOE obtained two new landslide victories on 22 June 1986 and 29 October 1989. This unique dominance of politics was largely explained by the lack of a clear challenging alternative.[44] Centre parties disintegrated and a great part of their electorate went over to the PSOE. UCD broke up in 1983. Suárez's own project, the CDS, survived a little longer but after failing to make clear headway also collapsed in 1991. Schisms in the PCE also benefited the Socialists. It was not until the second half of the 1980s that the Communists began gradually to recover part of the lost ground. By then the PCE was the leading force of an alliance of leftist groups, the United Left (IU), and was headed by the charismatic former Mayor of Córdoba, Julio Anguita. AP, entrenched as the main opposition force, seemed to have peaked in 1982. Its image, still dominated by the Francoist past, put off prospective moderate centrist voters. Thus the gradual erosion of the Socialist vote did not translate into Conservative ones, but rather benefited local nationalist forces. The most important was that of the Catalan Nationalists of the CiU, obtaining over fifteen deputies and emerging as a major force in national politics. The PNV, however, after an internal split, had to form a coalition with the PSOE from 1987 to retain control of the Basque government.[45] It was not until 1989 when Fraga finally retired to serve as President in his native homeland, Galicia, that a proper bipartisan system appeared. AP underwent a relaunch with a new image and a new name *Partido Popular* (PP). Most of the old figures of the past were replaced by a team of young Conservatives led by José María Aznar, a former tax inspector and President of the Autonomous Region of Castilla-León. Aznar's lack of humour and coolness could not be more distant from the image portrayed by Felipe González. Yet his efforts to modernize his party and move towards the centre of the political spectrum paid off in the 1990s.

There has been much positive in the PSOE's long period in power. The modernization of the country has been dramatic. Spain is no longer different but very much a modern European society in which democratic values are firmly rooted. One of the fundamental problems of the transition, *golpismo*, has been successfully eradicated. While there were still two more serious conspiracies in the 1980s, the first on the eve of the elections of October 1982 and the second in June 1985, they involved only a minority of hard-liners and were swiftly dismantled.[46]

Unlike UCD, the PSOE immediately dealt with the armed forces. Its strategy combined appeasement with the determination to stamp out revolt. Thus members of the army who espoused anti-democratic views were replaced by those known for their loyalty. At the same time, the defence budget remained very high so as to bring military pay into line with that of their civilian counterparts. Also, the PSOE's startling about-turn in favour of staying in NATO in the referendum of March 1986 was calculated not only to content the army but also to democratize military thinking through international contact. By the 1990s, after the retirement of the last batch of officers who had participated in the Civil War, it is no longer plausible to speak of a 'military threat'.[47]

Foreign policy proved to be the area of greatest success. In little more than a decade, Spain abandoned its peripheral role to occupy a central part in European and even world affairs. The new diplomacy constituted a total departure from the Francoist past. Under the dictatorship, Spain had been semi-ostracized in Europe and followed a pro-American and pro-Arab foreign policy. The Socialists pursued instead a European and Atlanticist strategy. In January 1986 Spain established full diplomatic relations with Israel. In the same month the long-sought objective of joining the EEC was fulfilled. Two months later a referendum confirmed membership of NATO.[48] Spain could follow a more independent line from that marked by the United States. Thus negotiations were successfully completed to reduce substantially the US military presence in Spain. Spanish diplomacy often differed from the Americans in Latin America. For instance, excellent relations were maintained with Castro's Cuba and Spain condemned the US-sponsored *Contras* in Nicaragua, instead endorsing the so-called Contadora Plan to find a negotiated solution in that country. In the 1990s, Spanish forces participated in two important world missions, the Gulf War and Bosnia. In 1991, Madrid held the crucial Arab–Israeli Peace Conference. The year 1992 marked the peak of Spain's new standing in the world. There were celebrations for the 500th anniversary of the discovery of America, Madrid was designated Europe's cultural capital, Barcelona staged the Olympic Games, and Sevilla the World Trade Exhibition. In late 1995, Javier Solana, then Foreign Minister, was appointed the new Secretary-General of NATO.[49]

Socialist handling of the economy produced more ambiguous results. When the PSOE assumed office, the structural weaknesses of Spain's economy remained unsolved. Public deficit had reached 5.4 per cent of GDP, inflation remained at around 15 per cent and the unemployment rate had risen to 16.5 per cent. Furthermore, throughout the Western world, Social-Democratic principles encompassing Keynesian demand management techniques, state interventionism and nationalization of key sectors, were being abandoned in favour of strict monetary regulations. Spanish Socialists swiftly embraced 'neo-liberal' market principles of privatization and dropped traditional socialist objectives of state control and high taxation to redistribute wealth. Emphasis was placed on sound finance, fighting inflation, modernizing the infrastructure and improving competitiveness. A Plan of Industrial Reconversion was soon introduced to establish an industrial base capable of competing internationally. The public sector was pruned of inefficient plants. This affected mainly the steel, iron and shipbuilding industries with many companies closed down or sold off.[50]

The economic restructuring programme was relatively successful if judged in terms of conventional macroeconomic indicators: the rate of inflation was halved and levels of productivity and efficiency greatly improved. Spain even experienced a small economic boom in the second half of the 1980s. The annual rate of economic growth, at almost 5 per cent, was the highest amongst the Western economies. After joining the EEC, Spain undoubtedly benefited from large inflows of foreign capital attracted by high interest rates, relatively low labour costs and a massive popular thirst for consumer goods. Yet like the rest of the world, the boom turned to bust by 1992. The economy showed no sign of picking up again until 1995. By then, the peseta had been devalued several times and interest rates cut from 14.3 per cent in March 1993 to 7.5 per cent in May 1994.[51]

The government's economic policy was lauded by the financial world and criticized by the organized labour movement. In fact, the brunt of the harsh adjustment measures was borne by the working classes. Modernization meant unpopular job-cutting policies which a right-wing party could never have got away with. The electoral promise of October 1982, the creation of 800 000 new jobs within the following four years, was not only dropped, but reconversion meant a notable increase in the numbers of unemployed. Between 1982 and 1996, the unemployment rate hovered around 20 per cent of the working population, the largest in western Europe. The government tried to soften this high social cost by increasing pensions, social security and protection for those on fixed-term contracts, and by turning a blind eye to the existence of an underground economy, estimated at about 25 per cent of the GDP. This was not enough to appease the trade unions. In 1988 Nicolás Redondo, the UGT leader, resigned his parliamentary seat, and his organization joined the CC.OO. in a general strike on 14 December. In the 1990s, the gap between PSOE and the labour movement widened. After signing the Maastricht Treaty, the government found itself further constrained by the need to meet the convergence criteria for economic and monetary union. Being in the first wave of nations to join a single currency meant a package of restrictive measures, including a tightening of fiscal policy and public cuts. New general strikes on 24 May 1992 and 27 January 1994 proved that the stage for confrontation remained open.[52]

Despite his achievements in government, Felipe González may not be seen as the great modernizer of Spanish politics. While his statesmanship is hailed in Europe, where he could be a strong candidate for the post of President of the European Union, his reputation at home has been severely tarnished. A succession of scandals ensured he will never achieve the same amount of respect that the king and Adolfo Suárez enjoyed.[53] Even if innocent of the many financial and political misdeeds, opinion polls suggest that the overwhelming majority of Spaniards believe he could not have been ignorant of the embezzlement, nepotism and bribery of his administration. Lack of executive accountability, corruption, nepotism and other crimes are not uniquely Spanish phenomena. Other countries such as France, Greece, and above all, Italy, were affected by comparable crises. Ironically, although revelations of widespread governmental misconduct strengthened the scepticism of the citizens towards the political class, they also in a subtle way confirmed the foundation of democratic politics in Spain. Had they emerged in the transition years, the new regime might have collapsed. However, in the 1990s not a single voice called for a return to the authoritarian past. Furthermore, the same audience, shocked by the degree of political depravity, was the first to recognize that under the old order it would never have come to light.

Under the leadership of Felipe González and Alfonso Guerra, the PSOE was transformed beyond recognition. It became a successful electoral machine but simultaneously, the austerity and honesty which had characterized the party founded by Pablo Iglesias was seriously compromised.[54] After the reforms of the party statutes in 1979, the PSOE became a highly centralized organization with its rank-and-file relegated to sanctioning the leadership's actions. The old working-class party was replaced by a group of middle-class professionals mostly interested in preserving their lucrative jobs. Lacking any serious political challenge, the government began to identify itself with the state. Felipe González gradually adopted a presidential stand, failing to attend a parliament which had become a rubber-stamp for governmental decisions and creating a 'royal court' around his headquarters at the Moncloa Palace.[55] The PSOE grew increasingly contemptuous of public opinion, arrogant towards any criticism and considered the public sector their possession. Clientelism and administrative patronage became an intrinsic part of Spanish Socialism. By 1994 at the XXXIII PSOE Congress 72 per cent of delegates held official positions.[56]

During these years, the Socialist constituency was also altered. In 1982, the PSOE had surged into power with the promise of change by the massive vote of the young and urban middle and working classes. Henceforth Spanish Socialism became a catch-all party based on a coalition of interests. In Cataluña and Euskadi, it maintained a substantial part of the vote by portraying itself as a progressive Spanish party. Memories of the Francoist past permitted the PSOE to conserve large sectors of its original Leftist constituency. Many whose first choice would be Communist ended up giving their 'useful' vote to the PSOE. Finally, a significant part of the PSOE's electoral support came from those quarters who benefited from governmental action: pensioners, public employees, and the massive rural vote in Andalucía and Extremadura. In these southern strongholds a clear example of clientelist politics would operate. Designated as poor regions, funds were set aside for development projects to give people work and improve conditions in villages. Anyone who could document working for sixty days would qualify to get community benefits for the entire year. In practice, with the complicity of local Socialist authorities, this scheme developed into colossal frauds. In some towns, different family members would succeed each other in different jobs doing the minimum time and all qualifying for benefits. In others, villagers would be credited with working on projects that never took place. As a result, one of the most vulnerable sectors of the Spanish population was able to get through hard times, but also provided a 'captive' vote for the Socialists.[57]

It is not surprising that the first monumental scandal erupted in Andalucía, the Socialist heartland. In December 1989, Juan Guerra, brother of the Deputy Prime Minister, seized the headlines. He was accused of *tráfico de influencias* ('influence-peddling'), having amassed a vast fortune in a series of shady deals from his office at the PSOE's headquarters in Sevilla. Under fierce criticism in parliament, Alfonso denied knowledge of any of his brother's misdeeds. Finally, he resigned from government but retained his key position in the party. Throughout 1991 and 1992 new scandals of *tráfico de influencias* rocked the government. The biggest uproar was caused by the discovery of a series of artificial consulting companies, in reality fronts for the PSOE, which had been receiving millions of pesetas from leading banks and industries in exchange for unknown services.

In March 1993, Felipe González visited the Central University in Madrid. Believing himself on safe ground among the students, he was shocked at being abused and called 'thief' by them. Seemingly moved by public opinion, González based the electoral campaign of June 1993 on the promise of fighting corruption. As a proof of his intention, he placed Baltasar Garzón, one of the most prominent judges, number two, behind him, on the party list for Madrid. The results gave the Socialists a fourth consecutive victory. However, the PSOE lost its overall majority and the Popular Party, for the first time, transcended its electoral ceiling of about 25 per cent of the vote by rising to 34.8 per cent. Given the existing hostility between the PSOE and IU, the government had to rely on CiU votes to remain in power.[58]

The fourth term in office soon turned into a nightmare. A frustrated Garzón resigned in early 1994 claiming he had been deceived. Despite all the executive attempts to obstruct judicial investigations, magistrates and journalists launched themselves into a relentless campaign which, similar to the high-profile cases emerging then in Italy and France, exposed a myriad of scandals that made front page news daily. The levels of political depravity reached nearly every area of the public administration (television, national railways, the Spanish Red Cross, local governments, banks, etc.). Leading political and financial personalities had to abandon their jobs and in some cases faced arrest. The more spectacular of these scandals were the imprisonment of the former Governor of the Bank of Spain, Mariano Rubio, accused of fraud, and the startling flight abroad of Luis Roldán, the first civilian head of the Civil Guard and favourite to be the next Minister of the Interior, charged with embezzlement of public funds, taking kickbacks on building contracts and laundering money across the world.[59]

Yet it was the judge Garzón who uncovered the most damaging affair for the reputation of the government, that of the GAL. Between 1983 and 1987, a mysterious organization, the so-called *Grupos Antiterroristas de Liberación* (GAL), murdered 28 members or sympathizers of ETA, mainly in its safe haven in south-west France. The GAL's accurate information and precision aroused the suspicion that they were part of a dirty war orchestrated by the authorities.[60] In 1988, two police inspectors, José Amedo and Michel Domínguez, were charged with the creation of the GAL and sentenced to 100 years in jail. For the next seven years, the affair was practically forgotten. Its re-opening by Garzón in 1994 proved a bombshell. His investigations revealed that Amedo and Domínguez were scapegoats in an operation engineered by top officials. In order to buy their silence, both policemen were still receiving salaries of half a million pesetas monthly, possessed secret accounts in Switzerland and had been promised a pardon. Under pressure, they implicated in their confessions the former Civil Governor of Vizcaya, Julián Sancristobal; the former chief of the anti-terrorist brigade, Francisco Alvárez; the Chief of Police in Bilbao, Miguel Planchuelo; the former Secretary of the PSOE in Euskadi, Ricardo García Damborenea; and a former Director of State Security, the number two in the Interior Ministry, Rafael Vera. Under interrogation all but the last implicated the senior officials in the PSOE, including José Barrionuevo, the former Minister of the Interior, and even Felipe González. Further investigations coinciding with the deportation and arrest of Luis Roldán brought to light the existence of a huge circuit of sleaze: hundreds of millions of pesetas of the so-called *fondos reservados* ('slush funds') of the Interior Ministry had been used for private deals or ended in Swiss accounts.[61]

The atmosphere of widespread political corruption was reminiscent of that of the notables in the first decades of the century. However, the difference now was that neither the rule of law nor public opinion could be ignored. In less than a year five members of the cabinet were forced to resign and dozens of top officials in the civil service, local government, party management and the police faced criminal charges or were under investigation. A new scandal erupted in the summer of 1995 – the secret services had been illegally monitoring the conversations of opposition politicians and even of the king. The Catalan Nationalists stopped supporting the PSOE in the chamber. Consequently, failing to pass the budget in autumn, the government had to dissolve parliament and call early elections for March 1996.

The electoral campaign was the most acrimonious in the democratic era. Fighting for his credibility, Felipe proved once more a formidable communicator. To constant accusations of corruption and sleaze, he claimed to be the victim of a slur campaign whose ultimate goal was to return to power the unreconstructed Right. Clever exploitation of memories of the dictatorship, appeals for tactical voting and Aznar's lack of personal magnetism favoured the Socialists. Ignoring the barrage of scandals, the electoral coalition which held the PSOE in power for 14 years remained mostly loyal. Thus far from being routed as in Italy and France, the Socialists returned 141 deputies. Those who had hoped that a crushing defeat for the PSOE would usher in a period of self-examination, reform and renewal within Spanish Socialism were disappointed. So too were IU, whose hopes of displacing the PSOE as the new hegemonic Leftist force, by focusing on the government's criminal and immoral activities, were shattered. IU's twenty-one seats, the best outcome since 1979, was far short of its objectives.

The electoral results of 1996 opened a new chapter in Spain's history. Although the political balance shifted from Left to Right, the latter was denied a blank cheque. The PP won a bitter victory. Far from achieving the massive swing that all the opinion polls had predicted, their 156 seats left them nineteen short of an overall majority and thus dependent on the Nationalist parties, CiU and PNV who, with sixteen and five deputies respectively, became the arbiters of politics.[62]

Initially, when polls closed, PP supporters chanted 'Pujol, you dwarf, now you will have to speak Castilian.' However, the results imposed political pragmatism over deeply rooted historical prejudices. It is this necessary collaboration between the PP and the Catalan and Basque Nationalists that offers an historic opportunity to end terrorism once and for all. Aznar and his party have been forced to moderate their entrenched centralism and it has been, paradoxically, his right-wing government that since 1996 has been responsible for the greatest degree of devolution in economic, cultural and administrative prerogatives to the regions. This shift from confrontation to co-operation between the centre and the peripheral nationalisms paves the way for dialogue and could lead to the isolation of those who pursue terrorist methods. Recent events, the rescue in July 1997 of a prison officer kept hostage for 18 months by ETA followed by the kidnapping and callous execution of a PP councillor in a small Basque village, have sparked the largest spontaneous mass mobilizations in Spanish history. For the first time, even sectors historically supportive of ETA, including some of its imprisoned members, have condemned the latest spate of violence. The PP can build on this momentum and seek a political solution on the wave of national outcries for peace. Only when central administrations in Madrid recognize the existence of distinctive nations within the Spanish state, and even accept their right to self-determination, can the last remaining ghosts of the Civil War be laid to rest.

NOTES

1 Introduction

1. D. Blackbourn and G. Eley, *The Peculiarities of German History* (Oxford: Oxford University Press, 1991), pp. 169–74.
2. G. Tortella, 'Agriculture: A Slow Moving Sector, 1830–1935', in N. Sánchez-Albornoz (ed.), *The Economic Modernization of Spain, 1830–1930* (New York: New York University Press, 1987), p. 45.
3. J. Nadal, 'The Failure of the Industrial Revolution in Spain, 1830–1914', in C. M. Cipolla (ed.), *The Fontana Economic History of Europe*, Vol. VI, Part Two: *The Emergence of Industrial Nations* (Hassocks: the Harvester Press, 1976), pp. 556, 567.
4. A. Shubert, *A Social History of Modern Spain* (London: Unwin Hyman, 1990), p. 60.
5. M. Tuñón de Lara, *Estudios de historia contemporánea* (Barcelona: Nova Terra, 1977), p. 98.
6. The disentailment of the land began in 1836 under the minister and financier Juan Alvarez Mendizábal. His main target was the expropriation of the property owned by the secular as well as the regular clergy. It was sold at public auction with payment in either cash or government debt. Common and municipal lands were for the time being only leased out. It was not until the passing of the so-called Law of General Disentailment by Pascual Madoz in 1855 that all the land not privately owned was sold at public auction.
7. The two main political factions were the so-called *Moderados* and the *Progresistas*. The *Moderados* were the party of the upper classes, who believed in a political sovereignty shared by the Crown and parliament and quickly re-established good relations with the Catholic Church. The *Progresistas* appealed more to the middle classes. They were more anti-clerical and supported parliamentary sovereignty, elected municipal governments and the establishment of citizens' militias under local control. Yet both models were essentially centralist and restricted the franchise to those with large property. The *Progresistas* granted the vote in 1837 to 2.2 per cent of the population which was later restricted by the *Moderados* in 1845 to just 0.8 per cent of the country. In 1856 the *Progresistas* extended the franchise to over 4 per cent of the population.
8. Nadal, op.cit., p. 541.

9. C. Trebilcock, *The Industrialization of the Continental Powers, 1780–1914* (London: Longman, 1981), p. 307.
10. Nadal, op.cit., pp. 549–53.
11. The Cuban revolt lasted 10 years between 1868 and 1878. General Prim, the strong man of the new regime, was killed in the streets of Madrid. It remains a mystery who was behind this assassination.
12. R. Herr, *An Historical Essay on Modern Spain* (Berkeley, CA: University of California Press, 1974), p. 110.
13. M. Tuñón de Lara, *Poder y sociedad en España, 1900–1931* (Madrid: Colección Austral, 1992), pp. 108-19, 202–11.
14. J. Varela Ortega, *Los amigos políticos: Partidos, elecciones y caciquismo en la Restauración, 1875–1900* (Madrid: Alianza Editorial, l977), pp. 359–66.
15. J. Romero Maura, 'El caciquismo: tentativa de conceptualización', pp. 19–22 and J. Varela Ortega, 'Los amigos políticos: funcionamiento del sistema caciquista', p. 55, both in *Revista de Occidente*, no. 127 (October 1973).
16. J. Nadal, 'A Century of Industrialization in Spain, 1833–1930', in Sánchez-Albornoz (ed.), *The Economic Modernization of Spain*, p. 64.
17. Nadal, *The Failure*, pp. 558–9.
18. Tortella, op.cit., p. 52.
19. R. Carr, *Modern Spain, 1875–1980* (Oxford: Oxford University Press, 1980), p. 20.
20. J. C. Ullman, *The Tragic Week: A Study in Anticlericalism in Spain, 1875–1912* (Cambridge, MA: Harvard University Press, 1968), p. 35.
21. F. Lannon, *Privilege, Persecution and Prophecy: The Catholic Church in Spain, 1875–1975* (Oxford: Clarendon Press, 1987), pp. 121–2.
22. M. Ballbé, *Orden público y militarismo en la España constitucional, 1812–1983* (Madrid: Alianza Editorial, 1985), pp. 247–8; J. Lleixá, *Cien años de militarismo* (Barcelona: Anagrama, 1986), p. 60.
23. R. Núñez Florencio, *El terrorismo anarquista, 1888–1909* (Madrid: Siglo XXI, 1983), pp. 45–60; F. Olaya Morales, *Historia del movimiento obrero español* (Madrid: Siglo XXI, 1994), pp. 631–65, 813–34.
24. C. Serrano, *Final del Imperio: España, 1895–1898* (Madrid: Siglo XXI, 1984), pp. 14–17.
25. J. Smith, *The Spanish-American War: Conflict in the Caribbean and the Pacific, 1895–1902* (London: Longman, 1994), pp. 2–3.
26. Serrano, op.cit., p. 12.
27. M. Golay, *The Spanish-American War* (New York: Facts on File, 1995), pp. 6–9; Smith, op.cit., pp. 28–30.
28. Cánovas was the first to make that speech in the *Cortes* in July 1891. Sagasta expressed himself in similar terms in March 1895.
29. Golay, op.cit., p. 4.
30. Smith, op.cit., pp. 13–14.
31. Smith, op.cit., pp. 30–47; Serrano, op.cit., pp. 32–3.
32. R. Pérez Delgado, *1898. El año del desastre* (Madrid: Tebas, 1976), pp. 292–4.
33. E. Moradiellos, '1898: A Colonial Disaster Foretold', *Association for Contemporary Iberian Studies (ACIS)*, 6, no. 2 (Autumn 1993), p. 36; J. Varela Ortega, 'Aftermath of Splendid Disaster: Spanish Politics before and after

the Spanish American War of 1898', *Journal of Contemporary History*, vol. 15 (1980), pp. 319–22; Serrano, op.cit., pp. 38–40.

34. Serrano, op.cit., p. 41; Varela Ortega, 'Aftermath', pp. 323–5.
35. Admiral Cervera, in charge of the Spanish fleet in the Atlantic, summed up the situation when he declared that the navy had been sacrificed 'because unlike the army, it was unable to stage a coup'.
36. Pérez, op.cit., pp. 363–4.
37. The United States offered a cash gift of 20 million dollars for the cession of the Philippines.

2 The Liberal Monarchy: The Politics of Notables, 1898–1923

1. Pérez, *1898*, pp. 394–5.
2. Tuñón, *España: la quiebra de 1898* (Madrid: Sarpe, 1986), p. 13.
3. Varela, 'Aftermath', pp. 332–9; J. Harrison, 'The Regenerationist Movement in Spain after the Disaster of 1898', *European Studies Review*, vol. 9 (1979), pp. 8–23.
4. A. Yanini, 'La manipulación electoral en España: sufragio universal y participación ciudadana (1891–1923)', in J. Tusell (ed.), *El sufragio universal* (Madrid: Ayer no. 3, 1991), p. 102.
5. Lerroux has historically been vilified by Socialist, Syndicalist and Catalanist authors. Modern historiography has, to a certain extent, rescued Lerroux's tarnished reputation by trying to find a balance between his opportunism and close collaboration with Liberal governments in Madrid with his ability to create a modern political party by mobilizing elements of the proletariat and petty bourgeoisie, formerly unrepresented within the Spanish political system. See J. Romero-Maura, 'La rosa de fuego'. *El obrerismo barcelonés de 1899 a 1909* (Madrid: Alianza Editorial, 1989); J. Alvarez Junco, *El Emperador del Paralelo: Lerroux y la demagogia populista* (Madrid: Alianza Editorial, 1990); J. R. Mosher, *The Birth of Mass Politics in Spain: Lerrouxismo in Barcelona, 1901–1909* (New York: Garland, 1991).
6. Some 121 000 workers, 80 000 of them in Andalucía, affiliated to the Spanish Regional Federation (1870–81), the Spanish section of the First International. At the Congress held at Seville in 1882, a new Regional Federation of Spanish Workers was created. It had a total of 57 934 members, almost 40 000 in Andalucía, most of the rest were from Cataluña. The Socialists could not have had more than 3000 members at the time. Internal divisions and state repression brought about the disappearance of the Anarchist organization in 1888.
7. D. Geary, *European Labour Protest, 1848–1939* (London: Methuen, 1984), pp. 112–13.
8. P. Heywood, *Marxism and the Failure of Organized Socialism in Spain, 1879–1936* (Cambridge: University Press, 1990), pp. 2–3; F. Pérez Ledesma, *El pensamiento socialista español a comienzos de siglo* (Madrid: Centro, 1974), pp. 27–34.
9. B. Martin, *The Agony of Modernization: Labour and Industrialization in Spain* (Ithaca: ILR Press, 1990), p. 98.

10. See J. J. Morato, *Pablo Iglesias: Educador de muchedumbres* (Madrid; UGT, 1926), pp. 121–2.

Pablo Iglesias and two other Socialists were elected as local councillors for Madrid in the local elections of 1905 by using forged ballot papers.

11. J. P. Fusi, *Política obrera en el País Vasco, 1880–1923* (Madrid: Turner, 1975), pp. 81–94; A. Shubert, *The Road to Revolution in Asturias: The Coal Miners of Asturias, 1860–1934* (Chicago, IL: University of Illinois Press, 1987), p. 108.

12. J. Alvarez Junco, *La ideología política del anarquismo español (1868–1910)* (Madrid: Siglo XXI, 1976), pp. 593–8.

13. Núñez, *Terrorismo*, p. 189.

14. E. González Calleja, 'La razón de la fuerza. Una perspectiva de la violencia política en la España de la Restauración', in J. Aróstegui (ed.), *Violencia y política en España* (Madrid: Ayer no.13, 1994), p. 97.

15. A. Bar, *La CNT en los años rojos, 1910–1926* (Madrid: Akal, 1981), pp. 54–9.

16. During his reign, political crises were known as *'orientales'* as they were produced and resolved at the Palace of Oriente, Alfonso's residence. See Varela, *Los amigos*, pp. 450–1.

17. C. Seco Serrano, *Militarismo y civilismo en la España contemporánea* (Madrid: Instituto de Estudios Econòmicos, 1984), p. 233. In 1900 there were 499 generals, 578 colonels and over 23 000 officers for some 80 000 troops (six times more officers than in France which had an standing army of 180 000 soldiers). This represented a cancer for the state which devoted over 40 per cent of its expenditure to defence. However, 70 per cent of the military budget went on officers' salaries, hence neglecting the modernization of the armed services.

18. Ballbé, *Orden*, pp. 272–7.

19. A. Balcells, *Catalan Nationalism* (London: Macmillan, 1996), pp. 55–8.

20. In February 1901 Maura warned that if the regime did not lead a revolution from above, it would be overthrown by an insurrection from below. See G. Maura and M. Fernández Almagro, *Por qué cayó Alfonso XIII* (Madrid: Ambos Mundos, l948), p. 40.

21. Maura had opposed the introduction of the Law of Jurisdictions by the Liberals in 1906. A certain mutual admiration and co-operation was sealed after 1907 between Maura and Cambó. Yet the *Lliga* refused to become the Catalan branch of the Conservative party.

22. The best analysis of the Tragic Week is Connelly Ullman, *The Tragic Week*; more recent is P. Voltes, *La semana trágica* (Madrid: Espasa Calpe, 1995). Ferrer Guardia hardly played any part in the Tragic Week. He was condemned for his historical position as leading Anarchist thinker and his possible part in the assassination attempt against Alfonso XIII in 1906. That action was carried out by Mateo Morral, a teacher in Ferrer's school. In 1907 he was tried but acquitted for lack of evidence. In 1909, Ferrer was used as scapegoat for the tragic events. A decisive factor in his sentence was the accusation of several Radical politicians that he had been the chief of the rebellion. In fact, they had more to answer for than Ferrer.

23. T. G. Trice, *Spanish Liberalism in Crisis: A Study of the Liberal Party during Spain's Parliamentary Collapse, 1913–1923* (New York: Garland, 1991), p. 26; Maura and Fernández, op.cit., pp. 154–5, 240–1.

24. They included regulation of working conditions, labour insurance, the right of religious freedom in public and the famous Padlock Law which halted the further growth of religious orders in Spain.

25. Romanones embodies probably better than anybody else the stereotype of leading dynastic notable of the era – a clear representative of the Castilian landed oligarchy, but also a financier, one of the largest investors in the Moroccan mines and a courtier. He was well known for his cynical approach to politics, lack of ideological principles and his ability to 'make' elections. The philosopher and novelist Miguel de Unamuno wrote that 'the limit of a semantic paradox was that Romanones was one of the leaders of Spanish Liberalism'.

26. M. Fernández Almagro, *Historia del reinado de Alfonso XIII* (Barcelona: Montaner, 1977), pp. 191–3.

27. Fernández Almagro, op.cit., pp. 257–60; M. J. González Hernández, *Ciudadanía y acción: el conservadurismo maurista, 1907–1923* (Madrid: Siglo XXI, 1990), pp. 39–40; F. J. Romero Salvadó, 'Maura, Maurismo and the Crisis of 1917', in *ACIS*, vol. 7, no. 1 (Spring 1994), pp. 17–18.

28. Bar, op.cit., pp. 176–207.

29. In 1910 the Radical Party still cashed in on the events of July 1909 to obtain a resounding electoral victory. Under a cloud of financial scandals, the Socialists expelled them from the *conjunción* in December. By 1914, the Radicals' popularity and credibility among Catalan workers was in clear decline.

30. Fusi, op.cit., pp. 297–301.

31. Maura and Fernández, *Por Qué*, pp. 472–3.

32. F. J. Romero Salvadó, 'Spain and the First World War: The Structural Crisis of the Liberal Monarchy', *European History Quarterly*, vol. 25, no. 4 (October 1995), p. 532.

33. G. Meaker, 'A Civil War of Words', in H. A. Schmitt (ed.), *Neutral Europe between War and Revolution, 1917–1923* (Charlottesville: The University of Virginia Press, 1988), pp. 6–7.

34. Unlike the UGT–PSOE, led by a partisan pro-Allied leadership, the CNT opposed any involvement in a 'capitalist' war.

35. Romero, 'Spain', pp. 533–4.

36. J. L. García Delgado, S. Roldán and J. Muñoz, *La formación de la sociedad capitalista en España, 1914–1920* (Madrid: CEIC, 1973); Instituto de Reformas Sociales, *Movimientos de precios al por menor durante la guerra* (Madrid: IRS, 1923).

37. J. A. Lacomba, *La crisis española de 1917* (Málaga: Ciencia Nueva, 1970), pp. 28–32.

38. A. Saborit, *Julián Besteiro* (México: P. Iglesias, 1961), pp. 87–8; Heywood, *Marxism*, p. 41.

39. Saborit, op.cit., pp. 92–4.

40. Alba's power base was Valladolid, the heart of the Castilian wheat lobby. The best study of Alba's economic programme is M. Cabrera, F. Comín and J. L. García Delgado, *Santiago Alba: un programa de reforma económica en la España del primer tercio del Siglo XX* (Madrid: Instituto de Estudios Fiscales, 1989), pp. 251–367; also see J. Harrison, *The Spanish Economy in the Twentieth Century* (London: Croom Helm, 1985), pp. 41–4.

41. F. Cambó, *Memorias* (Madrid: Alianza Editorial, 1987), pp. 223–4, 246.
42. C. P. Boyd, *Praetorian Politics in Liberal Spain* (Chapel Hill, NC: University of North Carolina, 1979), pp. 51–2.
43. B. Márquez and J. Capó, *Las juntas militares de defensa* (Barcelona: Porvenir,1923), pp. 22–4; J. Buxadé, *La bullanga misteriosa de 1917* (Barcelona: Bauzá, 1918), pp. 33–43.
44. Romanones, *Notas de mi vida, 1912–1931* (Madrid: Espasa Calpe, 1947), pp. 94–5.
45. Thirty-one Spanish vessels, 80 000 tons of Spain's merchant fleet, had been sunk by April 1917.
46. Romanones, op.cit., p. 103; Fernández, *Historia*, pp. 205–7. Alfonso aspired to the role of mediator in the Great War and even to organize a peace summit. To confirm that position, in 1915 he set up a bureau to deal with prisoners' conditions, missing citizens, humanitarian aid, etc. However, the Russian Revolution and the subsequent acceptance by the Allies of the new regime moved Alfonso towards the *Germanophile* camp.
47. F. Soldevilla, *El año político de 1917* (Madrid: Julio Cosano, 1918), pp. 164–8.
48. F. Soldevilla, *Tres Revoluciones (Apuntes y notas)* (Madrid: Julio Cosano, 1917), pp. 63–5; Buxadé, op.cit., pp. 43–59.
49. G. Meaker, *The Revolutionary Left in Spain, 1914–1923* (Stanford, CA: Stanford University Press, 1974), p. 69.
50. M. Burgos y Mazo, *Páginas históricas de 1917* (Madrid: Núñez Samper, 1918), p. 59; Lacomba, op.cit., p. 201.
51. On the Assembly see L. Simarro, *Los sucesos de agosto en el parlamento* (Madrid: UGT, 1918), pp. 365–79; F. Soldevilla, *1917*, pp. 325–39.
52. Between June and August 1917, Maura was constantly urged by his followers to take a decision. Some, such as the right-wing Catalan *Maurista*, Gustavo Peyrá, established links with the *Juntas*, and tried to convince Maura to seize power with their support. Others, such as Ossorio or Miguel Maura, encouraged him to join the Assembly and destroy the corrupt political system. They all ran into Maura's categorical opposition. He refused to support the Assembly as it was a subversive manœuvre against the legal order and opposed any contacts with the officers even leaving one of their messengers out in a heavy storm outside his holiday home in Santander. Correspondence between Maura and his followers can be seen in Maura and Fernández, op.cit., pp. 486–8, 492–5.
53. Tuñón, *Poder*, p. 262.
54. M. García Venero (*Melquiades Alvarez: historia de un liberal* (Madrid: Torrent, 1954), p. 350), claims that *agents provocateurs* initiated the transport conflict in Valencia. However, the Socialist Manuel Cordero (*Los socialistas y la revolución* (Madrid: Torrent, 1932), pp. 30–3, argues that the imprudence of local Republicans caused the strike.
55. Meaker, *Revolutionary*, pp. 83–4; Buxadé, op.cit., pp. 23, 218–30; García Venero, op.cit., pp. 344–5.
56. Simarro, op.cit., p.167.
57. Saborit, op.cit., pp. 100–2.
58. On the August revolution see Lacomba, op.cit., pp. 213–84; A. Saborit, *La huelga de agosto de 1917* (Mexico: P. Iglesias, 1967), pp. 67–74;

192 Notes

NotesNotes

F. Soldevila, *1917*, pp. 363–404; J. Serrallonga, 'Motines y revolución. España en 1917', in F. Bonamusa (ed.), *La huelga general* (Madrid: Ayer, 1991), pp. 169–94.

59. Márquez and Capó, op.cit., pp. 68, 216–22.
60. T. Carnero, 'Política sin democracia en España, 1874–1923', *Revista de Occidente*, no. 83 (April 1988) p. 53.
61. On the role played by Cambó during the crisis of October 1917, see J. Pabón, *Cambó* (Barcelona: Alpha, 1952), vol. I, pp. 570–2; Lacomba, op.cit., pp. 318–21; Saborit, *La huelga*, p. 83.
62. Cierva was not chosen by Alhucemas but was imposed by the officers and the personal intervention of the king. See J. de la Cierva, *Notas de mi vida* (Madrid: Reus, 1955), pp. 188–9.
63. T. Carnero, 'Modernització, desenvolupament politic i canvi social: Espanya (1874–1931)', *Recerques*, no. 23 (1989), p. 79.
64. Boyd, op.cit., p. 102–4.
65. Márquez and Capó (op.cit., pp. 104–5) argue that there was a military plot to create a government presided over by Cierva with eight colonels. This opinion is shared by Fernández (op.cit., pp. 259–60) and Seco (*Militarismo*, p. 277).
66. By August 1918, over sixty Spanish vessels, a quarter of the merchant fleet had been sunk by German submarines. More than a hundred sailors had been killed.
67. J. Tusell, *Antonio Maura: Una biografía política* (Madrid: Alianza Editorial, 1994), pp. 183–8.
68. Fernández, op.cit., pp. 267–8.
69. IRS, op.cit., pp. 10–11. Overall prices between 1914 and 1918 had shot up by 72.8 per cent in the cities and 61.8 per cent in the countryside. Salaries over the same period had increased by a mere 25.6 per cent and 35.1 per cent, average male and female worker respectively.
70. Meaker, *Revolutionary*, p. 125.
71. Martin, op.cit., p. 195.
72. In fact, the first proper Communist Party had been formed in April 1920 by a group of the Socialist Youth in Madrid. Both Communist parties merged in November 1921.
73. F. J. Romero Salvadó, 'The Views of an Anarcho-Syndicalist on the Soviet Union: the Defeat of the Third International in Spain', *Revolutionary Russia*, vol. 8, no. 1 (June 1995), pp. 26–103.
74. J. Díaz del Moral, *Historia de las agitaciones campesinas andaluzas* (Madrid: Alianza Editorial, 1976), pp. 267–73; J. Maurice, *El anarquismo andaluz. Campesinos y sindicalistas, 1868–1936* (Barcelona: Crítica, 1990), pp. 329–47; A. Barragán, *Conflictividad social y desarticulación política en la provincia de Córdoba, 1918–1920* (Córdoba: Posada, 1990), pp. 75–126.
75. Bar, op.cit., pp. 359–431.
76. A. Balcélls, *El sindicalismo en Barcelona* (Barcelona: Nova Terra, 1965), pp. 73–82.
77. Martin, op.cit., p. 218.
78. On the social violence of these years see L. Ignacio, *Los años del pistolerismo. Ensayo para una guerra civil* (Madrid: Planeta, 1981); C. Winston, *Workers*

and the Right in Spain, 1900–1936 (Princeton, NJ: Princeton University Press, 1984).

79. A. Comalada, *El ocaso de un parlamento* (Barcelona: Peninsula, 1985); Boyd, op.cit., pp. 177–82.

80. T. González Calbet, 'La destrucción del sistema político de la Restauración: El golpe de septiembre de 1923', in J. L. García Delgado (ed.), *La crisis de la Restauración: España entre la primera guerra mundial y la segunda Republica* (Madrid: Siglo XXI, 1986), pp. 101–20; J. Tusell, *Radiografía de un golpe de estado: El ascenso al poder del General Primo de Rivera* (Madrid: Alianza Editorial, 1987), pp. 21–8.

3   From Dictatorship to Republic, 1923–31

1. H. Graham and P. Preston (eds), *The Popular Front in Europe* (London: Macmillan, 1987), p. 1.

2. J. L. Gómez Navarro, *El régimen de Primo de Rivera: Reyes, dictaduras y dictadores* (Madrid: Cátedra, 1991), pp. 53–5, 487–8.

3. Ballbé, *Orden*, p. 306.

4. Gómez, op.cit., p. 66.

5. For a detailed narrative of the events surrounding the coup see J. Tusell, *Radiografía de un golpe de estado: El ascenso al poder del General Primo de Rivera* (Madrid: Alianza Editorial, 1987).

6. S. Ben-Ami, *Fascism from Above: The Dictatorship of Primo de Rivera in Spain, 1923–1930* (Oxford: University Press, 1983), pp. 80–1.

7. Colectivo de Historia, 'La Dictadura de Primo de Rivera y el bloque de poder en España', *Cuadernos Económicos de Información Comercial Española*, no. 6 (1978), pp. 191–2.

8. There were among others Puig i Cadafalch, President of the *Mancomunidad*, the Marquis of Alella, Barcelona's Mayor, the Marquis of Comillas, ultra-Catholic magnate and ship-owner, the Viscount of Cusso, President of the industrialists' confederation *Fomento del Trabajo Nacional*, and Cambó's right-hand man, Juan Ventosa.

9. Boyd, *Praetorian*, p. 262.

10. C. Navajas Zubeldia, *Ejército, estado y sociedad en España, 1923–1930* (Logroño: Instituto de Estudios Riojanos, 1991), p. 37; Ben-Ami, op.cit., pp. 63–4.

11. S. Ben-Ami, *The Origins of the Second Republic in Spain* (Oxford: University Press, 1978), pp. 8–9; Boyd, *Praetorian*, pp. 270–1; Gómez, op.cit., pp. 126–9.

12. G. Cardona, *El poder militar en la España contemporánea hasta la guerra civil* (Madrid: Siglo XXI, 1983), pp. 41–3.

13. Maura and Fernández, *Por qué*, p. 533; M. Maura, *Así cayó Alfonso XIII*, 7th edn (Barcelona: Ariel, 1995), p. 39.

14. Ben-Ami, *Fascism*, p. 26.

15. Colectivo, op.cit., p. 187; Tuñón, *Poder*, p. 290.

16. Ben-Ami, *Fascism*, pp. 56–8.

17. Gómez, op.cit., p. 209.

18. Ben-Ami, *Fascism*, p. 163.
19. J. H. Rial, *Revolution from Above: The Primo de Rivera dictatorship in Spain* (London, Associated University Press, 1986), pp. 79–80.
20. Ibid., pp. 81–2.
21. Heywood, *Marxism*, pp. 95–7; Martin, *Agony*, pp. 267–8. An ailing Pablo Iglesias had, since 1917, been effectively succeeded by Julián Besteiro as leader of the Socialist Party. Iglesias finally died on 9 December 1925, followed two days later by the demise of Antonio Maura.
22. Gómez, op.cit., pp. 412–31.
23. Martin, op.cit., pp. 281–4.
24. Ben-Ami, *Fascism*, pp. 299, 308.
25. Colectivo, op.cit., p. 201.
26. Tusell, *Radiografía*, pp. 34–5.
27. S. E. Fleming and A. K. Fleming, 'Primo de Rivera and Spain's Moroccan problem, 1923–27', *Journal of Contemporary History*, vol. 12 (1977), pp. 87–8.
28. Ibid., pp. 90–3.
29. Many *Mauristas* welcomed and supported the dictatorship assuming that Primo was putting into practice Maura's message of revolution from above. However, Maura, a Liberal, first and foremost, until his death in 1925 made clear his distance and dislike for the new regime. See Fernández, *Historia*, p. 362; Maura, op.cit., p. 119.
30. Ben-Ami, 'The Dictatorship of Primo de Rivera: A Political Reassessment', *Journal of Contemporary History*, vol. 12 (1977), pp. 67–70.
31. For an analysis of the social and political membership of UP and its evolution see Gómez, op.cit., pp. 207–60.
32. Ben-Ami, *Fascism*, p. 172.
33. Gómez, op.cit., pp. 303–4, 519.
34. Fernández, op.cit., pp. 357–8.
35. Ben-Ami, *Fascism*, p. 101.
36. Fernández, op.cit., pp. 415–17.
37. González, 'La razón', pp. 106–7.
38. S. Payne, *Los militares y la política en la España contemporánea* (Madrid, Ruedo Ibérico, 1968), pp. 193–4; Navajas, op.cit., pp. 53–7, 137–49.
39. Payne, op.cit., pp. 201–2.
40. González, op.cit., pp. 108–9. Typical of Primo's eccentric character was that after failing to obtain a condemnation of Sánchez Guerra, he commuted the death sentences of several artillery officers involved in the revolt.
41. Harrison, *Spanish Economy*, pp. 69–70.
42. R. Carr, *Spain, 1808–1975* 2nd edn (Oxford: Oxford University Press, 1982), p. 587.
43. Ben-Ami, *Fascism*, pp. 342–3.
44. Tuñón, *Poder*, p. 342; Heywood, op.cit., pp. 101–4.
45. Carr, *1808*, p. 590.
46. Ben-Ami, *Fascism*, pp. 176–7.
47. Maura, op.cit., p. 17.
48. Navajas, op.cit., p. 61.
49. Ibid., pp. 70–1.

50. Maura, op.cit., pp. 44–5, 53.
51. Ben-Ami, *Fascism*, p. 390.
52. Ben-Ami, *Origins*, p. 23.
53. S. Ben-Ami, 'The Republican 'Take-Over': Prelude to Inevitable Catastrophe?', in P. Preston (ed.), *Revolution and War in Spain, 1931–1939* (London: Methuen, 1984), pp. 15–16.
54. For an excellent analysis of the disarray of the dynastic politicians see S. Ben-Ami, 'The Crisis of the Dynastic Elite in the Transition from Monarchy to Republic, 1929–1931', in P. Preston and F. Lannon (eds), *Elites and Power in Twentieth-Century Spain: Essays in Honour of Sir Raymond Carr* (Oxford: Oxford University Press, 1990); also see M. Suárez Cortina, *El reformismo en España* (Madrid: Siglo XXI, 1986), pp. 295–9.
55. Ben-Ami, *Origins*, p. 31.
56. Ben-Ami, 'Republican', pp. 17–18.
57. Ben-Ami, *Origins*, pp. 47–55, 68–76.
58. Ibid., pp. 56–7.
59. Maura, op.cit., pp. 69–72.
60. Martin, op.cit., p. 293.
61. Being aware of Galán's intentions, the provisional government sent one of its members, the Galician Republican Casares Quiroga, to stop him but he arrived too late.
62. The exception was Lerroux, raising once more questions about his political dealings, as although a prominent member of the provisional government, he was not arrested. According to M. Maura (op.cit., p. 105), the police informed him that Lerroux was not to be molested! The other Republicans could never conceal their distrust for the Radicals and their shady reputation. In San Sebastian, they agreed not to give them any portfolios with economic responsibilities.
63. J. Aróstegui, 'El insurreccionalismo en la crisis de la Restauración', in J. L. García Delgado (ed.), *La Crisis de la Restauración: España entre la Primera Guerra Mundial y la II República* (Madrid: Siglo XXI, 1986), pp. 92–3.
64. Ben-Ami, *Origins*, pp. 202–5.
65. Maura, op.cit., pp. 121–4.
66. Tuñón, *Poder*, pp. 367–9.
67. Due to a grave illness, Cambó, the *Lliga*'s leader, remained on the sidelines for over a year. In the meantime, his party, following in its traditional footsteps of accidentalism and opportunism, left all doors open. The decision to join the cabinet in March and bet on the continuity of the regime, proved a serious miscalculation which only accelerated the decline of the *Lliga* in Catalan politics. Both *Mauristas* and the *Lliga* founded a new group in March, the *Centro Constitucional*, as the foundation of a modern conservative party. It never really took off and came too late to save the monarchy.
68. Maura, op.cit., p. 126.
69. Cierva, *Notas*, pp. 342–3.
70. Seco, *Militarismo*, pp. 370–1; Maura, op.cit., pp. 132–7.
71. Ben-Ami, 'Crisis', pp. 81–3.
72. Maura and Fernández, *Por qué*, p. 387.
73. Ben-Ami, 'Crisis', p. 86.

74. According to Maura (op.cit., pp. 145, 152, 180–1), the Republicans initially welcomed the results as the perfect step in order to win the forthcoming general elections, but feared the possible announcement of martial law and their subsequent arrest. They were genuinely surprised but took advantage of the Monarchist disintegration during the next twenty-four hours.
75. Fernández, op.cit., pp. 469–70.
76. Gómez, op.cit., pp. 526–7.
77. Ben-Ami, *Origins*, pp. 238–47; Maura, op.cit., pp. 165–6.
78. Maura, op.cit., p. 189.

4   The Second Republic: A Brief Exercise in Democracy, 1931–6

1. Rial, *Revolution*, p. 233.
2. M. Tuñón de Lara, *La II República* (Madrid: Siglo XXI, 1976), vol. 1, p. 76.
3. E. Malefakis, 'Peculiaridad de la república española', *Revista de Occidente* (November 1981), pp. 25–7.
4. Lannon, *Privilege*, pp. 179–82.
5. S. Juliá, *Manuel Azaña: Una biografía política* (Madrid: Alianza Editorial, 1991), pp. 98–110; Cardona, *Poder militar*, pp. 159–66.
6. P. Preston, *The Coming of the Spanish Civil War: Reform, Reaction and Revolution in the Second Republic* (London: Routledge, 1994), pp. 80–1; E. Malefakis, *Agrarian Reform and Peasant Revolution in Spain* (London: Yale University Press, 1970), pp. 166–8.
7. M. Cabrera, *La patronal ante la II República: Organizaciones y estrategia, 1931–1936* (Madrid: Siglo XXI, 1983), pp. 15, 253.
8. M. Cabrera, 'Las cortes republicanas', in S. Juliá (ed.), *Política en la Segunda República* (Madrid: Ayer no. 20, 1995), p. 17.
9. Preston, *The Coming*, pp. 38–40. M. Blinkhorn, *Democracy and Civil war in Spain, 1931–1939* (London: Routledge, 1988), pp. 13–16.
10. S. Payne, *Spain's First Democracy: The Second Republic, 1931–1936* (London: University of Wisconsin Press, 1993), pp. 121–2.
11. Maura, *Así*, pp. 298–304; Lannon, op.cit., p. 188.
12. Lannon, op.cit., pp. 163–4.
13. Preston, *The Coming*, pp. 50–1.
14. Cabrera, *Patronal*, p. 19.
15. Ibid., pp. 275–8.
16. Malefakis, *Agrarian*, pp. 166–70; Schubert, *Social History*, p. 101.
17. P. Preston, 'The Agrarian War in the South', in P. Preston (ed.), *Revolution and War in Spain, 1931–1939* (London: Methuen, 1984), p. 159.
18. The total UGT membership grew from less than 300 000 in December 1930 to more than a million in June 1932. The sudden growth of the FNTT was greatly out of proportion with the overall growth of the UGT. The FNTT constituted about 10 per cent of the total UGT membership in 1930, two years later it was nearly 40 per cent.
19. Lannon, op.cit., pp. 166–9; Cabrera, *Patronal*, pp. 63–5.

20. Preston, *The Coming*, pp. 2, 77–80; Preston, 'Agrarian', pp. 160–1, 165–7.
21. Martin, *Agony*, pp. 310–11.
22. There were insurrections all over the country, but the worst outcome was in Sevilla where in the general strike of July more than twenty people were killed.
23. Tuñón, *La II República*, vol.1, pp. 70–1.
24. Malefakis, 'Peculiaridad', p. 31.
25. The Catholic Minister of the Interior, Miguel Maura, praised the spirit of compromise and the lack of feelings of revenge which presided over the members of the Republican government. He singled out for their moderation and sense of responsibility the Socialist Indalecio Prieto and Fernando de los Ríos. Maura also stressed the subversive and conspiratorial activities of influential elements in the Church's hierarchy leaving him with no option but to expel them from the country. See Maura, op.cit., pp. 82, 210, 217–22, 246–62, 296–305.
26. Ibid., pp. 84–8.
27. Ben-Ami, *The Coming*, pp. 289–91.
28. S. Juliá, 'Sistema de partidos y problemas de consolidación de la democracia', in Juliá (ed.), *Política*, p. 125.
29. The role played by Lerroux during these events is ambiguous. It seems that the Radical leader had been in close touch with Sanjurjo before the coup, but the Azaña cabinet preferred to avoid investigating these contacts that if exposed could have a devastating effect on public opinion. See E. Ucelay-Da Cal, 'Buscando el levantamiento plebiscitario: insurrecionalismo y elecciones', in Juliá (ed.), *Política*, pp. 71–2.
30. Juliá, *Azaña*, p. 183.
31. Preston, *The Coming*, pp. 60–3.
32. The best analysis of the agrarian reform can be found in Malefakis, *Agrarian*, pp. 172–257.
33. Ballbé, *Orden*, pp. 357–8.
34. Malefakis, *Agrarian*, pp. 258–60.
35. G. Esenwein and A. Shubert, *The Spanish Civil War in Context, 1931–1939* (London: Longman, 1995), pp. 13–14; Preston, *The Coming*, pp. 7–37, 106–17; Heywood, *Marxism*, pp. 110–26.
36. J. Avilés Farré, *La izquierda burguesa en la II República* (Madrid: Espasa-Calpe, 1985), pp. 191–6.
37. Juliá, 'Sistema', pp. 125–6.
38. At the Thirteenth Congress of the PSOE in October 1932 the followers of Largo Caballero and those of Prieto collaborated in defeating Besteiro, and Largo Caballero became the PSOE's President. The *Besteiristas* were finally ousted from the UGT in January 1934 when a new executive dominated by *Caballeristas* was appointed.
39. Tuñón, *La II República*, vol. 2, pp. 12–15.
40. Payne, *Spain's First*, p. 185.
41. Cabrera, 'Cortes', pp. 33–5.
42. Cabrera, *Patronal*, p. 132.
43. Juliá, 'Sistema', pp. 130–1.

44. Avilés, op.cit., pp. 238, 246–7.
45. Blinkhorn, *Democracy*, pp. 23–4.
46. Cabrera, *Patronal*, pp. 21–2; Malefakis, *Agrarian*, pp. 321–9; Esenwein and Shubert, op.cit., p. 18.
47. Malefakis, *Agrarian*, pp. 333–4.
48. José M. Macarro, 'Sindicalismo y política', in Juliá (ed.), *Política*, pp. 160–1, 163–4.
49. Preston, 'Agrarian', pp. 174–6.
50. Companys had become President of the *Generalitat* and leader of the *Esquerra* after the death of Francesc Maciá in December 1933.
51. Balcells, *Catalan*, pp. 107–8.
52. Cabrera, *Patronal*, pp. 173–5.
53. Preston, *The Coming*, pp. 66–70.
54. Ibid., p. 126.
55. Ballbé, *Orden*, pp. 371–3.
56. Luis Sirval, a journalist who dared to report the brutalities committed in Asturias was assassinated by members of the Foreign Legion.
57. Tuñón, *La II República*, vol. 2, pp. 78–98.
58. Preston, *The Coming*, p. 184.
59. Malefakis, *Agrarian*, pp. 347–61; Cabrera, *Patronal*, pp. 169–72.
60. Ballbé, op.cit., pp. 378–82; Preston, *The Coming*, pp. 188–91.
61. The so-called *straperlo* gambling fraud exploded in October and involved the collusion of several ministers and even Lerroux's step-son with an international swindler, the Dutchman Daniel Strauss. One month later a new scandal appeared affecting the misappropriation of public funds by other Radical ministers.
62. Preston, *The Coming*, p. 200.
63. Payne, *Militares*, p. 270.
64. Juliá, *Azaña*, p. 345.
65. Ibid., pp. 411–19.
66. For the schisms in the Socialist movement see Juliá, *Azaña*, pp. 421–8; Preston, *The Coming*, pp. 211–38; Heywood, op.cit., pp. 146–71.
67. The POUM was a small group of dissident Communists concentrated in some small areas of Cataluña. It had been created in November 1935 by the merging of two groups led by two former Anarcho-Syndicalists, Joaquín Maurín's Workers and Peasants Bloc (BOC) and the Communist Left (IC) of Andreu Nin, Trotsky's former secretary.
68. Tuñón, *La II República*, p. 166.
69. Preston, *The Coming*, pp. 242–4; Payne, *Militares*, pp. 272–3.
70. Malefakis, *Agrarian*, pp. 375–81.
71. Preston, *The Coming*, p. 247.
72. Cabrera, *Patronal*, pp. 44–7.
73. H. Graham, 'The Spanish Popular Front and the Civil War', in Graham and Preston, *The Popular Front*, p. 110.
74. For Miguel Maura, op.cit., p. 222, the Socialist veto on Prieto was a catastrophe which inevitably sealed the end of the Republic; see Preston, *The Coming*, pp. 241, 261–4.
75. Preston, *The Coming*, p. 265.

5 A Modern Crusade: The Spanish Tragedy, 1936–9

1. S. Juliá, 'El fracaso de la República', in *Revista de Occidente* (November 1981), pp. 199–200.
2. Graham and Preston (eds), *The Popular Front*, p. 1.
3. H. Thomas, *The Spanish Civil War*, 3rd edn (Harmondsworth: Penguin, 1986), pp. 215–57, 327–33; G. Jackson, *The Spanish Republic and the Civil War, 1931–1939*, 5th edn (Princeton, NJ: Princeton University Press, 1972), pp. 231–46.
4. P. Preston, *A Concise History of the Spanish Civil War* (London: HarperCollins, 1996), p. 98.
5. T. G. Powell, *Mexico and the Spanish Civil War* (Albuquerque, NM: University of New Mexico Press, 1981), pp. 58–60, 71–5, 96–9.
6. *L'Ouvre de Léon Blum* (Paris: Albis Michel, 1965), vol. IV, 2, pp. 373–5; W. L. Shirer, *The Collapse of the Third Republic* (London: Cox & Wyman, 1970), pp. 272–4; J. Lacouture, *Léon Blum* (New York: Holmes & Meier, 1982), pp. 305–7; H. Haywood Hunt, 'The French Radicals, Spain and Appeasement', in M. S. Alexander and H. Graham, *The French and Spanish Popular Fronts: Comparative Perspectives* (Cambridge: University Press, 1989), pp. 38–49; J. Avilés Farré, *Pasión y farsa: Franceses y Británicos ante la Guerra Civil Española* (Madrid: Eudema, 1994), pp. 2–10.
7. See the works by E. Moradiellos: *Neutralidad Benévola: El gobierno británico y la insurrección militar española de 1936* (Oviedo: Pentalfa, 1990), pp. 77–103, 117–33, 147–88, 211–14; 'The Origins of British Non-Intervention in the Spanish Civil War: Anglo-Spanish Relations in Early 1936', *European History Quarterly*, vol. 21 (1991), pp. 339–61; 'British Political Strategy in the Face of the Military Rising of 1936 in Spain', *Contemporary European History*, vol. 1, no. 2 (1992), pp. 123–9; 'The Gentle General: The Official British Perception of General Franco during the Spanish Civil War', in P. Preston and A. L. Mackenzie, *The Republic Besieged: Civil War in Spain, 1936–1939* (Edinburgh: University Press, 1996), pp. 2–9; *La Perfidia de Albión* (Madrid: Siglo XXI, 1996), pp. 18–51, 58–64; see also Avilés, op.cit., pp. 4, 9–14; J. Edwards, *The British Government and the Spanish Civil War* (London: Macmillan, 1979), pp. 80–100.
8. M. Alpert, *A New International History of the Spanish Civil War* (London: Macmillan 1994), pp. 54–5; Thomas, op.cit., p. 360.
9. Britain was the main investor in Spain with 687.5 million pesetas, followed by France with 439.6 million. Germany's capital investments amounted only to 10.3 million pesetas.
10. A. Viñas, *La Alemania nazi y el 18 de julio* (Madrid: Alianza Editorial, 1977), pp. 13–14, 322–96; R. H. Whealey, *Hitler and Spain: The Nazi Role in the Spanish Civil War, 1936–1939* (Lexington: The University Press of Kentucky, 1989), pp. 5–9, 28–9; C. Leitz, 'Nazi Germany's Intervention in the Spanish Civil War and the Foundation of HISMA/ROWAK', in Preston and Mackenzie (eds), *The Republic*, pp. 55–63.
11. I. Saz, *Mussolini contra la II República* (Valencia: Alfons el Magnánim, 1986), pp. 39–210; P. Preston, 'Mussolini's Spanish Adventure: From Limited Risk to War', in Preston and Mackenzie (eds), *The Republic*, pp. 31–45.

12. Thomas, op.cit., p. 376.
13. Ibid., p. 374.
14. Leigh, op.cit., pp. 63–4; Whealey, op.cit., p. 14.
15. Preston, *Concise*, pp. 99–100; Lacouture, op.cit., pp. 312–13.
16. Shirer, op.cit., pp. 251–2, 281–5; Lacouture, op.cit., pp. 322–9.
17. Moradiellos, *La perfidia*, pp. 66–72.
18. Moradiellos, *Neutralidad*, pp. 189–210, 285–8.
19. Moradiellos, *La perfidia*, pp. 81–7, 111–14; M. Kitchen, *Europe between the Wars* (London: Longman, 1988), p. 249.
20. For personal accounts of members of the International Brigades, see among others, B. Alexander, *British Volunteers for Spain* (London: Lawrence & Wishart, 1986); J. Gurney, *Crusade in Spain* (Devon: Faber, 1974); A. Landis, *The Abraham Lincoln Brigade* (New York: Citadel Press, 1967).
21. D. Smyth, 'We Are with You: Solidarity and Self-Interest in Soviet Policy towards Republican Spain, 1936–1939', in Preston and Mackenzie (eds), *The Republic*, pp. 88–100; Alpert, op.cit., pp. 10–11, 49–52.
22. Thomas, op.cit., p. 432.
23. Jackson, op.cit., pp. 319–32.
24. P. Preston, *Franco: A Biography* (London: HarperCollins, 1993), pp. 205–6.
25. Whealey, op.cit., pp. 48–50.
26. Avilés, op.cit., pp. 52–6.
27. A. Viñas, 'Gold, the Soviet Union and the Spanish Civil War', in M. Blinkhorn (ed.), *Spain in Conflict, 1931–1939: Democracy and its Enemies* (London: Sage, 1986), pp. 222–43.
28. Leigh, op.cit., pp. 65–72; Whealey, op.cit., pp. 74–93.
29. P. Preston, *Franco*, pp.1–144; J. Tusell, *Franco en la Guerra Civil: Una biografía política* (Madrid: Tusquets, 1993), pp. 15–33; A. Reig Tapia, *Franco Caudillo: Mito y Realidad* (Madrid: Tecnos, 1995), pp. 68–75.
30. There were several attempts to rescue José Antonio, but Franco's half-hearted support served to undermine them and so helped secure his execution. See Preston, *Franco*, pp. 193–6.
31. Thomas, op.cit., pp. 258–67; Preston, *Franco*, p. 146; Reig, op.cit., pp. 192–3.
32. Cabanellas in Zaragoza was the only army commander in one of the eight military regions who joined the insurrection. A majority of division and brigadier generals remained loyal to the government. However, most colonels and junior officers revolted against the Republic. Cardona, *El poder militar*, pp. 307–9.
33. Tusell, op.cit., pp. 40–9.
34. Preston, *Concise*, pp. 83–4.
35. Thomas, op.cit., pp. 408–13.
36. Preston, *Franco*, pp. 175–84; Tusell, op.cit., pp. 52–6; S. Ellwood, *Franco* (London: Longman, 1994), p. 85.
37. Thomas, op.cit., pp. 414–16; Preston, *Concise*, pp. 158–60.
38. P. Preston, 'Francisco Franco: Política y estrategia en la Guerra Civil', *Revista de Extremadura* (September–December 1996), pp. 3–27.
39. Thomas, op.cit., pp. 598–604.
40. Preston, *Franco*, pp. 242–7.
41. Ibid., pp. 292–4.

42. Thomas, op.cit., pp. 797–803.
43. Preston, *Franco*, pp. 248–74.
44. Tusell, op.cit., pp. 69–75.
45. Preston, *Concise*, pp. 148–53.
46. I. Saz 'Salamanca, '1937: los fundamentos de un régimen', *Revista de Extremadura* (September–December 1996), pp. 82–105.
47. Preston, *Franco*, pp. 285–300.
48. Thomas, op.cit., pp. 219–230.
49. G. Cardona, 'La sublevación de Julio', in *Socialismo y Guerra Civil: Anales de la Historia*; vol. 2 (1987), p. 29.
50. J. Casanova, 'Anarquismo y Guerra Civil: del poder popular a la burocracia revolucionaria', pp. 73–8; M. Tuñón de Lara, 'Los mecanismos del estado en la zona republicana', pp. 124–6, both in *Socialismo y Guerra Civil*.
51. Jackson, op.cit., pp. 276–83; Martin, *Agony*, pp. 383–91.
52. Preston, *Concise*, pp. 145–7, 168–9.
53. Thomas, op.cit., pp. 268–79; Preston, *Concise*, pp. 168–9; Reig, op.cit., pp. 188–95.
54. F. Fernández Bestarreche, 'La estrategia militar republicana durante la guerra civil', in *Socialismo y Guerra Civil*, pp. 50–1.
55. Thomas, op.cit., pp. 400–8.
56. Jackson, op.cit., p. 341.
57. S. Juliá, 'De la división orgánica al gobierno de unidad nacional', in *Socialismo y Guerra Civil*, pp. 240–4.
58. Martin, *Agony*, pp. 400–1; Jackson, op.cit., pp. 360–1.
59. The POUM cannot be termed a Trotskyist group. Some of its leaders had once been disciples of Trotsky, and the party secretary, Andreu Nin, had been his private secretary in the past. Yet Trotsky cut links with the POUM after that group decided to join the Popular Front and his criticisms increased as the war went on. See L. Trotsky, *The Spanish Revolution*, 4th edn (New York: Pathfinder, 1986), pp. 207–21, 245–50.
60. For a personal, but one-sided account of the May events see G. Orwell, *Homage to Catalonia*, (Harmondsworth: Penguin, reprinted 1988) and A. Souchy *et al.*, *The May Days: Barcelona 1937* (London: Freedom Press, 1987).
61. H. Graham, *The Spanish Socialist Party in Power and Crisis, 1936–1939* (Cambridge: University Press, 1991), pp. 107–97.
62. S. Juliá, 'Partido contra sindicato: Una interpretación de la crisis de mayo de 1937', in *Socialismo y Guerra Civil*, pp. 343–6.
63. This view can be seen in the works by B. Bolloten, *The Spanish Revolution: The Left and the Struggle for Power during the Civil War* (Chapel Hill, NC: University of North Carolina Press, 1979), pp. 451–76 and 'Negrín: el hombre de Moscú', *Historia 16*, no. 117 (January 1986), pp. 11–24.
64. R. Miralles, 'Juan Negrín, resistir, para qué?', *Historia 16*, no. 253 (May 1997), pp. 10–12.
65. H. Graham, 'War, Modernity and Reform: The Premiership of Juan Negrín', in Preston and Mackenzie (eds), *The Republic*, pp. 180–93.
66. Miralles, op.cit., p. 9.
67. Preston, *Concise*, p. 171.
68. Miralles, op.cit., pp. 14–18; Graham, *Spanish Socialist*, pp. 132–7.

69. Graham, 'War', p.193.
70. Preston, *Concise*, pp. 4, 190.
71. Avilés, op.cit., pp. 104–8; Alpert, op.cit., p. 144.
72. Moradiellos, *Perfidia*, pp. 179, 206–7; Lacouture, op.cit., pp. 342–5.
73. Moradiellos, *Neutralidad*, pp. 363–80.
74. Moradiellos, *Perfidia*, pp. 186–8, 197–200, 221–40.
75. *L'ouvre*, pp. 395–400; Lacouture, op.cit., pp. 346–9.
76. Moradiellos, *Perfidia*, pp. 258–81.
77. Thomas, op.cit., p. 820.
78. Ibid., pp. 835–44.
79. Preston, *Franco*, pp. 307–8.
80. Moradiellos, *Perfidia*, p. 321.
81. Soviet aid had begun to diminish by the summer of 1937. Still, in December 1938 Negrín secured $100 million worth of arms. Most of them reached Spain too late to be deployed. Alpert, op.cit., p. 166, 168.
82. Thomas, op.cit.,pp. 852–5.
83. Avilés, op.cit., p. 177.
84. Thomas, op.cit., pp. 869–82.
85. Moradiellos, *Perfidia*, pp. 381–5.
86. Miralles, op.cit., p. 19.
87. Preston, *Franco*, pp. 318–20.
88. Thomas, op.cit., pp. 886–94; On Besteiro see P. Preston, 'A Pacifist in War: The Tragedy of Julián Besteiro', *Tesserae*, vol. 2 (Winter 1996), pp. 179–202.
89. M. Tuñón de Lara, 'El final de la guerra', in E. Malefakis (ed.), *La guerra de España, 1936–1939* (Madrid: Taurus, 1996), pp. 623–33; Thomas, op.cit., pp. 900–15.

6 Franco, Regent for Life, 1939–75

1. Preston, *Concise*, p. 217.
2. R. Carr and J. P. Fusi, *Spain: Dictatorship to Democracy*, 2nd edn (London: Unwin Hyman, 1981), p. 50; Ellwood, *Franco*, pp. 114–16; Shubert, *Social History*, pp. 206–7; Harrison, *Spanish Economy*, pp. 121–2; A. Carreras, 'Depresión económica y cambio estructural', pp.12–32, and C. Barciela, 'La España del estraperlo', pp. 106–31 both in J. L. García Delgado (ed.), *El Primer Franquismo: España durante la Segunda Guerra Mundial* (Madrid: Siglo XXI, 1989).
3. P. Preston, *The Politics of Revenge: Fascism and the Military in 20th Century Spain* (London: Routledge, 1995), p. 37.
4. A larger figure of 200000 executions is given by Jackson, *The Second Republic*, p. 538. For more details on post-war repression see M. Richards, 'Civil War, Violence and the construction of Francoism', in Preston and Mackenzie (eds), *The Republic*, pp. 195–239; Ballbé, *Orden*, p. 405; J. P. Fusi, *Franco: Autoritarismo y poder personal* (Madrid: El País, 1985), pp. 78–9; Reig, *Franco*, pp. 198–200, 205–9.
5. Reig, op.cit., pp. 186–7; Ellwood, op.cit., p. 112.
6. Ellwood, op.cit., pp. 113–14; Reig, op.cit., p. 78, 225–38.

7. J. Tusell, *Franco, España y la II Guerra Mundial: Entre el Eje y la Neutralidad* (Madrid: Temas de hoy, 1995), p. 13.
8. J. Tusell and G. García Queipo de Llano, *Franco y Mussolini* (Barcelona: Planeta, 1985), pp. 51–60; Ellwood, op.cit., p. 121.
9. Tusell, op.cit., pp. 43–9.
10. Preston, *Franco*, p. 341.
11. Tusell, op.cit., pp. 59–61.
12. S. Hoare, *Ambassador on Special Mission* (London: Collins, 1946), pp. 21–5, 29–36, 44–7, 60–4; Tusell, op.cit., pp. 172–84; Ellwood, op.cit., p. 121.
13. M. Séguéla, *Franco-Pétain: Los secretos de una alianza* (Barcelona: Prensa Ibérica, 1994), p. 53.
14. Tusell, op.cit., pp. 85–8, 132–9; Preston, *Franco*, pp. 361–2, 377–80, 387.
15. Preston, *The Politics*, p. 60.
16. Séguéla, op.cit., pp. 81–8, 98, 115; Fusi, op.cit., pp. 80–1.
17. Preston, *Franco*, pp. 393–5.
18. Tusell, op.cit., p. 13; Séguéla, op.cit., p. 111.
19. Preston, *Franco*, pp. 395–9; Tusell, op.cit., pp. 158–64.
20. Preston, *Franco*, p. 400.
21. Tusell, op.cit., pp. 164–71.
22. Preston, *Franco*, pp. 415–16.
23. Tusell, op.cit., pp. 262–9; Fusi, op.cit., p. 84.
24. Hoare, op.cit., p. 122; Preston, *Franco*, p. 442.
25. Preston, *The Politics*, pp. 51–2.
26. Preston, *Franco*, pp. 465–71.
27. Preston, *The Politics*, p. 53.
28. Preston, *Franco*, p. 431.
29. S. Payne, *The Franco Regime, 1936–1975* (Madison, WI: University of Wisconsin Press, 1987), p. 293.
30. C. J. H. Hayes, *Wartime Mission in Spain* (New York: Macmillan, 1945), pp. 86–94; Tusell, op.cit., pp. 315–16, 357–61.
31. Reig, op.cit., p. 201.
32. Hoare, op.cit., pp. 184–5, 197–204, 249–56.
33. Tusell and García, op.cit., pp. 235–6.
34. Hayes, op.cit., pp. 187–230; Hoare, op.cit., pp. 259–63.
35. Hoare, op.cit., p. 267.
36. Séguéla, op.cit., p. 311; Hoare, op.cit., pp. 272–3.
37. First noticed by the US ambassador (Hayes, op.cit., p. 242) in his meeting with Franco on 6 July.
38. Hoare, op.cit., pp. 282–4, 300–6.
39. Preston, *Franco*, p. 531.
40. F. Portero, *Franco aislado: La cuestión española, 1945–1950* (Madrid: Aguilar, 1989), p. 33.
41. Preston, *Franco*, p. 546.
42. Portero, op.cit., pp. 104–6, 128.
43. Q. Ahmad, *Britain, Franco Spain and the Cold War, 1945–1950* (London: Garland, 1992), pp. 15–16, 20–1, 33–8, 110; Portero, op.cit., pp. 79–82, 115–16, 233–6.
44. Ahmad, op.cit., p. 60

45. Ahmad, op.cit., pp. 41–2; Portero, op.cit., pp. 99–101, 137–54; Séguéla, op.cit., pp. 317–18.
46. B. Pollack, *The Paradox of Spanish Foreign Policy: Spain's International Relations from Franco to Democracy* (London: Pinter, 1987), pp. 35–6; Ahmad, op.cit., pp. 65–7, 72–3; Portero, op.cit., pp. 237–250.
47. Ahmad, op.cit., p. 63.
48. R. Gillespie, *Historia del Partido Socialista Obrero Español* (Madrid: Alianza Editorial, 1991), pp. 74–117; P. Preston, 'La oposición antifranquista: La larga marcha hacia la unidad', in P. Preston (ed.), *España en crisis: La evolución y decadencia del régimen de Franco* (Madrid: Fondo de cultura económica, 1977), pp. 217–35.
49. Séguéla, op.cit., p. 295; Tusell, op.cit., pp. 608–9; Preston, 'La oposición', pp. 231–5.
50. Preston, *The Politics*, pp. 101–8; Tusell and García, op.cit., pp. 222–6; Payne, op.cit., pp. 325–32.
51. C. Powell, *Juan Carlos of Spain: Self-Made Monarch* (London: Macmillan, 1996), p. 7.
52. Preston, *The Politics*, p. 106; Ellwood, op.cit., p. 142–6.
53. Lannon, *Privilege*, p. 215; Payne, op.cit., pp. 362–3.
54. P. Preston, 'Franco y la elaboración de una política exterior personalista, 1936–1953', p. 208, and F. Portero, 'Artajo, perfil de un ministro en tiempos de aislamiento', pp. 213–14 both in *Historia Contemporánea*, no. 15 (1996).
55. Preston, *Franco*, pp. 527–8.
56. Ellwood, op.cit., pp. 146–50.
57. Preston, *Franco*, pp. 577–80.
58. Pollack, op.cit., p. 22; Ahmad, op.cit., pp. 79–80, 91–6, 102–3.
59. Ahmad, op.cit., p. 103.
60. Portero, *Franco*, p. 363.
61. Ahmad, op.cit., pp. 212–13.
62. Shubert, op.cit., pp. 234–5.
63. Preston, *Franco*, pp. 622–3; Fusi, op.cit., pp. 118–21.
64. Preston, *Franco*, pp. 644–650.
65. Payne, op.cit., pp. 405–6, 409.
66. Lannon, op.cit., pp. 225–9.
67. Harrison, op.cit., pp. 132–4.
68. There were three Plans for Economic Development. The first covered the period 1964–7, and the second and third, 1968–71 and 1972–5, respectively. Their aim was planning and targeting resources to bring about growth while social concerns were neglected. Redistribution of wealth and income was never an objective and the age-old gap between the stagnant interior rural provinces and the industrialized regions of the north and east widened.
69. Harrison, op.cit., pp. 144–54; Shubert, op.cit., pp. 207–10.
70. Harrison, op.cit., pp. 154–7; Carr and Fusi, op.cit., pp. 57–8.
71. Ellwood, op.cit., pp. 176–7.
72. Preston, *Franco*, pp. 739–42; Powell, op.cit., pp. 37–42.
73. V. M. Pérez-Díaz, *The Return of Civil Society: The Emergence of Democratic Spain* (Cambridge, MA: Harvard University Press, 1993), pp. 12–13; P. Preston, *The Triumph of Democracy in Spain* (London: Methuen, 1986),

pp. 11–13; D. Gilmour, *The Transformation of Spain: From Franco to the Constitutional Monarchy* (London: Quartet, 1985), p. 33.

74. N. Cooper, 'La iglesia: de la cruzada al cristianismo', in Preston (ed.), *España*, p. 107; Lannon, op.cit., pp. 232–6.

75. E. Mujal-León, *Communism and Political Change in Spain* (Bloomington, IN: Indiana University Press, 1983), pp. 1–2, 57–66.

76. Carr and Fusi, op.cit., pp. 79–86; Preston, *The Politics*, pp. 28–9.

77. Pérez-Díaz, op.cit., pp. 16–17; Carr and Fusi, op.cit., pp. 146–9.

78. Balcells, *Catalan*, pp. 145–51, 164–5.

79. J. Sullivan, *ETA and Basque Nationalism: The Fight for Euskadi* (London: Routledge, 1988), pp. 70–110; R. P. Clark, *The Basques: The Franco Years and Beyond* (Reno, NV: University of Nevada Press, 1979), pp. 153–87; J. L. Hollyman, 'Separatismo Vasco Revolucionario: ETA', in Preston (ed.), *España*, pp. 364–76; Fusi, op.cit., pp. 165–6, 199.

80. Lannon, op.cit., pp. 5–6, 46–9, 247–51; Cooper, op.cit., pp. 107–40.

81. Mujal-León, op.cit., pp. 19–20.

82. Preston, *The Triumph*, p. 16; C. Powell, 'The Tácito Group and Democracy', in F. Lannon and P. Preston (eds), *Elites and Power in Twentieth-Century Spain* (Oxford: Oxford University Press, 1990), pp. 247–56.

83. Carr and Fusi, op.cit., p. 184.

84. Juan Vilá Reyes, a member of the Opus Dei and a manufacturer of machinery for the textile industry, MATESA, was alleged to have obtained some ten billion pesetas in export credits under false pretences, with the connivance of people in the government.

85. Payne, op.cit., pp. 542–6.

86. Preston, *The Politics*, pp. 127–8, 167–70; Preston, *The Triumph*, pp. 41–2.

87. Preston, *Franco*, p. 762.

88. Ibid., pp. 763–4.

89. Gilmour, op.cit., pp. 69–70.

90. Powell, *Juan Carlos*, pp. 64–8.

91. The most dramatic ETA action was the blowing up of the Cafeteria Rolando in Madrid, a place frequented by policemen, which left thirteen dead and seventy injured in September 1974.

92. Preston, *The Politics*, pp. 183–8.

93. Preston, *Franco*, p. 776.

94. Preston, *The Triumph*, pp. 75–6; Powell, *Juan Carlos*, pp. 74–8.

7   The Triumph of Democracy, 1975–98

1. Pérez-Díaz, *The Return*, pp. 34–5.

2. P. Aguilar Fernández, *Memoria y olvido de la Guerra Civil española* (Madrid: Alianza Editorial, 1996), pp. 34–5, 47, 56–7.

3. Powell, *Juan Carlos*, p. 46; Carr and Fusi, *Spain*, p. 208.

4. Powell, op.cit., pp. 82–4.

5. Mujal-León, *Communism*, pp. 53, 135–8; Powell, op.cit., pp. 64–5.

6. Gillespie, *Historia*, pp. 280–318.

7. Gilmour, *The Transformation*, p. 138.

8. Aguilar, op.cit., pp. 234–5.
9. Preston, *The Triumph*, pp. 79–80; Powell, op.cit., p. 86.
10. Gilmour, op.cit., p. 147; Powell, op.cit., p. 104.
11. R. Tamames, *La economía Española: De la transición a la unión monetaria* (Madrid: Temas de hoy, 1996), pp. 103, 108.
12. Gilmour, op.cit., pp. 143–4.
13. Powell, op.cit., pp. 106–11.
14. Preston, op.cit., pp. 89, 94–5.
15. Ibid., pp. 97–8.
16. Carr and Fusi, op.cit., pp. 224–5.
17. Ibid., p. 224.
18. Aguilar, op.cit., pp. 315–16.
19. Mujal-León, op.cit., pp. 151–3.
20. Aguilar, op.cit., pp. 336–7.
21. Tamames, op.cit., pp. 130–62.
22. Balcells, *Catalan*, pp. 169–75.
23. Clark, *The Basques*, pp. 267, 272–81; Sullivan, *ETA*, pp. 154–80; Preston, op.cit., pp. 104–5, 125–7.
24. Sullivan, op.cit., pp. 200–5, 227–8.
25. P. Heywood, *The Government and Politics of Spain* (London: Macmillan, 1995), pp. 37, 51; Pérez-Díaz, op.cit., pp. 21–2.
26. Heywood, op.cit., pp. 46–52.
27. Gilmour, op.cit., pp. 207–10.
28. Heywood, op.cit., pp. 92–3; Carr and Fusi, op.cit., pp. 257–8.
29. Harrison, *The Spanish Economy*, p. 177.
30. Preston, op.cit., p. 145.
31. M. Sánchez Soler, *Los hijos del 20-N: Historia Violenta del Fascismo Español* (Madrid: Temas de hoy, 1993), pp. 165–203, 210–53; J. L. Rodríguez Jiménez, *Reaccionarios y golpistas: La extrema derecha en España: del tardofranquismo a la consolidación de la democracia, 1967–1982* (Madrid: CSIC, 1994), pp. 224–5, 229.
32. Clark, op.cit., p. 377.
33. Rodríguez, op.cit., pp. 278–9.
34. Preston, op.cit., pp. 148–9.
35. Carr and Fusi, op.cit., pp. 250–1.
36. Gilmour, op.cit., p. 249.
37. S. Juliá, 'The Ideological Conversion of the Leaders of the PSOE, 1976–1979', in Lannon and Preston (eds), *Elites*, pp. 273–82.
38. Gilmour, op.cit., p. 251.
39. Rodríguez, op.cit., pp. 286–9; Preston, op.cit., pp. 195–201; Powell, op.cit., pp. 168–72.
40. Powell, op.cit., p. 173.
41. Gilmour, op.cit., pp. 263–4.
42. Mujal-León, op.cit., pp. 200–22.
43. Gilmour, op.cit., p. 267.
44. R. Gillespie, 'Regime Consolidation in Spain: Party, State, and Society', in G. Pridham (ed.), *Securing Democracy: Political Parties and Democratic Consolidation in Southern Europe* (London: Routledge, 1990), p. 126.

45. The PNV split in 1986 when the former *Lehendakari* Carlos Garaikoetxea broke away to lead his own party, *Eusko Alkartasuna*.
46. In the second coup the conspirators apparently planned to assassinate the king and leading figures in the government by blowing up the official stand at the Armed Forces Day military parade in La Coruña on 1 June 1985. Sánchez, op.cit., pp. 267–8; *El País* (23 February 1981 and 17 February 1991).
47. Gillespie, 'Regime', pp. 131–2; Heywood, op.cit., p. 65.
48. The PSOE's change of mind was decisive to turn the vote in favour of NATO membership. The Socialists had fought the 1982 elections with the slogan *'OTAN. De entrada No!'* ('NATO. No entry yet!'). About 53 per cent voted to stay in NATO and 39 per cent to withdraw.
49. A. Viñas, 'Dos hombres para la transición externa: Fernando Morán y Francisco Fernández Ordóñez', *Historia Contemporánea*, no. 15 (1996), pp. 257–88; R. Cotarelo, 'La política exterior', in J. Tusell and J. Sinova (eds), *La década socialista: El ocaso de Felipe González* (Madrid: Espasa, 1992), pp. 224–33.
50. J. Harrison, *The Spanish Economy: From the Civil War to the European Community* (London: Macmillan, 1993), pp. 48–9; K. Salmon, 'Spain in the World Economy', in R. Gillespie, F. Rodrigo and J. Story (eds), *Democratic Spain: Reshaping External Relations in a Changing World* (London: Routledge, 1995), pp. 72–84.
51. Salmon, op.cit., pp. 78–80; Heywood, op.cit., pp. 222–40.
52. V. Pérez-Díaz, *España puesta a prueba* (Madrid: Alianza Editorial, 1996), pp. 148–52; C. Rodríguez Braun, 'De la agonía a la agonía', in J. Tusell and J. Sinova (eds), op.cit., pp. 51–4, 56–60.
53. Pérez-Díaz, *España*, p. 90.
54. J. Pradera, 'Las pasiones del poder: el PSOE tras diez años de gobierno', in Tusell and Sinova, op.cit., pp. 273–5.
55. Cándido, *La sangre de la rosa: El poder y la época, 1982–1996* (Madrid: Planeta, 1996), p. 14.
56. Pérez-Díaz, *España*, p. 40.
57. Pérez-Díaz, *The Return*, p. 149; P. Castellano, 'El Parlamento y el gobierno', in Tusell and Sinova (eds), op.cit., p. 144.
58. The PSOE obtained 159 seats, PP 141, IU 18, CiU 17 and the PNV 5.
59. For a list of scandals see *El Mundo* (29 December 1994); Tamames, op.cit., pp. 291–322.
60. Sullivan, op.cit., pp. 254–5.
61. *El Mundo* (27–30 December 1994, 9 March 1995), *Diario 16* (9 March and 25 July 1995). The arrest of Luis Roldán was initially presented as proof of the government's determination to investigate official corruption, but turned into another disaster when it was discovered that the former chief of the Civil Guard, allegedly arrested in Laos, had been residing in France and accepted being extradited from Laos on condition that he could only be tried on limited charges.
62. Pérez-Díaz, *España*, pp. 172–4.

INDEX